ARTIC CIRCLE
the North
HUDSON'S BAY
Goose Lake
Swan Lake
Swan River
Carribou River & Lake
River & Lake
English River
Carrying Place of 200 Yards
3 Carrying Place
Mineront
called by the French
Carrying Place
Churchill Fort
Churchill River
CHRISTINEAUX
Road to Churchill
York Fort
Beaver Lake
Middle Road to Hudsons Bay
Lake
Cumberland House
MASKAGO'S
Where Fort Bourbon was
Lake Bourbon
Great Rapids
South Road to Hudson's Bay from L. Winipique
Part of the CLINCHINO'S
Lac Folleavoine
Lac du Carpe
Lake Alone
Albany River
Flat Lake
L. Lake Winipique
G. Lake Winipique
L. Minitopa
River Winipique
Back road from L. la Pluis to L. du Bois
CHIPOWAY or by
Lake Nipigon
Lac du Bois
Lac la Pluis
Sturgeon Lake Chain of Lakes
the French SAULTEURS
G. Portage
LAKE SUPERIOR
Rr. St. Louis
Red River
R. Montgomery
Fort Epinett
Assinipoil River
Red Lake
Bear Lake or Winipique
White Bear Lake
Rib River
Rib Lake
Ravens wing River
St. Croix Lake
Godlards R.
SNAKE INDIANS
NOTTOWASES or SIOUS
St. Peters River
Papin Lake
Chipoway R.
Green River
Fox River
Mississipi
Here upon the Branches of the Missury live the Maundiens, who bring to our Factory at Fort Epinett, on the Assinipoil River Indian Corn for sale. Our People go to them with loaded Horses in twelve Days

THE ELUSIVE MR. POND

ALSO BY BARRY GOUGH

The Royal Navy and the Northwest Coast of North America, 1810–1914

To the Pacific and Arctic with Beechey

Distant Dominion

The Northwest Coast: British Navigation, Trade and Discoveries to 1812

Gunboat Frontier: British Maritime Authority and Northwest Coast Indians

First Across the Continent: Sir Alexander Mackenzie

HMCS Haida*: Battle Ensign Flying*

Fighting Sail on Lake Huron and Georgian Bay: The War of 1812 and Its Aftermath

Through Water, Ice and Fire: Schooner Nancy *of the War of 1812*

Fortune's a River: The Collision of Empires in Northwest America

Historical Dreadnoughts: Arthur Marder, Stephen Roskill and Battles for Naval History

Juan de Fuca's Strait: Voyages in the Waterway of Forgotten Dreams

THE ELUSIVE MR. POND

THE SOLDIER, FUR TRADER AND EXPLORER WHO OPENED THE NORTHWEST

Barry Gough

DOUGLAS & MCINTYRE

1 2 3 4 5 — 18 17 16 15 14

Douglas and McIntyre (2013) Ltd.
P.O. Box 219, Madeira Park, BC, V0N 2H0
www.douglas-mcintyre.com

Edited by Audrey McClellan
Jacket design by Anna Comfort O'Keeffe
Text design by Mary White
Indexed by Ellen Hawman
End papers detail from "A print of Peter Pond's map presented to Lieutenant-Governor the Honourable Henry Hamilton in 1785, and showing Western and North-Western Canada and the whereabouts of Indian tribes," courtesy of Library and Archives Canada.
Printed and bound in Canada

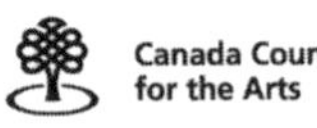

Douglas and McIntyre (2013) Ltd. acknowledges financial support from the Government of Canada through the Canada Book Fund and the Canada Council for the Arts, and from the Province of British Columbia through the BC Arts Council and the Book Publishing Tax Credit.

Cataloguing information available from Library and Archives Canada
ISBN 978-1-77162-039-0 (cloth)
ISBN 978-1-77162-040-6 (ebook)

To the Memory of
F.W. Howay and Margaret Ormsby,
Historical Pathfinders

The story of the Nor'Westers, though not without its darker pages, is a brilliant chapter in the history of Canada. No braver or more picturesque band of adventurers ever put it to the touch, to gain or lose it all. Some of them were French Canadian traders and voyageurs, the sons of those who had followed La Vérendrye to the rivers and prairies of the West in the dying days of the French regime. Others were American frontiersmen who had served their apprenticeship in the fur-trade in the valleys of the Ohio and the Mississippi and in the north country that Americans call the Old Northwest. Most of them were Scottish Highlanders, the sons of those who had come to Canada in Wolfe's army or as United Empire Loyalists and refugees from the American Revolution...These men were hardy, courageous, shrewd, and proud. They spent a good part of their lives traveling incredible distances in birch-bark canoes, shooting rapids, or navigating inland seas. They were wrecked and drowned. They suffered hunger and starvation. They were robbed and murdered by the Indians, and sometimes by one another. They fell the victims of smallpox, syphilis, and rum. Yet they conquered half a continent, and they built up a commercial empire, the likes of which North America at least has never seen.

—W. Stewart Wallace,
Introduction to *Documents Relating to the North West Company* (1934)

Contents

Author's Preface		xiii
Illustrations		xxi
Timeline		xxii
1	Peter Pond and the Riddles of History	1
2	Crucible of War	8
3	Wilderness Tangles: Robert Rogers, Jonathan Carver, and the Northwest Passage	35
4	Trader and Emissary to the Sioux	49
5	Among the Canadians on the Saskatchewan, and the Rivals from Hudson Bay	75
6	Athabasca Odyssey	93
7	Maps, Dreams, and Empire	119
8	The Outlier Returns	148
	Epilogue: In Pond's Tracks, a New Athabasca	172
Acknowledgements		185
Notes		189
Bibliography		210
Index		222

Overleaf: London-based Aaron Arrowsmith marked the imperial progress of trade and discovery with his up-to-date maps. A detail from this 1814 edition displays the explorations of Sir Alexander Mackenzie, who had been mentored by Peter Pond. LIBRARY OF CONGRESS, GEOGRAPHY AND MAP DIVISION

A MAP
Exhibiting all the New Disc
in the Interior Parts of
NORTH AMER
Inscribed by Permission
To the Honorable Governor and Company of Adv
TRADING INTO HUDSONS BA
In testimony of their liberal Communi
To their most Obedient
and very Humble Servant, A. Arr
THE SEA
THE SEA
120 W
N O R T H P A C I F I C O C
R U P

s of England
DAVIS STRAIT
HUDSONS
BAY
LABRADOR
LOWER
OCEAN

Author's Preface

Like many another personal oddity from the past, Peter Pond continues to speak to us from his grave. He is an elusive character. Angular and quixotic, tough and enigmatic, this colonial American of Puritan heritage opened Canada's and North America's greatest fur preserve, the vast and untamed Athabasca. He has always been a ghostly presence haunting the margins of the continent's history. His is a North American story of the late eighteenth century, a time when political identities and loyalties shifted or stiffened with the winds of war and the whims of fate. Strangely, he holds no secure place in American history and no firm place in Canada's either. One authority on the history of the North West Company, who will remain unnamed, told me "he really was not one of us."

Was Pond truly an outsider? He gets at least some notice or vague mention in any serious history of Canada or the fur trade. In a unique way, Pond was a forerunner of Canada's transcontinental grasp: the enormous confidence that drove him also laid the foundations for the North West Company's fur empire of Athabasca, of which the Mackenzie River basin formed the heart. He also lit the way for that greatest of fur trading explorers, Sir Alexander Mackenzie, who by the time Pond's star was on the wane was making his two stupendous and justly famed voyages to the Arctic and Pacific Oceans. Mackenzie penned a magnificent account of his voyages and thereby won literary laurels and earned himself a knighthood. Pond's near contemporary Alexander Henry, a fellow colonial American, wrote a commendable work, *Travels and Adventures in Canada and the Indian Territories*, that assured him a permanent position in historical letters. Pond, by contrast, was disadvantaged when it came to gaining renown in his own time. His crowded early life left him little opportunity for formal education. His near illiteracy thus posed a permanent barrier to his entry into North American letters in many genres—travel, discovery, fur trade history, and even ethnography. He was not a Scot, one of those said to have created Canada. But he was a notable figure in the creation of the empire of the St. Lawrence, and it is tempting to go so far as to call him a father of confederation. His greatest achievement lay at the very extremity of the Laurentian or Precambrian Shield. He opened trade in the far distant Arctic watershed, of which the Athabasca River was the headwater. He also lived at the edge of truth, on the margins of respectability, and it is no surprise that many wicked stories were circulated about him in his time. He's a literary oddity, his story often half-told. He deserves better.

In his pioneering biography *Peter Pond: Fur Trader and Adventurer* (1930), fur trade scholar Harold Innis explains that he wrote the biography so as to elucidate the history of the North West Company. In its day that biography was a considerable achievement. But, truth to tell, Innis rushed it into print and subsequently had to publish a number of articles correcting, retracting, or defending his positions, especially against his detractor, Professor Arthur Silver Morton, noted historian of Western Canada. Parts of Innis's Pond biography were shown to be unreliable, and it also left many questions unanswered. One such was Pond's relationship to Mackenzie, whose life I wrote.[1] Mackenzie's story was doubtless Pond's in inception, but Mackenzie never could give credit where credit was due. It was not just anti-Americanism (Pond being a Connecticut Yankee): Mackenzie similarly slighted his "lieutenant" on his great North American canoe and land voyages, the consequently unheralded Alexander McKay. It seems as if explorers of that age wanted to claim the entire prize for themselves.

In the end, as will be seen, Pond fought hard to preserve his own reputation as a pioneer explorer and cartographer. In the end, too—and sad to relate—he was outflanked or cast aside by those who had gained so much from his enterprises. Possibly impoverished and perhaps disillusioned about the so-called august majesty of the British Empire, for which he had fought during the Seven Years' War (the French and Indian Wars, as Americans call it), he passed from the pages of history unnoticed. He died in the place of his birth, Milford, Connecticut, uncelebrated and unknown. Mackenzie, by contrast, makes more than cameo appearances in Pond's story. He flits in and out of our later pages, especially those chapters that focus on northwestern discoveries and on the Athabasca trade immediately after Pond's pioneering venture. And he had more success in navigating the stormy seas of British mercantile trade and regulation, accomplishing as Pond could not an influential direction in fur trade policy in Canada.

In its own peculiar way, Pond's life follows the rise and fall of what some have called the First British Empire. He played a small role in the imperial expansion that brought Canada under the Union Jack. He saw the British Empire in America at flood tide. He lived to see the hard-won imperial fabric torn in twain by colonial revolt. He witnessed the imposition of an international boundary separating the infant United States from the British North American provinces, and a reordering of rivals vying for control of the lands and fur trade of the Northwest. This rise and fall of the old empire—with the conquest of New France and the remaking of the First Nations alliance from the French to the British—provides the context of the political and military changes that Pond found himself caught up in. An equally important set of circumstances, all compelling to Pond, was the fabulous prosperity of the northwest fur trade in the formative decades after the capitulation of New France. While Pond could have no control over the political maelstrom that split the old empire, in the fur trade he rose to become a master, and unquestionably one of the giants, of the northwest trade.

All his achievements occurred against a background of Native or aboriginal North America. All fur traders depended on their Native trading allies and customers and, to a degree, lived on sufferance in the Native world. They had powerful links with women of chiefly lineage, lived in the custom of the country, and sired early generations of the Métis nation. Accordingly, I have given specific attention to such intercultural relations. It is clear that Pond lived easily among First Nations and was a master of diplomacy with them; these characteristics, coupled with innate inquisitiveness and love of wilderness adventure, gave him undoubted advantages as an explorer and cartographer.

The thirty-six–sheet memoir or narrative that Pond wrote, which I have exploited heavily in the early chapters of this book, is a literary legacy for the 1770s history of the fur trade of the upper Mississippi River, especially lands near Green Bay, Wisconsin. That memoir, a curious example of orthography, is also much in demand nowadays as a representation of the way in which a colonial American, without much formal education, might speak. In this book I have ventured reasons why he wrote this memoir, and who prompted him to do so. In reading his story we (to our delight) can almost hear him speaking in his rough and antiquated tongue. It is to be regretted that so little of this work has survived (what we have ends in 1775), and the yawning gaps that he left for later years have inspired some of the most creative writers to imagine what was left out.[2]

In addition to the problem left the biographer by an incomplete memoir of the subject is the unfortunate paucity of letters to and from Pond. His correspondence regarding Great Slave Lake, though known at the time, has disappeared, lost forever. Adding to this is the furtive and fragmentary documentation about the North West Company and its Canadian rivals. Any historian working on such subjects as a biography of Pond or, for that matter, of Mackenzie will not fail to curse the archival holocausts that have all but eradicated the documentary trail which we must follow to recreate such lives. But new material comes to light, such as the *English River Book*, noted below. It may be fashionable nowadays to engage in creative non-fiction, but I can assure the reader that I have declined this seduction, save where I have speculated on Pond's appearance.

In the course of researching this book it became alarmingly clear to me that a giant void exists about the Mackenzie River system, particularly concerning details of historical geography of the late eighteenth century. Historical and geographical atlases of North America and Canada have yet to be compiled that will provide a researcher or biographer dedicated to authenticated history with adequate works of reference on that region in that era.

As with Pond's memoir, so, too, his maps. These he drew without sufficient scientific knowledge to make them authentic, but even so they remain subjects of wonder and fascination. They contain many details about place names, Native tracks and war trails, rivers and lakes, historical particulars about posts occupied (and when), and similar. Let us then embrace Pond's maps as being in the category of the last phase of pre-scientific cartography. They provide added details appropriate to my narrative and analysis. I like to think of Pond's maps as a representation of the man himself and of his life's work in the northwest. In that sense, his maps served his purpose and were, charmingly, his own unique creation. They remain enigmatic and incomplete, much like Pond himself.

Peter Pond had high expectations of making an exploration west of the Continental Divide to link up with the Russians at Cook Inlet. He then hoped to travel to Kamchatka, cross Russia, and find his way to the Russian court. Pond drew this map with the intention of presenting it to the empress of Russia. GLENBOW ARCHIVES NA-789-53

Pond's later years in the fur trade were crowded ones in international history. They were also crowded years in Pond's progress through time and space. Readers must remember that not only was there a dog-eat-dog rivalry between the North West Company and the Hudson's Bay Company, but also an equally strong fight for commercial autonomy between the Nor'Westers and other Montreal-based rivals. A Spanish rivalry existed on the southern margins of the Canadian trade in the continental interior, though in only a faint way and from distant St. Louis and New Orleans, while the American contest for the fur trade coming west from Ohio and into Illinois was a considerable threat. During the time of Pond's Athabasca prominence, the maritime fur traders were prosecuting the sea otter trade of the North Pacific. Spain's northern frontier was about to be checked at Nootka Sound on Vancouver Island. The Russian traders were coming south out of the fog and mists of Kamchatka and Alaska. Pond had pressed into a vast quarter of the continental interior that Samuel Hearne of the Hudson's Bay Company had only touched upon in his discoveries. The Northwest Passage had yet to be fully disclosed, or disproved, in these latitudes. No reliable maps existed as to the general lay of the lakes and rivers of these million square miles. The pull of the Pacific Coast, with all its possible wealth in the sea otter trade and links to the fabulous China market, could not have escaped the notice of the energetic and hard-driving Pond, who would have known, too, about the discoveries of Captain James Cook on his third voyage to the Pacific Ocean. And Pond would also have been well aware that trade connections with Russia could be used to get into the China trade.

Pond was a secretive fellow. Ice seems to have run through his veins. He gave away no secrets. Mystery, even duplicity, surrounds his later years, and Pond may have deliberately misled those he informed of his travels. But by his actions and achievements, Pond was an attention-getter. The crowded last years of his life in the Canadian fur trade brought him to the attention of highly placed imperial strategists as well as jealous trading rivals. I have sought to trace his influence in the halls of power, but the average reader will likely be unaware of the complications of imperial statecraft as it was worked out in these days. Accordingly, I have attempted an explanation of this statecraft even though we cannot always follow the process to its final results (if achieved). I have also included a chronology as an aid to readers.

A few more prefatory points need to be made. There exists rich material in Pond's narrative about the Sioux. Would it were thus with other tribes and nations. If there were more surviving details about Pond's relations with indigenous trading partners, I would have included them. I draw the reader's attention to the comprehensive surveys of these Native nations that exist in such studies as June Helms's *Smithsonian Handbook of North American Indians*, vol. 6: *Subarctic*, and in the materials listed in the bibliography of that work. George C. Davidson, in *The North West Company*, did successful detective work on Pond's progress as told in his maps. This work is highly recommended. The evaluation of Pond's maps as cartographic history is best analyzed in the work of G. Malcolm Lewis. On Pond's memoir as literary work, the analysis of Bruce Greenfield (see bibliography) repays close study. Statistics of battle casualties (killed, wounded, or missing) are always subject to verification. I have given what I regard to be as authentic a figure as possible from available evidence. All longitudes mentioned are based on the Prime Meridian, Greenwich, England. When I refer to canoes I often mean not only the vessels themselves but also the trading cargoes that they carried inland. Many variants exist of the place name *Michilimackinac*, though this spelling is historically accurate for that era. In consequence, even though that spelling is not used today, I have used it here. I have not sought to correct it, or standardize it, in the various documents quoted. This word, I have on reliable authority, is now generally pronounced *Mackinaw*, irrespective of its spelling and whether it is referring to the fort, town, or strait.

Barry Gough
Victoria, British Columbia

Illustrations

Map of North America by Aaron Arrowsmith, 1814	x–xi
Map by Peter Pond intended for the empress of Russia, 1787	xvii
Portrait of Alexander Mackenzie	4
Carte de l'Amérique septentrionale (map of North America), 1754	15
Map of the area around Fort Carillon (Fort Ticonderoga)	21
Portrait of Sir William Johnson	27
Portage La Loche	37
Portrait of Jonathan Carver	44
Canadian voyageurs walking a canoe up a rapid	54
Portrait of Daniel Harmon	55
Shooting the rapids	62
Map of the main waterways of the Canadian fur trade	76–77
Portrait of Alexander Henry (the Elder)	83
North West Company trading tokens	90
Map of the Methye Portage	95
Post at Île à la Crosse	116
Map of western North America by Peter Pond, 1785	124
Map presented to the Honourable Henry Hamilton by Peter Pond, 1785	128–29
Map by Peter Pond published in *Gentleman's Magazine*, 1790	144
Map of Peter Pond's travels by Ezra Stiles, 1790	149
Fort Chipewyan	174
Map of Mackenzie's journey from Fort Chipewyan to the North Sea	177

Timeline

1740 Birth of Peter Pond in Milford, Connecticut

1756 Pond enlists in 2nd Connecticut Regiment

1758 Pond enlists again, fights at Battle of Fort Carillon (Ticonderoga)

1759 Pond, now a sergeant, enlists in Suffolk County Regiment of the New York Provincial Army and is present at the fall of Fort Niagara

1760 Ensign Pond serves under the commander-in-chief, General Amherst, and is at the capitulation of Montreal

1761 Pond takes his first trading voyage to the West Indies

1762 Susanna Newell marries Peter Pond in Milford

1763 By the Treaty of Paris, France relinquishes sovereignty of New France to Britain

1765 Peter Pond, following in his father's footsteps, commences trading westward, based on Detroit

1771 Pond accepts an invitation from Felix Graham to trade west from Michilimackinac

1772 Pond makes a second voyage to the West Indies

1773 Pond resumes trade from Michilimackinac, visits Montreal to obtain supplies, travels to the Sioux as emissary of the Crown, and acts as peacemaker among warring tribes

1774 Pond brings Sioux chiefs to the commandant's grand council of tribes at Michilimackinac. The Quebec Act extends the province's boundaries and administrative responsibilities in the northwest

1775 Pond trades on the lower Saskatchewan River and winters at Fort Dauphin

1776 Pond goes to the forks of the Saskatchewan and winters above the forks on the North Branch

1778 An association of traders, forerunner of the North West Company, gives Pond control of the trading venture to Athabasca. This is a prelude to a momentous event in Canadian history. Leaving Sturgeon Lake, he crosses Methye Portage into waters flowing to the Arctic. Late that year, at the onset of winter, he erects on the Athabasca River a post called Athabasca Post, later called Pond's House

1779 Pond comes out of Athabasca in the spring. He arrives at the yearly traders' rendezvous at Grand Portage with the first half of his Athabasca furs

Seven small partnerships and two individual merchants enter a co-partnership called the North West Company; Pond holds one of sixteen shares

The recently formed North West Company sends Waden to take over trade in the Athabasca region opened by Pond

1780 Pond returns to Grand Portage late this year

Smallpox begins its deadly ravages among northern tribes

1781 Pond leads a fur trading expedition from Grand Portage and winters at Lac la Ronge, which was established by Waden in 1779

1782 Waden dies of a gunshot wound, and suspicion hangs heavily over Pond's head

Another trading expedition to Athabasca, perhaps involving Pond, makes inconclusive trading results owing to the aboriginal population being diminished by smallpox

1783 A reorganized North West Company is established. Pond, dissatisfied, refuses to take a share offered to him. Pond returns to Athabasca Post for a third winter, probably directly from where he had wintered at Île à la Crosse.

The first British Empire comes to an end, with the recognition of the United States as a sovereign power by the Treaty of Versailles

1784 Pond returns to Grand Portage and Montreal. He commences drawing his map of the Northwest

1785 Pond becomes a charter member of the Beaver Club. He presents his memorial to the Lieutenant Governor of Quebec, the Honourable Henry Hamilton. His map and memorandum are presented to Congress

1787 Rival trader John Ross is murdered; Pond is implicated, and suspicion hangs even more heavily over his head

1788 Fort Chipewyan, the first of the name, is constructed on Lake Athabasca; in consequence, Pond's House is abandoned

1789 Alexander Mackenzie follows *De Cho*—the Mackenzie River—to the Arctic Ocean and returns to Fort Chipewyan

Pond is in the town of Quebec to present his findings to Governor Dorchester and consults with well-informed and interested persons

1790 News of Pond's discoveries becomes the subject of speculation and discussion in London. A map of his discoveries is first published in *Gentleman's Magazine,* a London periodical

Pond retires from the fur trade, sells his share, and is not included in the North West Company reorganization of that year

Pond returns to Milford, goes to Yale University, and is quizzed by President Ezra Stiles about his distant discoveries. Stiles prepares a version of Pond's map. Pond begins to write his memoirs

1793 Mackenzie crosses "the sea of mountains" to the Pacific Ocean near Bella Coola and makes his return to Fort Chipewyan

Captain Pond is employed by General Henry Knox of the War Department in Ohio

1801 Mackenzie's *Voyages from Montreal* is published to acclaim

1807 Pond dies in Milford

1812 The beginning of the Anglo-American War

1814 The Treaty of Ghent ends the War of 1812

1818 By the Convention of 1818, the boundary west of the Lake of the Woods to the "Stoney Mountains" is set at the 49th parallel

1820 Mackenzie dies in Scotland

1821 The North West Company and the Hudson's Bay Company unite under the name of the latter

1

Peter Pond and the Riddles of History

Much has been written by historians of discovery concerning official—that is to say, state-sponsored—voyages, whether by sea or by land, and the consequences of these to the evolution of trade, to the enlargement of geographical knowledge, and to the progress of national ambitions and imperial rivalries. Less is known about the contribution to these same fields of human endeavour by individual persons unsupported by government, learned societies, or corporations. It is governments and statesmen who have left the largest paper trail for the historian to follow. People like Peter Pond, who are marginally literate and largely unskilled in the scientific principles of cartography, pose a daunting challenge to the historian and biographer. In consequence, their lives can only be tracked, so to speak, like the intermittent flashes of a firefly on a summer's night. Here and there we see rare illuminations, but in between lie large blank spaces.

We are left to wonder what those blank spaces contain. The historian—unlike the poet or the novelist—works at what can be described as a second-rate trade, and can only fashion for posterity that which is finite and derives from the past's documentation. We do the best we can. Many voids remain, not by choice but of necessity.

As a class, merchant traders merit attention as discoverers and mapmakers. Samuel Hearne, John Meares, Simon Fraser, and David Thompson are four such. They were pathfinders in the unique sense that they were expanding the sphere of business capitalism. They were searching out promising new areas of commerce. In certain cases, largely unappreciated, they were pioneers or heralds of empire. As John S. Galbraith, the historian of the Hudson's Bay Company's role as imperial agent, puts it unerringly, the energies of the mercantile class were largely responsible for British imperial expansion. "Far more important to the shaping of British Imperial policy than the secretaries and under-secretaries of state often credited with its formation," he writes, "were hundreds of men in the commercial community, most of them unknown to history, who created the conditions upon which that policy was based."[1]

The fur traders of North America contributed markedly to the exploration of the continent, especially its river basins, mountain passes, and portages. Fur traders were necessarily inquisitive. They were observant. They were pathfinders in so many ways, and the names of many of them and their achievements are lost to history. Moreover, they existed largely on sufferance of the Native peoples, and their profits as well as their survival depended on the people among whom they travelled and traded. They learned of the land's resources and opportunities and how to survive in unimaginably difficult wilderness conditions. They questioned the petty circuit traders who were part of the network of commerce in the interior, they interrogated the Native peoples and the mixed-bloods now known as Métis, and they took notes. They learned of Native tracks and war trails, shortcuts and avenues of Native commerce. They built trading posts, their compressed bastions of power and influence. They established amazingly workable networks of communications, so beneficial and necessary to their trade and their survival. They took Native women "in the fashion of the country," establishing many ties of enduring length, fathering numerous children, and contributing to the evolution of the Métis as an independent people. Easy as it would be to dismiss these fur traders as "unscientific," they led lives on the frontier that required a pragmatic disposition. They lived for the moment and for the trading season, it is true, but they also cast an eye to the future years of trade and Indian diplomacy. As the American scholar of frontier exploration William H. Goetzmann states of fur traders as explorers, "They were seriously engaged in the process of empirical information gathering, and their very lives depended upon the testing of geographical hypotheses formed for very practical reasons."[2]

Throughout North America's river valleys and mountain passes, fur traders enlarged the world's knowledge about hitherto inaccessible or little-known peoples and places. The vastness of the continent made the dynamic of discovery a piecemeal process. The Northwest Passage was still a subject of speculation. Fur traders held few grand designs of this sort. They lived workaday lives. Some, however, stood above the others. Of an adventurous and inquisitive nature, Peter Pond was, besides, aggressive and courageous. He was necessarily competitive and would brook no rivals. "Pond was in many ways admirably fitted for the arduous work of a trader in the wilderness, and it may also be said of him that he was, in a truer sense than many of his contemporaries, an explorer." So wrote Lawrence J. Burpee, Canadian historian of western discoveries, and to this he added these distinctions:

> The Frobishers and [Alexander] Henry looked upon exploration solely as a means to an end. First and always they were fur traders. They penetrated the unknown west, paddled over unexplored waterways, discovered portages that led them into new river systems, but all with an eye to the possibilities that each new field offered in the way of peltries. Pond, too, was a fur trader, but he seems to have been equally, or even more, a pathfinder. He was possessed by that *Wanderlust* that after all had been at the bottom of most of the world's exploration—the passion for discovering what may lie beyond the uttermost bounds of the known, that has carried men across untravelled seas to the shores of unknown lands, to the heart of great continents; and that neither arctic cold nor tropic heat could dampen.[3]

Pond, as is argued in this book, ranks high on the list of fur trade explorers of the North American Northwest deserving to be better known. He frequently stands in the shadow of the Nor'Wester Sir Alexander Mackenzie, who made two great journeys in search of a route to the Pacific from Lake

Alexander Mackenzie, the bonnie Scot from near Stornoway, made two fabulous expeditions and opened the greater northwest to geographical knowledge. His famed book *Voyages from Montreal* (1801) sparked the American statesman Thomas Jefferson to mount the Corps of Discovery led by captains Lewis and Clark to find a passage to the Pacific. Mackenzie used Pond's discoveries without giving credit where credit was due. LIBRARY AND ARCHIVES CANADA

Athabasca, the first of which took him to the Arctic and the second of which carried him, despite greater obstacles, to his destination. Pond also stands in the shadow of the fur trading surveyor David Thompson, who, when in the employ of the North West Company, unlocked the secrets of the upper Columbia River system. Pond also receives less due than the feisty, self-preoccupied Simon Fraser, who traced the river named after him from near its upper waters to its mouth at Pacific tidewater at Musqueam, the north arm of the Fraser River near present-day south Vancouver. Comparisons, as it is often said, are invidious. Pond stands firm as a geographical pioneer, for this resilient, violent, and ambitious man made a significant contribution to opening the trade of Athabasca to the nascent North West Company based in Montreal.

Detractors might claim, with some justice, that his work was hardly sensational and was more often than not prosaic. But it can also be said that he reformulated the world of the fur trader in three ways. First, his forceful actions compelled trading rivals to enter into a partnership, a revised North West Company, which by 1790 constituted the most aggressive trading concern in North America west and south of the Hudson's Bay Company's Rupert's Land. Second, he added to the trading domain of that concern, which under Mackenzie extended its interests into Athabasca and throughout the Mackenzie River valley and later to the Pacific Coast of what eventually became Canadian territory. Pond's accomplishments rested on his discovery and use of the Methye or La Loche Portage, linking two of the continent's main river systems, the Churchill and the Mackenzie. More than any other trader he broadened the links of the Canadian-based trade, filled out its margins, so to speak, and gave promise to its final enlargement in and after the era of Mackenzie. Third, he made unique contributions to cartography. His skills as a mapmaker were largely unscientific, and disdain has been heaped upon him by later generations on this score. Such judgments are harsh and often ahistorical. "After the event, any fool can be wise," wrote Homer. Pond's maps are tributes to his time and reflect the limits of his scientific and cartographic abilities. Even so, his maps of the northwestern regions of North America remain among the principal visual references for our knowledge of the river systems and trading posts for the last quarter of the eighteenth century. In Pond's hands, maps were historical documents on which detail of place, tribes, and commerce could be recorded.

If Pond's life seems one of paradox, we must remember that so, too, were the times in which he lived. His wilderness career spanned those unsettled years that witnessed a phenomenal turnaround in North American history and is commensurate with much of the second half of the eighteenth century. We are introduced to a very young Pond fighting as a British colonial soldier in an important and seemingly endless struggle against the French and First Nations for the control of Canada. We see him next as a chosen emissary to the Sioux and, by definition, other tribes of Wisconsin and Minnesota. His role in discoveries in Minnesota places him high as an explorer there. Then we follow his rapid progress as a merchant trader, mapmaker, and political geographer in what would become the Canadian northwest under the security of the British Empire. Finally we view him in retreat from that same empire, partly engulfed by the rivalry, jealousy, and suspicions of others, and ultimately dismissed by government authorities as a native-born American of dubious loyalty. David Thompson, in part because of his suspicious nature and dark personality, chose Pond as his target of blame. Thompson's pen has portrayed Pond as a black hand guiding U.S. diplomats in shaping the Canadian–American boundary west via the Great Lakes to the Lake of the Woods. The idea that Pond was a scapegoat, and that British diplomats had fallen down in boundary negotiations, was not something Thompson could ignore, but he liked to cite that which the celebrated Edmund Burke put on record: "There is a fatality attending all the measures of the British Ministry on the North American Colonies." In every transaction with the United States government concerning matters of territory and boundaries, said Thompson, Canada and British North America always suffered, for their American counterparts outwitted the British diplomats.[4]

Pond is best seen as an outlier, an extraordinary person standing apart from others, a mover and a shaker. Much has been made of the concept of American exceptionalism. Pond fits the concept by virtue of the age in which he lived and the tight and controlled yet expansionistic polity that was New England—specifically, in his case, Connecticut. He came from a nonconformist, dissenting tradition. He was a product of his past but he was hoping to escape its bounds for it offered no excitement for him, no promise. He found both in the West and in the North. "Eighteenth-century Americans," writes historian Jack Sosin, who authored a work recounting British imperial purposes in the Old Northwest at the time Pond made his entry into the fur trade, "were a highly individualistic breed. Jealous of their rights and privileges, but not overly concerned perhaps with their responsibilities, they tended to resent any restrictions imposed on them by a distant government."[5] The love of the wilderness and the freedom of the forest, the opportunities of migration and the prospects of carving out a home on the frontier or of making a living by trading there also fired their concepts of independence and liberty. Many colonists or provincials saw little reason not to exploit the fur trade or not to take lands from the aboriginal people. London stood against them. The imperial program of setting up garrisons, licensing the fur trade, and guarding aboriginal interests impeded the path of the ambitious and independent-minded American settlers and thereby set up tensions between Whitehall and the wilderness. "New Englanders, I have heard it claimed [Robert Rogers is said by his biographer Kenneth Roberts to have stated], are tight-lipped and tight-fisted: as close as the bark on a tree, and cold as a brass doorknob."[6] It was that way with Peter Pond, which helps explain how difficult it is for the biographer to get below the surface of his personality and character. All the same, we follow him by his actions as he moves through time and space.

With characteristic Yankee shrewdness, Pond shifted from the Albany and Detroit trade south and west of Michilimackinac to that of what is now the Canadian West and, later, into the far Northwest. In these later locales he found himself in much richer territory for the fur trade.

There, too, the fruits of exploration offered themselves to a fertile mind, a vigorous body, and a dogged constitution such as he possessed. He took advantage of circumstances that presented themselves. But he had to battle the views of conniving rivals for pre-eminence and fame, and these rivals were prepared to sweep him away by categorizing him as of an old and less scientific breed than they were. It is an old story, and victims stalk the stages of history, reminding us that winners should not always write the great chronicles.

2

Crucible of War

No oil portrait survives to give us even a rosy hint of his appearance. There is not so much as a sketch of the man. Nor did anyone who encountered him have the wit to write down details of his visage or of his stature. Was he nondescript? Perhaps, but if I were asked to draw from my imaginings, and what I know of the details of his remarkable life, what I think Peter Pond looked like, I would say the following. Knowing as I do that his family was English and hailed from East Anglia, I would say that he was of Anglo-Saxon features. Most probably he had light brown, straight hair and a fair complexion, though because of his years out of doors he would have a decidedly weathered countenance. Also, I would say that he was of modest, wiry build. I know him, too, to be a fast runner and to have almost limitless energy. So I do not see him as rotund or overweight but lithe and sinewy. He does not present himself as a genial chap, a "hail fellow well met," but rather the reverse. He is of single mind and purpose, a man of action and determination and of a solitary disposition. He is not shy. Neither is he modest. In fact, he is rather egotistical, something possibly derived from continuing success in the face of adversity. Hesitation is unknown to him. It is this, and his boundless energy and insight into the prospects of an individual empire based on commerce and his own immense labour, that has gained him an ascendancy over his fellow traders, who, because they are also men of action, though of a lesser sort than Pond, are somewhat envious of his capabilities and achievements. He was, in all, a formidable character—ardent, urgent, and imperative—and he was one who ought not to be crossed. Rivals were necessarily on the alert. Pond was to be avoided or given a wide berth, or at least treated with the greatest of care. He could handle himself in a fight, and he was handy with a gun: he had been blessed with good eyesight and quick responses, essentials for being a good shot.

I see him dressed in the garb of his era on the frontier, with a broad-brimmed felt hat, a stained silk scarf around his neck, a shirt and vest beneath, and some sort of military-style cloak with large, bulging pockets. A broad leather belt made by his own hand keeps up his trousers. He sports leather leggings above woollen hose and is shod in stout, supple boots. He has a dagger about his person at all times, and probably a pistol, too. Not far from his reach are his rifle, fowling piece, and ammunition. His satchel holds notebooks, ledgers, scribblers, family letters, correspondence files and works of reference, a bible, writing implements, a telescope, and even a chronometer or other devices of navigation. He carries very little food and probably less drink, for he can get those when required from those with him who do the heavy hauling at his behest. In a small red chest, or cassette, he keeps his other essentials. His seemingly is a charmed life, one that somehow carries him through dangers and difficulties and that in the end gives him legendary status. In his own way, he is an outlier, a person of exceptional capacities.

Born in the Town of Milford, County of New Haven, Connecticut, on 18 January 1740, Peter Pond was the third of eleven children of Peter Pond and Mary Hubbard.[1] He saw himself as a member of the warrior class. He was born, he writes with pride, into a family well known from the fifth generation downward as "all waryers [warriors] Ither by Sea or Land and in Dead [deed] Both."[2] By fifth generation he means that particular one after the arrival of his ancestors in America.

Others have reconstituted his lineage and from it we glean the following highlights.[3] Although the date of the first Pond's arrival in America is not known, it seems likely that he was one of two sons of William Pond, a neighbour of John Winthrop of Groton, Suffolk, England, leader and first governor of the Massachusetts Bay Colony, who arrived with the great fleet of 1630. Within ten years nearly twenty thousand Puritan immigrants were to arrive. Peter Pond's lineage descends from one of William Pond's sons, Samuel, who settled in Windsor, on the Connecticut River, not later than 1642. They had been drawn south from Massachusetts Bay to take advantage of the rich soils of the Connecticut River valley, but from there they had to fight the Dutch and vanquish the Pequot tribe. They were part of the association that formed the Colony of New Haven, a federative ecclesiastical republic, in 1638.

God-fearing and righteous, progressive and commercially minded, and boasting good managerial skills, these religious nonconformists, including the Ponds, were freeborn Englishmen zealously protective of their rights and liberties. These entitlements were private in nature and included the right of association. Many of these immigrants had formed corporations for trade and settlement, such as the Massachusetts Bay Colony, and these were regarded as much like the corporations of the City of London or of Bristol, which were self-governing and self-controlling, though they did not exercise sovereignty. Most of the emigrants to New England were middle-class farmers, tradesmen, and artisans. Independent yeomen and workmen formed the backbone of the community, along with strong and God-fearing women, the goodly portion of whom were raising children. The Puritans put no stigma on manual labour. In a New England town you could readily find a blacksmith, wheelwright, or carpenter, a joiner, tanner, or ironworker, or a spinner, weaver, or other to make things that Virginia, Carolina, or Georgia at that era had to import from the old country.

The Ponds had done well in the New World. Peter Pond's father, also Peter, was a shoe and boot maker, and thus solidly of the artisan class. The shoemaker would have known many if not all of the townsfolk who came to him for his valued services. He was a necessary part of village life, and one wonders if his busy life lent credence to the proverb that a cobbler's children often go barefoot. Making and repairing shoes and boots, then as now, was a whirlwind occupation, meeting the needs of the day as they arose. We can imagine that Peter's father kept a workshop and store, making and selling shoes, boots, and leatherwear. The location was near the village green, and there was a planting lot for growing crops. The clapboard house, typical of this period, would have had high-peaked gables and leaded-glass casement windows. Perhaps there were bedrooms above the shop or in one of those typical extensions added on behind. In the house's architecture as in the village layout, cleanliness was a partner of austerity. Fecundity was also a feature of New England families of those days, and the shoemaker had a very large family. The crowded, boisterous, and hungry household that young Peter grew up in demanded increasing responsibilities for him as eldest son and apprentice to his father.

Connecticut colony law required parents to provide schooling for their children, but this mandatory stricture was only as good as the time and resources the parents had to devote to their offspring. In larger communities, schools were provided by levy. Peter Pond came to possess a rudimentary elementary education, perhaps obtained at home or at the town school. He could read and write but only at a limited level or quality. His spelling was invariably phonetic and erratic, and when we read his text we can hear his nasal speaking tone, typical of New Englanders. We thus have, delightfully, an audio transcript of the colonial tongue of Massachusetts and Connecticut. His narrative retains a characteristic charm because of his quirky spelling (for example, the word "parents" becomes *parans*, and "voyageurs," *voigers*). Nowadays, not surprisingly, scholars of philology and linguistics, especially of colonial American English, rush to study Pond's text and do so with relish. The narrative, at least that part that survives, provides the only insights we have into Pond's early life. What he wrote was entirely autobiographical, a rough memoir written in the less pressing days of retirement.

We can imagine that as a child and youth Peter attended the Congregational church in Milford, now known as First Church, and even now we can see him sitting there, erect in the family pew, flanked by brothers and sisters, all dressed in sombre clothes, as well kitted out on a Sunday as was possible in a cash-strapped family. Among these Congregationalists, scripture offered the guide to everyday life. There would have been a Sunday school for him to attend and the rituals of the Sabbath to observe, too, including quiet Sunday afternoons of prayer, scripture reading, and reflection. It would be stretching it to say that when he grew into a man he was as God-fearing as were so many of the Puritans from whose stock he derived—no evidence survives to support such a view. But, then again, there is no evidence to proclaim him an idolater, drunkard, or heretic. He was not a blasphemer, and no record survives of his use of alcohol.

Milford was typical of the several river towns of Connecticut that were close to the sea, almost overlooking Long Island Sound. The settlement bestrode the Wepawaug River, and a plan of the town that bears the date 1646 shows how house lots were placed so as to take advantage of access to the river and to creeks. Roads and tracks led down to waters where ships and boats could ply. As was familiar in New England, there was a great common, rectangular in shape. Formerly a palisade provided a secure perimeter, while an old fort stood as a guardian to the approach from the sea. Here clapboard-sided houses and shops faced right out on the street. In all it was a tight little community of hardly more than a thousand persons. The population of Milford was solidly of English stock, and the census of 1790 reported 96.2 percent of the people to be English, most by this time of local birth.

Peter Pond and his immediate family were of this born-in-America breed, powerful in their sense of place and virtue, hardened by the seasonal shifts of climate, inured to the wilderness at their back doors, and mindful of the menacing revenge threatened by the vanquished and dispossessed Connecticut Natives, the Pequots, whose military power they had quelled by sword and musket.

In early colonial days, Connecticut society exhibited a close alliance between church and state, the established church being that of the Congregationalists. The theocratic character of the government is revealed in the strict enactments and decisions known as the "Blue Laws"—which included the death penalty for adultery or for conspiring against authorized power, strict observance of the Sabbath, and heavy fines for concealing or entertaining Quakers "or other blasphemous heretics." The governing classes recognized the importance of education, the rights of local government, and the necessity of religious freedom, and the result was rigid adherence to a strict, severe family life. Religious spirit and general moral earnestness were dominant forces in this homogeneous society. In 1661, following the restoration of Charles II, the colony obtained a royal charter; however, given the nature of local government and political order, the colony was virtually independent except in name, and it had the power to choose its own governor. How this unusually favourable charter came to be was on account of the connections that John Winthrop Jr. had at the English court. But there was controversy, because the New Haven Colony, of which Milford was a part, was abolished and made part of the Connecticut Colony. In Milford there was dissatisfaction at this change of arrangements, and a number of people left and founded a new settlement at Newark, New Jersey. Much later, when the revolution against King George III occurred, Connecticut joined the rebel cause without any considerable difficulty, so tightly knit, and already largely independent, was the state-to-be of the new Union.

Connecticut, though not a place of marked agricultural promise except in small holdings, was a place of commercial and industrial innovation, and the peddler sold Connecticut housewares throughout the settled portions of New England and the Atlantic states. The Connecticut Yankee had many skills to go with an inventive mind, and, not least, energy with a purpose. Shipbuilding was a burgeoning economy, and colonial merchants looked outward for trade links and profits, building up credits for the purchase of dry goods and specialty items from Britain. Milford and its surrounding area produced clothing and shoes, while in nearby New Haven cottons, tools, machinery, and firearms were manufactured; throughout Connecticut a great mixed industrial base was being built up, and in Peter Pond's time the foundations of this were very much in evidence.

Five generations had separated young Pond from the transatlantic voyage of his ancestor Samuel Pond. From the beginning of English colonization inland from tidewater, the frontier, with its demanding existence and wars among Native tribes, had shaped the attitudes of his forebears and his contemporaries. Settlement was still largely confined to the coast. But the main wealth of New England was to be made on the sea, in maritime trades.

Trade with the West Indies was the main feature of local prosperity in those years. New England fared well under the protective measures of the Acts of Trade and Navigation—and with the corresponding rise of sugar plantations in the British West Indies. When the New Englanders turned to trade with the French West Indies, for the production of molasses in the British West Indies alone could not keep pace with English demand, the government passed the Molasses Act in 1733, prohibiting English colonies from buying molasses from the French West Indies. This encouraged smuggling. The colonials regarded freedom of trade as a natural liberty or right as Englishmen. They traded with the French and the Spanish as it suited them, mindful that they had to do this by stealth and subterfuge, for the Royal Navy was the enforcer of the Navigation Acts. In their sleek and swift American-built brigs and ketches, sloops and schooners, usually sixty to one hundred tons, New England merchant captains and their crews shipped refuse, or low-grade, cod as food for the slaves working the plantations. They also freighted pickled mackerel, salt beef and pork, vegetables, flour, lumber, staves, and masts, as well as horses needed to work the mills grinding the sugar cane. The vessels made the homeward passage laden with molasses, rum, sugar, coffee, hardwoods, and sometimes, in a pinch, indigo. Much of Connecticut's seaborne trade was coastwise, to Boston or, closer, to New York. In later years, Connecticut ports developed some long-range merchant trades by sea, and nearby Stonington became famous for its seal hunting in the Falkland Islands.

With the sea at his very doorstep, an able-bodied young lad such as Peter Pond might, if the opportunity presented itself, slip away to sea, perhaps joining the Royal Navy or signing on to one of the numerous merchant ships engaged in coastal trading or voyaging to the West Indies. A West Indies voyage might include, in the first instance, St. Eustatius, a Dutch colony and entrepôt, there to gather information as to where the best prices were to be gained for products shipped (and where the best prices might be had for molasses and other products for the homeward leg). Jamaica, understandably, was a choice target for trade, for it was among the largest, but a sailor might well find himself at San Domingo or Hispaniola. Altogether it was an exotic if demanding cruise. Although merchant captains were hard-driving fellows of a ruthless nature, a young hand sailing before the mast (or under the captain's protection) could experience a warmer world in winter than the ice-bound and damp life at home in Milford or some other Connecticut river town. Typically such a cruise would take four or five months, beginning in November.

If the Atlantic and Caribbean offered commercial promise, so did the pull of the frontier. Connecticut towns backed on to seemingly limitless forests. The rivers that ran down to the sea here drained a hinterland, and beyond that again lay the Hudson River, the Mohawk Valley, and the traverse to Lake Ontario. At the back door of Connecticut and to the northwest, therefore, lay the powerful Iroquois nations and also the Roman Catholic heartland, New France, which was under the sovereignty of a hated foreign king. During much of the eighteenth century, Britain and its colonies had been at war with France. The control of Quebec, its agricultural lowlands, but above all its prized fur trade, on which the profits of the communities of Montreal, Trois-Rivières, and the administrative and military town of Quebec turned, offered attractive possibilities. In the continental interior a trader was free from the social restrictions of a New England community. The freedom of the forest alone was enticing, if a living could be made in the fur trade. But the sexual attractions of the country upriver and in the interior beyond the Great Lakes were limitless, for here a trader bearing wealthy commodities and promises of more to come had remarkable influence. This was a time of great change and flux. In all, Peter Pond knew intimately the pull of sea and of frontier, a common feature of Connecticut life. Indeed, his younger brother, Charles, became a sea captain and is noted in Milford history. (It was he who ferried the local militia to New York in August 1776 for the fighting there against King George III's forces, most notably in the Battle of Long

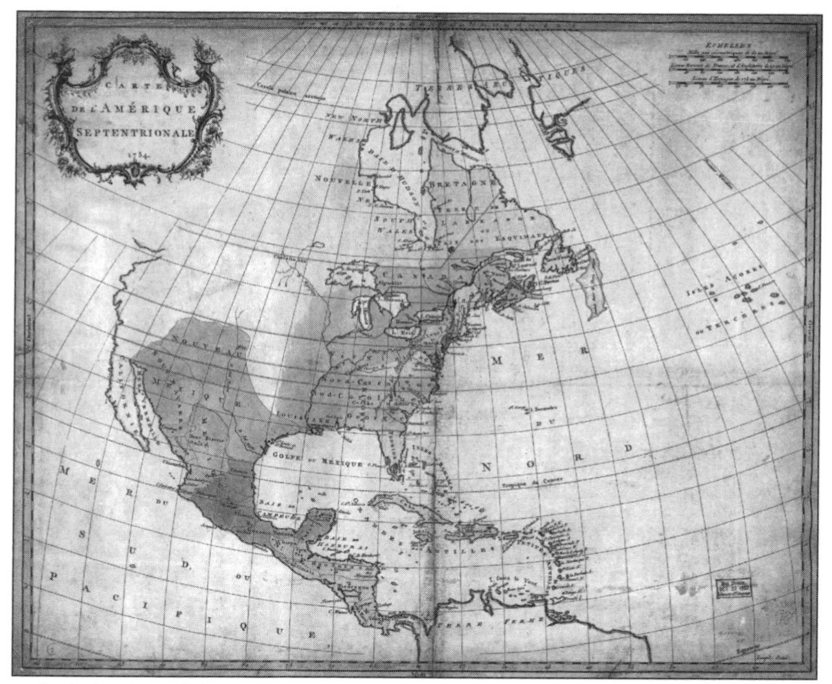

In the mid-eighteenth century, the interior of North America was largely unknown except by occasional traders and travellers. This was the general state of geographical knowledge at the time that Peter Pond, Alexander Henry, Jonathan Carver, and others penetrated the wilderness to reach the interior. They were at the leading edge of fact-finding based on commercial enterprise. Fur traders were the first geographers, though the First Nations already knew the land's secrets. LIBRARY OF CONGRESS, GEOGRAPHY AND MAP DIVISION

Island. More famously, it was Charles Pond who took Nathan Hale across Long Island Sound on his ill-fated espionage expedition.)

At the time of Peter Pond's arrival on the world stage, Britain and colonial America were in the third of four great Anglo-American wars. In 1713, by the Treaty of Utrecht, France had been forced to withdraw from Newfoundland, and in Acadia that country was restricted to Cape Breton Island, with its sedentary fishery. In 1745, when Peter Pond was age five, a great force had been raised in the English colonies in America, principally from the New England colonies led by powerful Massachusetts, the object of which was to take Louisbourg, the French bastion of power, at Cape Breton. That place, founded in 1729 as a marine and fishing base, was a thorn in the side of the Commonwealth of Massachusetts, with its own great coastal maritime interests. The attack and victory were mainly a provincial affair, which not only hardened American colonial hatreds against the French but also built up the military power of the colonial or provincial regiments, including those of Connecticut.

To the shock and anger of the American colonists, Louisbourg had been returned to France at the peace. The government of France was resolved to keep Canada, and the defences of New France were strengthened. Louisbourg was rebuilt. New posts were thrown up so as to secure the water approaches to Montreal, Quebec, Fort Frontenac, and elsewhere. These developments were seen as detrimental to American provincial interests and future expansionist possibilities westward, and it seemed clear that war might resume. All the while the French nurtured their alliance with various tribes, and the gift-giving to the King of France's allies was generous and effective. But those who directed French policy must have wondered how this state of affairs might be sustained, for New France was not self-sufficient and depended on security and supplies that could only come by sea—across the vastness of the Atlantic and by way of the St. Lawrence River to the heartland of the colony. These were the unenviable circumstances facing French imperial statesmen precisely at the time Pond, a bit player in this great war of empire, makes his appearance on the stage of history.

Few young men of his age or station could resist the call to arms, unless they were conscientious objectors, and the king's needs were mighty and also attractive. The French from Canada had built Fort Duquesne at the strategic forks of the Ohio, where the Allegheny joins the Monongahela, and forced the surrender of a small British expedition under Major George Washington at nearby Fort Necessity on 3 July 1754. This was two years before the formal declaration of war in Europe, but here in this backwoods of colonial British America, the French from Canada and the English from Virginia were fighting for control of the rich Ohio Valley. For the next five years—except when winter prevented all but minor skirmishes—the finally decisive struggle between the British and French in North America was waged on three fronts: first, in the west, in the Ohio country and around Lakes Erie and Ontario; second, in the mid-country, where the Hudson–Champlain–Richelieu waterway constituted the so-called great warpath of nations; and, third, in the northeastward approaches to Canada, the Gulf and River St. Lawrence, including Louisbourg and the Chignecto Peninsula.

Pond was not involved at the outset of this undeclared conflict. In July 1755, Major General Edward Braddock, the British commander-in-chief, was ambushed when marching from Fort Cumberland to Fort Duquesne. His larger force was severely mauled by adroit French, Ottawa, and Potawatomi forces that had taken up concealed positions on the flanks of the approaching British. London was hot to avenge Braddock's defeat. Late that year the British attacked but failed to capture Fort St. Frédéric (Crown Point). Only in the low-lying causeway that joins present-day New Brunswick with Nova Scotia did the British succeed; there they took Fort Beauséjour and subsequently expelled the Acadians, who refused to take an oath of allegiance to the Crown.

The next year, 1756, Britain declared war on France. The French army made early gains in America. By late summer the French commander in North America, the Marquis de Montcalm, had captured and destroyed Fort Oswego (Chouaguen) at the southeastern end of Lake Ontario. That trading post had been fortified by the British military in 1724, under concession from the Iroquois. It acted as a counterweight to the French fortification, Fort Niagara, which was built in 1720 at the other end—that is, the western corner—of Lake Ontario. Oswego in British hands had been a thorn in the side of the French, for it allowed furs to be diverted south to New York via the Mohawk and Hudson Rivers. It had disadvantaged the economy of Canada. Now by their military power the French had ended the British threat there. They left Oswego a shadow of its former self. The Iroquois confederacy faced two intruding sovereignties on the south shore of Lake Ontario and was, therefore, the subject of special favour from the two competing powers. Pond was drawn into this particular theatre of the war.

Toward spring of 1756, Connecticut, in answer to the imperial call to arms and also in an act of self-interest that characterized this jurisdiction (for it often excelled itself in comparison to other British colonies in America on the percentage of the male population it could provide the military cause), began to raise provincial troops. The object was to join the British army for the ensuing campaign against Crown Point under the command of General John Winslow, a native of Massachusetts. Patriotic fervour was swelling in the American colonies, especially New England. From time to time, novelist Nathaniel Hawthorne tells us, regimental and militia units paraded through town to raise forces for King George. There were abundant reasons to wage "a just war," said the proponents of same: to fight against the hated Roman Catholic French in the Ohio Valley and their dreaded Native allies in the Old Northwest, and to secure Canada for the British Empire.

The piercing shrill of the fife, the dire thump of the drum, and the fervent appeals of the regimental recruiting sergeant were irresistible to some lads. Peter Pond was one such. In the army he could be expected to be clothed and fed, perhaps better so than in civilian life. How long the call to arms tugged at him we do not know. Military service for a common soldier in a colonial regiment was on a campaign-by-campaign basis, and once one was finished a soldier's pay ended and he would return to winter quarters—his father's door. One authority who knew the Pond family, a Mr. Prudden, also born in Milford, told an inquirer that when the war in America began, one after another of the Pond brothers answered the call to arms. "The [Pond] Boys were all enterprizing, bold & adventurous."[4]

So strong was the propensity for the army, Peter Pond recounts of his own feelings at the time, that he could not withstand its temptations. One evening in April 1756, the drums and instruments of music were employed to such a degree that they charmed him. He repaired to a tavern where mirth and jollity ran high. There he found many lads of his acquaintance who had decided to go into the service. Pond spoke to Captain David Baldwin, the recruiting officer, and then enlisted as a private in the Connecticut Regiment under Baldwin. Pond had defied his parents in one of those familiar tugs-of-war between parents and sons. Peter had told them of his strong desire to be a soldier and of his determination to enlist under officers from Milford. "But they had for bid me and no wonder as my father had a Larg & young famerley I Just Began to be of Sum youse to him in his affairs." However, as Pond writes, he was then age sixteen, apparently an eligible age for him to enlist in the colonial militia. He had the law on his side. To the pull of the old family tradition of being warriors, either by land or by sea, Pond added his own quest for personal independence. "My Parans was so angry that thay for[bid me] making my appearance at Home."

Pond's mother and father must have thought him headstrong as well as selfish, which indeed he was. But it is also true that he was one of countless young Americans who answered the call to arms. He had swapped his old cloth jacket for a dazzling regimental coat, a profitable exchange, Pond thought. Barred from his childhood home, he tarried about the town with his fellow soldiers. Before long it was time to report. Pond recalls that he "came on Smartly," for he had some of his bounty money with him and did not want for ginger bread and small beer. He soon forgot, for it had apparently plagued him, that he had left his parents, who were exceedingly "troubled in mind" for his welfare. Peter Pond, like many before and since, had "gone for a soldier," leaving loved ones behind in a state of anxiety.

In June, Pond and his regimental company embarked at Milford and sailed for New York port, seventy miles distant. From there they proceeded north, up the Hudson River, to a place known as the Half Moon (beyond Albany), where the regiment gathered with others like it. This was the assembly point for a descent on the new, recently erected French stronghold of Fort Carillon, on the rocky Ticonderoga peninsula at the southern end of Lake Champlain. That fort, later known as Ticonderoga, had been built to guard against a British advance on Canada by protecting the famous carrying place between Lake Champlain and Lake George known as The Portage. In the event, the British force in which Pond was engaged was premature in its action: winter intervened, and the regiment was dispersed and went into winter quarters. As poet Robert Frost put it poignantly, home is a place they have to take you in. And so it was that Pond found himself back at hearthside with his parents, brothers, and sisters, in the peace and security of Milford. He was now content to be a bystander, at least for a time.

In 1757, Pond recalls, he tarried at home with his parents, with the benefit that he escaped the misfortune of a number of his countrymen, who were captured when Montcalm came against Fort William Henry and seized it. That was only half the story, as Pond explains, for as the American colonial troops marched to Fort Edward, complying with the terms of surrender, Montcalm's Native allies fell upon them and made "grate Havack."

If 1757 was the year that France made continual successes in North America, the circumstances of the war soon began to change. At the outset of that year's campaign, British fortunes seemed most desperate in consequence of the loss of Fort Oswego and other defeats in America. The French threat had become more material and more menacing to the frontiers of Maine, New Hampshire, Massachusetts, and Connecticut, besides many other provinces and colonies. This was no distant war; it was at the back door of the colonies. While Pond, for reasons unknown, did not enlist but, rather, awaited the next season's campaign, diplomats in Europe sought new allies and pondered diplomatic solutions, invariably dealing with a question of choosing the lesser evil, for not only were North American issues at stake (Acadia's western boundary, control of the St. Lawrence River, and the Ohio country generally) but also a whole mix of concerns involving European security and interests. William Pitt the Elder's rise to political authority at this time brought new zeal to British military planning and effort, with consequences for British military activities in America in which Pond played a part.

Pond takes up the story. In 1758, he recalls, the safety of British America required that a large army should be raised to act with the British troops against Canada. Once again the drum and bugles sounded through the towns and hamlets. Pond found tarrying at home "too inactive a life." He therefore joined many of his old companions a second time under the command of Colonel Nathan Whiting, an experienced and competent frontier fighter. It was a difficult year for raising colonial troops, and the royal province of New York offered larger bounties, drawing off some who would normally join the Connecticut units. Even so, that colony raised five thousand men. Once again the object was to capture Fort Carillon.

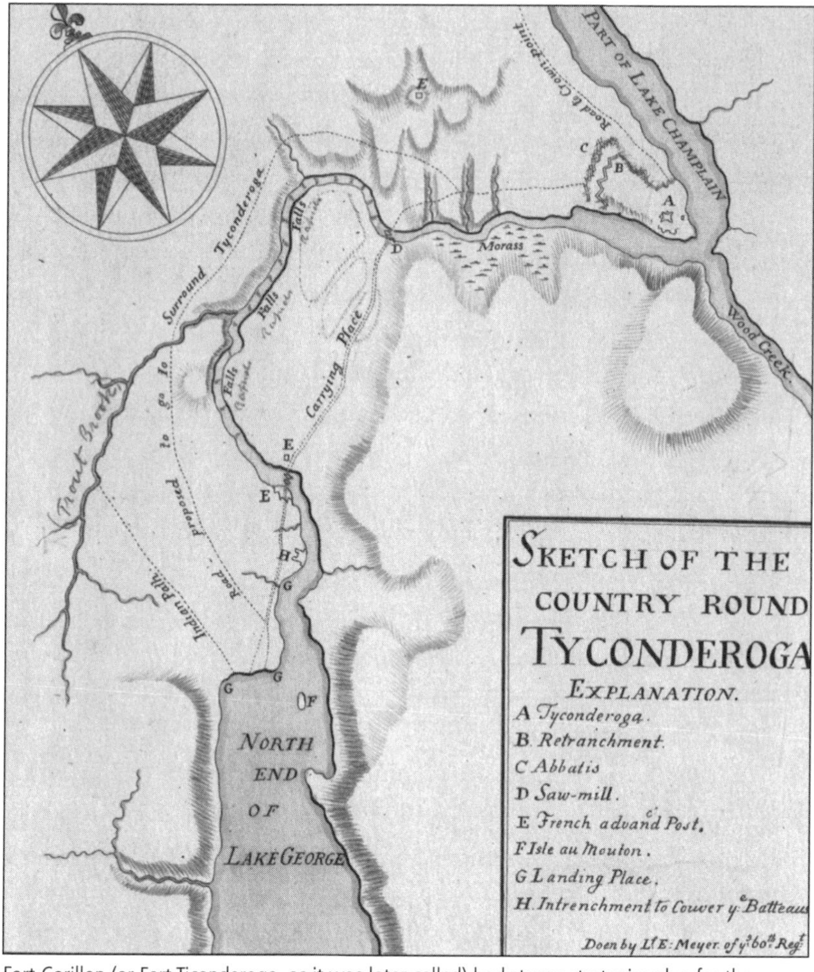

Fort Carillon (or Fort Ticonderoga, as it was later called) had strong strategic value for the military force powerful enough to take and hold it. It was much prized by the French as a means of controlling access to New France and Quebec. It proved a thorn in the side of the British Empire until it was eventually captured as part of the British victory over the French in North America. HARVARD MAP COLLECTION

The British campaign against the fort was an operation of vast scale, as Pond recounts. In the spring his regiment embarked to join the army at Albany, and there they arrived both safely and in timely fashion. The first task was to forward supplies to the place of need. Pond and his regiment were among those employed in the toil of moving provisions to Fort Edward for the use of the service. Fort Edward was at the south end of Lake George. Fort Carillon lay on a rocky neck of land between Lake George and Lake Champlain. The force needed to cross Lake George and then approach Fort Carillon from the landward side. When all was ready for the crossing, the army embarked.

It has been estimated that forces under the Union Jack amounted to fifteen thousand men—six thousand British regulars and nine thousand provincials. They embarked in about 1,200 watercraft, an odd and irregular armada that included whaleboats, floating batteries on rafts, flatboats carrying field pieces, row-galleys (the French called them *radeaux*), and gunboats. It was a massive armada, and a show of force that the numerically disadvantaged French, with a force of somewhat less than four thousand, would have to contend with. This battle pitted two experienced generals against one another: the British general James Abercrombie (or Abercromby) was thought to be a master of organization, and he had assembled a great force; but he also had a reputation for vacillation, and his troops called him Mrs. Nanny Cromby. His opposite, Montcalm, a brilliant tactician, was keen on the advantages of the defence but also, when possible, could take the war to the enemy.

"The next day we arrived at the north end of Lake George and landed without opposition," Pond recalls. The French who had been encamped at that end of the lake fled at the appearance of the British, falling as far back as Fort Carillon. There they joined their commander, Montcalm. Fort Carillon's defences were in a state of disrepair, and in consequence he devised a system of defence designed to confuse and trap the enemy. Montcalm dispatched five hundred soldiers to oppose the landing or at least obstruct the British and Americans in their march so that "he might put his camp in some sort of defense," as Pond writes, before the army could fall upon it—and his men succeeded most completely in a perfect execution of orders. Unaware of what lay before them, the British drew themselves up in order, Pond says. They were divided into columns and then ordered to march toward Montcalm and the fort.

Pond states that the British force, regulars and provincials, had marched no more than a mile and a half before they met the forlorn hope, "for such it proved to be." The British regulars kept to the road in one column; the Americans marched through the woods on their left; and to the right of the British flowed the La Chute River, which empties from Lake George into Lake Champlain. The British stumbled into the French force of five hundred. They were taken by surprise because of the unevenness of the ground and the fact that the enemy could not easily be seen in the distance.

According to Pond, Lord William Howe held the second place in command, and being at the head of the British troops with a small sidearm in his hand, he ordered the troops to form a line to the left to attack the French. While this was in process, the French opened fire and his Lordship received a ball and three buckshot through the centre of his breast. He "expired without spekeing a word." Thus died the young Howe, a field officer much loved by those serving under him, and an experienced wilderness fighter who had got caught in the crossfire of the moment. His death was greatly regretted, and he is memorialized in Westminster Abbey.

"The french pade dear for this bold attempt," Pond writes, and in a short time they found themselves surrounded by the whole of the American provincial troops. In dire straits, those that did not leap into the rapid stream in order to regain their camp were made prisoners or killed, and those that did were pulled down by the rapid current and drowned. According to the best information Pond could gather from French informants he quizzed on this matter, only seven of the five hundred French escaped.

Misfortune now befell Abercrombie's Army. In the course of chasing the French through the woods, the Americans also became so dispersed they could not find their way back to their boats at the landing in order to regroup. Darkness came on all too suddenly, and a large party of Americans spent the night in the woods, barely half a mile from the enemy lines, without knowing where they were until morning. Pond was not in that party. Rather, with about twelve men of his acquaintance, he had wandered in the woods before finally coming upon the road about a mile north of where the first shot had been fired. The road provided an easy path toward the boats but, it still being dark, the soldiers made a stumbling business of it, tripping on dead bodies that were strewn thickly on the ground for some distance. At length Pond and the others got to waterside just before the break of day. Whatever could be found of the troops was assembled and brought into a semblance of order, and they set off once again, marching to the same rapid stream and crossing it, leaving it now on their left. The road on that side was good, the going easy, and ed toward the French camp to a distance of one mile. There the night lying on their muskets.

while, the delay in attack had given Montcalm time to secure , a measure Pond describes as well executed. The next day the ere prepared to mount an attack, and at about eleven o'clock in the morning the army was set in motion, the regulars leading. They were drawn up before the hastily erected but strong breastwork, in such a crowded space that the 4,500 of them had no room for easy manoeuvring. They were now enveloped in what might be described as a spider's web, and to this was added a lack of artillery, for although the army had lots of field pieces, none had been brought up to this site. The job was left for infantry, unassisted by cannon or cavalry. The British regulars, with bayonets fixed, intended to march over the defence emplacement—that was the well-intentioned plan. But the French, in frantic preparation, had cut down a great number of pines in front of their camp, giving themselves an open field of fire. While some of the French had been entrenching, others had been cutting off the limbs of trees and sharpening them at both ends for what is called a *cheval de frise*; still others were cutting large logs and hauling them to make the massive breastworks. At length they were ready for our reception, says Pond sardonically. And what a reception it proved to be. Thomas Jeffery's map of the town and fort of Carillon shows the Connecticut and New Jersey troops forming the rearguard behind British line regiments disposed before the attack was made on the retrenchments that Montcalm had built on the heights west of Carillon.

About noon on 8 July 1758 the parties began firing, and the British began to march, with bayonets fixed, over the breastworks. But the limbs and treetops were stuck hard in the ground, creating a fearsome obstacle that the British could not penetrate. Tree trunks, piled to a height of eight feet, impeded their progress, and Pond says that "three forths" of the regulars were killed in the attempt. Meanwhile, the greater part of the army lay in the rear, "on their faces," until nightfall, while the British continued to batter at the makeshift breastwork that in places was nine logs thick. This was done while the artillery, as fine as could be expected in an army of fifteen thousand men, says Pond, stood idly by. At sunset, Abercrombie came from left to right at the rear of the troops and, having had enough, ordered them to beat a retreat. This was effected, leaving about 1,900 killed, wounded, or missing. The enormity of the event began to sink in.

One of the greatest armies ever assembled in North America had been destroyed.

The men were ordered to return to the boats. This was done, but only after travelling all night, and so slowly, says Pond, that they fell asleep by the wayside. About nine or ten in the morning came the order to embark. The result was a scene of confusion. The soldiers could not find their own boats and, expecting the French at their heels any moment, grabbed the first available watercraft. They crossed the lake to the head of Lake George unopposed. In a short time all were back at the encampment, which was well fortified. For a while they were safe from the French and from any Native Americans rumoured to be in the area. But all that summer and well into late fall—indeed, until the army broke up and the provincials returned to their respective colonies—the French harried the lines of supply to Fort Edward, cutting off hauling teams, destroying provisions, and killing the work parties and their escorts.

This battle—Carillon as it is now known (though Pond refers to it as Ticonderoga, for that, to repeat, was the name later given to the fort)—was one of the bloodiest battles of this American war and one of the key events of the Seven Years' War. Connecticut troops under Major General Lyman had carried on with great credit. They were prepared to entrench and to fight on. But that was not the British general's plan. Pond never suffered fools gladly and he does not hold back his disgust at the outcome: "Thus ended the most ridicklas campane eaver hard of." As for Abercrombie, he retired to Britain and later became a Member of Parliament who supported a coercive policy toward the revolting American colonies. History has not been kind to him, but some of the blame must go to engineers who advised him before the assault on Carillon that French defences were not as strong as they proved to be.[5]

Elsewhere that year—and farther west—the British destroyed Fort Frontenac (present-day Kingston, Ontario), forced the French to evacuate Fort Duquesne (Pittsburgh), and took Louisbourg fortress in Cape Breton, under the command of Brigadier General Jeffrey Amherst, General James Wolfe, and Admiral Edward Boscawen. The tide was beginning to flow in favour of the British and the American colonials.

On 17 April 1759 Pond enlisted yet again, this time as a sergeant, giving his occupation as shoemaker. He joined the Suffolk County Regiment of the New York Provincial Army at Long Island, New

York, part of an army raised to attack Fort Niagara, near present-day Youngstown, New York. All in that unit were volunteers. The force also included two regular regiments and the Royal Americans. Commanding this expedition was Brigadier General John Prideaux, an able and experienced officer fresh from European campaigns.[6] Pond suited up in the yellow drab jacket and natural leather belt of the New York Provincials, and wore a hat with a brim cut down to two and a half inches and no longer "cocked." This was the new style. He was about to be engaged in the final decisive struggle in the west.

A great shift had occurred in British diplomacy with the various Native nations, and the tribes' old alliance with the French was tottering and soon to collapse. In 1758, at Easton, the British had made a treaty with certain tribes whereby Pennsylvania's governor promised to restrain settlements in Indian territory (a forerunner of the Proclamation of 1763), and the western Delawares contentedly went home with agreements for their own council to ratify. French forces having withdrawn from the defence of Fort Duquesne, that place soon fell to British arms. The conquerors renamed it Fort Pitt, after the great British minister of war who was directing military and naval affairs from London. Added to this was the reintroduction of the covenant chain, an expression of peace and alliance between the Six Nations of the Iroquois and the British. The chain had been broken in the early 1750s, but its repair was now encouraged by Colonel Sir William Johnson. The Iroquois responded in such a way that Johnson concluded—not without reason, for he was a tangible factor in the whole enterprise of making and keeping Native alliances—that the Six Nations would make no military alliance with the French. It is the view of historian William Fenton, acknowledged authority on Iroquois history, that Johnson had remade the confederacy; certainly he had shifted its alliance away from the French, and now it was about to tip in the direction of the British.[7] Other Native nations, always acting in their own interest, were re-evaluating their military alliance with the French—deciding in some cases to remain neutral, and in others determining to back the British cause, which seemed to most benefit their own cause and their people. Johnson, helped by Seneca and Shawnee warriors, and aided also by Onondaga diplomacy, now put in place the last stroke of the war for victory in the west. A major amphibious operation was planned to oust the French from Fort Niagara, their only remaining western stronghold of any prominence.[8]

By now the force in which Pond served had ascended the upper Hudson River to Albany and Fort Schenectady; marched or voyaged by boat, barge, or canoe on the Mohawk River to the Great Carrying Place, where they crossed to Oneida Lake; then continued down the Oneida River to Oswego on Lake Ontario. That locale, as noted, had been destroyed by the French three years previous. The force of about 3,500 men reached Oswego with little opposition on 27 June. A thousand men were left to refurbish the fort and fortifications. Amherst planned to put up a royal dockyard there and build two sloops for operations on Lake Ontario so as to acquire command of the lake and then advance, when the right moment presented itself, on Montreal. Prideaux's force, meanwhile, would advance along that same shore at the west end of Lake Ontario where the Niagara River joins the lake.

A key personality at this turn of events was Colonel Sir William Johnson, second in command to Prideaux. Johnson, the seasoned British authority who ran the Superintendency of the Six Nations, was an Irishman by birth. His ambition was only matched by his high-minded view of himself, and seldom has an individual exhibited such power in such a vast wilderness inhabited by tribes. By moral suasion and shrewd diplomacy he held the tenuous British control of western New York, northern Pennsylvania, and eastern Ohio. He was the Crown's man on the frontier. Many years of diplomacy with the Delawares, Iroquois, and others had given him a self-interested position—he was a man who stood between two worlds, and he liked it that way. He inhabited an ambiguous space, knowing full well that it benefited British policy to

Sir William Johnson, the Irish-born superintendent of Indian affairs, built up an empire that grew wealthy in land and trade. He helped cement the Iroquois nations as British allies in the Seven Years' War. Pond was with him at the taking of Fort Niagara. COURTESY OF THE LIBRARY OF CONGRESS, LC-USZ62-2695

keep the various tribes, Iroquois and other, in an alliance, but not so close an alliance as to eradicate internecine rivalries. He might be described as a fixer. He was responsible for remaking the pan-Indian alliance but, again, ensuring it worked on the maxim of divide and rule. His headquarters was Johnstown in the Mohawk Valley, one of the heartlands of the Iroquoian kingdom, which lay west of the New York colonial capital, Albany, and south of the New France trading base, Montreal. For the current campaign, Johnson had brought a large body of armed Iroquois warriors—estimated to be as many as 600—up from Fort Stanwix on the Mohawk River to Fort Oswego. With them were 2,300 troops, 100 officers, and a detachment of artillery.[9] Johnson, using Senecas as informants, provided Amherst with critically important military intelligence.

Fort Niagara presented a formidable object to an attacking force: it was a stone fortification, rare in this regard (built in 1725 by order of the King of France). A young French military engineer of immense talents, Captain the Chevalier Pierre Pouchot, had arrived with orders in early 1759 to strengthen the fort and make ready for its defence. To his way of thinking, a view sustained by subsequent events, the enemy would attack from the east, for water approaches from the lake or the river could be easily countered. Thus he arranged for a fortification exactly suited to its geographical requirements, triangular in shape and bounded on two sides by the waters of the Niagara River and Lake Ontario.[10] It stood on an imposing, commanding site, with good visibility and a range of fire that could seemingly protect it on all sides. On the landward ramparts, a moat and earthworks had been thrown up to guard against any sudden approach or even a determined attack. Now, in late June, Captain Pouchot readied his men, 515 troops and some Ottawas, for attack. He knew that he could not hold out forever against a determined siege by the enemy, so he sent urgently to various distant forts—Detroit, Presque Isle, and Le Boeuf—for reinforcements.

Amherst's "Enterprise against Niagara," as he himself styled it, called for an overland expedition from the Mohawk Valley and a coordinated coastwise amphibious operation from Oswego. At Fort Oswego, Colonel John Johnston of the New York Provincials singled out Pond to be with him as they coasted along the shore, past where Rochester is today, to near Niagara. On 1 July the armada of boats and bateaux (they were all specifically numbered and had formed up in precise order) left

Oswego, favoured with calm weather and convoyed by British warships. It arrived at Four Mile Creek (Johnson's Landing, Pond calls it), four miles from Fort Niagara, on 6 July in the evening, and all landed and deployed in readiness. The British had planned to attack Fort Niagara on the 7th, but unexpected accidents led to delays.

Pond answered directly to an Orderly Sergeant named Bull. "I was kept so close to my dutey that I got neither sleape nor rest for the armey was down at Johnsons landing four miles from the acting part of the armey. I was forced to run back and forth four miles nite and day til I could not sarve eney longer. I sent to Mr. Bull to releave me by sending another sargint in my plase which was dun and I gind my friends agane and fought in the trenches aganst the fort." Pond was a small actor on a very large stage, and the memory of what had happened to the defeated British soldiers, wives, and children at the hands of Natives at Fort William Henry in 1757 would have been clear in his mind, as it was for all who prepared to attack the French in their far western fastness.

The attackers, under cover of artillery fire, dug a long zigzag trench running parallel to the eastern flank of Fort Niagara. Each day the range closed between the advancing British guns and the fort's artillery, and on the 19th the British opened their relentless bombardment. Under cover of this fire, pickets advanced to support the trenches, taking gabions and fascines to line trenches, fill ditches, and carry out other military engineering purposes. There was much grumbling about the poor trench engineering, and officers had orders to command the working parties and see that the work was done correctly. Gradually the batteries were moved forward, closing the range on the French, and by the 23rd an eight-gun battery "played with considerable success" within 150 yards of the fort, according to Sir William Johnson. All this time the British and New York regiments formed up in lines in the rear, near their camps, with men sent ahead to do the trenching and related work.

It was during this stage that Mr. Bull sent Pond to attend General Prideaux. For a time Pond was privy to the general's movements and to the messages that he sent or received. He may also have witnessed the general's death. The fellow was unfortunate, Pond says in reference to the British commander: in fact, on the 20th, General Prideaux was killed instantly by a fragment of an English shell that burst prematurely as it left the coehorn, the small field gun. That same day saw other mortal losses: Colonel John

Johnston—"my friend," Pond calls him—died in the trenches, shot through the leg by a musket ball, and Lieutenant Colonel Michael Thodey of the New York Regiment of Provincials was also killed. The loss of three brave officers in one day was a great one to "our small armey," notes Pond. "I was faverd—I got but one slite wound dureing the seage."[11] As was so often the case during his life, Pond was blessed by good fortune, and he was aware of the fact.

The spirited siege was kept up under Sir William Johnson, who assumed command upon Prideaux's death. On 24 July a body of French and Indians, about 1,200 in total, hastening to the defence of Fort Niagara at the urgent order of Pouchot, made their appearance. They attacked the British outside the fort, but the British gave them a warm reception and entirely defeated them. Thus, at the end of twenty-five days, the fort capitulated, and the French garrison left it with the honours of war, laying down their arms on the beach, where they were to embark in boats for Schenectady under escort. The prisoners were sent to New York, then to England and France.

The British campaign for Niagara ended triumphantly, with the western rim of empire secured, at least temporarily. Johnson rightly worried that without a proper naval presence, Fort Niagara in British hands could be subject to attack from French naval forces, then known to be superior on the lake. He set about building a few gun-carrying vessels and made two others found at Niagara into serviceable gunboats.

From Fort Niagara, Pond returned with his regiment to Oswego. Now, with the ring tightening around Montreal, it was time to make ready a huge camp to hold about ten thousand troops that would assemble there before the assault on that sole remaining French stronghold. As the officer commanding, General Amherst never did things by halves: he preferred the large battalions and a good fleet to carry them. At Oswego, Pond helped to rebuild the old Fort Ontario, nearby. But winter was fast approaching, and Pond (and others of his kind) returned home for the season. The shipbuilders were left to do their work, constructing a sizeable armada that would not only remove French naval power on Lake Ontario but also proceed downriver from Oswego, overcome any resistance met along the way, and then, in combination with other forces, take Montreal. That was the British plan for the next season's campaign.

Pond passed the winter of 1759–60 quietly in Milford, where a number of French prisoners were billeted. It was probably at this time that he learned French. In early 1760 he entered the army for the fourth time. He received a commission in the New York Provincial Army and was made ensign. His days as a lowly private, corporal, and sergeant were over. He now donned the red regimental coat of all officers, with blue or green facings and gold lace—and looked very much a British regular officer, except that his belt was of natural-coloured leather.

He went first to Albany, and then west to Oswego to join Amherst, commander-in-chief, who himself had come up via the Mohawk River. At Oswego in July the army gathered preparatory to its movement down the St. Lawrence River to Montreal.[12] Amherst's army consisted of no less than 10,142 men—more than half a division by World War I terms—including two battalions of the famous Black Watch (Royal Highland Regiment), plus 700 Native warriors under Johnson.[13] Pond's regiment was selected to guard General Amherst and work in close cooperation with him.

By 10 August the great armada was proud upon the water. It presented a spectacular sight to an observer standing on the shore of eastern Lake Ontario—a colourful concentration of military might, all afloat and in motion, its destination known to all, for no other ultimate prize presented itself except Montreal, last holdout of French ascendancy in America. Three schooners, including the flagship *Onondaga* (22 guns), formed the central firepower of this vast and colourful flotilla, accompanied by five shallow-draft row-galleys or gunboats and myriad bateaux and whaleboats, all carrying troops and their implements of war. The gunboats pressed ahead to identify safe channels, and the heavily gunned ships followed in their wakes. By the 15th the armada had reached La Présentation, a mission otherwise known as Oswegatchie, or La Galette, near present-day Ogdensburg. Amherst sent five gunboats to capture the French armed brig *Outaouaise*, which posed a danger to Amherst's bateaux and whaleboats. In doing so, the British vessels took some heavy firing from the French guns afloat and ashore. But for unexplained reasons the French brig struck the colours, and before long the British had run up the Union Flag.

Near the head of the rapids, the armada came to a mid-channel post called Fort Lévis, on Île Royale (now Galop Island), east of Prescott, Ontario, commanded by none other than the military engineer the Chevalier Pouchot, late commandant at Niagara, who after having been made a prisoner there had been exchanged. Pouchot had come to Fort Lévis the previous March and had busied himself in boosting its fortifications in preparation for the attack he knew would come. He was ready for the British armada that descended upon the island, and the French gunners acquitted themselves brilliantly, doing a good deal of damage to British vessels. But time was against him, and although his garrison put up stiff resistance, it eventually succumbed on 25 August. Pouchot had been taken twice within the year. The British vessels parading past saluted the vanquished Chevalier, whose military career was all but over. He retired to Corsica to live out his last days.

"Now began the critical part of the expedition, the descent of the rapids," writes historian Francis Parkman, who was describing a chapter of what might be called white-water warfare. "The Galops, the Rapide Plat, the Long Saut, the Côteau du Lac were passed in succession, with little loss, till they reached the Cedars, the Buisson, and the Cascades, where the reckless surges dashed and bounded in the sun, beautiful and terrible as young tigers at bay."[14] Boat after boat coursed through this cascade, and many were broken up completely or otherwise damaged. The human toll was gruesome: eighty-four men were lost to the dangerous rapids. Eventually the flotilla, or what remained, reached the placid waters of Lac St. Louis and took refuge at Île Perrot.

The next morning, 6 September, back in the boats, the force descended on Montreal and landed unopposed at Lachine, nine miles from the city.[15] About the same time, two other British armies, one from downriver at Quebec and another from Lake Champlain, marched on Montreal, a combined host of seventeen thousand men. Against them, and behind Montreal's walls, was the remaining French force in Canada, numbering about 2,200 regulars plus some colonial forces. The epic struggle for the control of North America, which had pitted British and French forces against one another, was about to end.

Amherst's opposite was the Marquis de Vaudreuil, the Canadian-born governor of New France. The game was up, and Vaudreuil knew it, though he fought hard to defend French civil and religious rights he feared might soon disappear. Amherst's response to the demands of his opposite was that they become subjects of the British king and be at his pleasure.

Pond witnessed Montreal's surrender on 8 September 1760, when the final capitulation of New France took place. Another observer, Major Robert Rogers of the Rangers, gave an appreciation of the significance of the victory: he said it was "a conquest perhaps of the greatest importance that is to be met with in the British annals, whether we consider the prodigious extent of the country we are hereby made masters of, the vast addition it must make to trade and navigation,...the security it must afford to the northern provinces of America,...the irretrievable loss France sustains hereby, and the importance it must give the British crown among the several states of Europe."[16]

The fall of French Canada marked a decisive turning point in young Pond's life. He expressed not a whiff of puffed-up enthusiasm for the imperial acquisition: to him it was a military campaign brought to a successful conclusion after seven long years. "All Cannaday subdued," Pond writes laconically of the conquest and the end of French power there. "I thought thare was no bisnes left for me." Indeed, a colonial militiaman, even one holding a commission, would not likely be employed in the garrison and the military regime that had been put in place by the British Crown. In any event, he was far too restless for such an assignment. He had not yet taken up any private commercial pursuit, so once again he found himself back home in Milford for the winter, apparently to resume his connections with his family.

But shoemaking offered too parochial a pursuit for this bold adventurer. In 1761 he therefore turned his attention to seafaring, thinking to make it his profession. He sailed, presumably from a Connecticut port, on a voyage to the West Indies. At the end of this voyage, on his return to Milford, he discovered that his mother, age thirty-seven, had died of a fever on 16 June 1761. He also learned, perhaps to his surprise (though he gives no hint of it), that his father had gone to Detroit on a fur trading venture—we know nothing of the details of this or any other connections in the trade. Some of his brothers, who like him had become acquainted with the wilderness and the fur trade during the war, had also taken up this occupation, trading from Albany and supplied out of New York. These seem to have been summer trading voyages, on circuit, as it were, with winters spent in Milford.[17] Fur trading seems to have become a family line of work.

All of this left the family in a desperate condition. Not knowing if or when his father would return, Pond gave up seafaring, took charge of the numerous children, and stayed in Milford for three years. He writes, in rather typical if complicated fashion, that "I bent my mind after differant objects and tared [tarried] in Milford three years." He says nothing about his marriage, but we know that he was joined in wedlock, probably in 1762, to Susanna Newell, by whom he had at least two children. These years in Milford, he later wrote, were the longest time between the ages of sixteen and sixty that he stayed in one place.

How it came to be that he, like his father, entered into the fur trade is not specified. But the lure of the western wilderness, recounted in the next chapter, proved irresistible. It clearly suited the likes of Pond, a young man, a former soldier in the King's service, a seasoned mariner capable of sailing inland seas such as the Great Lakes, a self-reliant fellow with an adventurous, even all-consuming disposition bent on making a career for himself. He now entered a world of commercial hard knocks, of unremitting toil, and of near and present dangers. But it was also a world being transformed by a British policy that regulated the fur trade with the tribes, garrisoned the key posts, protected aboriginal title to land, and offered the first faint measures of justice and law. Here was a forerunner of Canadian dominion. The evolution of this policy marched hand in hand with Pond's western progression, and to this we now necessarily turn.

3

Wilderness Tangles: Robert Rogers, Jonathan Carver, and the Northwest Passage

To the victor go the spoils, and so it was for the British after the conquest of Quebec and its subsequent capitulation. The British gave a new name to New France: the Province of Quebec. This jurisdiction, so different in its populace and its institutions from the American colonies, now lay uniquely under British military control, with General Jeffrey Amherst the all-powerful governor and commander-in-chief. A new order was instituted, but in many ways it followed older patterns of French administration and control.

The French fur trade inherited by the British was of inestimable value, the lifeblood of the colony and its principal means of revenue and trade. The war had not been fought in America for the fruits of the fur trade, but rather to provide security to the northern British colonies, especially Massachusetts, whose governor, Thomas Hutchinson, had championed the cause, proclaiming that the American colonies could never be secure as long as France held Canada. However, in subduing Canada, to employ Pond's description of the crushing defeat of French arms in North America, the British had inadvertently subverted the special place that the tribes had so long maintained as allies of the King of France. Security, commerce, and missionary endeavour all lay at the root of this alliance, but now its time had run out.

The early trade for fancy furs prized for beauty, warmth, and lustre had drawn the French farther west. Native peoples acted as middlemen, with a continuous and growing demand for European goods. Beaver was their currency of exchange. Intertribal friction accompanied the extension of the fur trade north and west across the continent. But the farther west the trade, the greater the cost of, and the more difficult, the transportation. The waterways of Canada offered no easy avenue of riverine commerce. Numerous portages of difficult character required transshipment—and the light canoes plus brawny backs to carry the cargoes inward and outbound.

The rivalry among traders induced a trend toward monopolistic control and the combining of goods, risks, and profits. The Dutch aided the Iroquois on the southern frontier at Albany and west toward Niagara, deflecting the French and Huron north. On the Ottawa and French Rivers and the North Channel toward Michilimackinac or to Sault Ste. Marie and up to Lake Superior, the Ottawa became middlemen, familiar with routes and canoes. In 1670 the English established the Hudson's Bay Company (of which more presently), and this provided an easier sea route to Europe. Always the St. Lawrence River system posed problems of easy trade access and communication. Canals could be built and were, but on the southern margin, where the English supplanted the Dutch in 1664, cheaper English goods favoured the advancement of trade with the Iroquois.

The French built Fort Frontenac (Kingston) in 1673, Niagara (1679), and Detroit (1686); farther west, in the next century, they threw up a fort on the Wabash designed to maintain their trade in the Mississippi region; in the 1720s they erected posts and depots at Sault Ste. Marie and Kaministiqua (later Fort William).They were now at the gateway to the fabulous, high-quality-fur-producing area of the northwest. La Vérendrye systematically opened up the interior west of Lake Superior by establishing forts at Rainy Lake, Lake of the Woods, and then on the Red and Assiniboine Rivers. He even went as far north as

The Methye Portage, or Portage La Loche, the passage between waters flowing eastward and those flowing to the western Arctic, was a back-breaking crossing between watersheds. This was a grand theatre of nature. Pond was the first to exploit the rich fur lands to the north, leading an expedition to set up the first post on Athabasca River. New dreams of empire were soon set in motion. LIBRARY AND ARCHIVES CANADA, ACC. NO. 1955-102-25

Cedar Lake, near the mouth of the Saskatchewan River, all the while improving the canoe routes so that larger canoes could be used. Once again the quality of furs coming out of this area increased because the higher transportation costs meant traders discriminated in their selection of furs, accepting only the best.

With this western expansion came governmental control: individual traders were licensed and trading posts were leased to the highest bidder. The greatest freedoms were granted to the individual traders who went into the interior, for here their costs, and their risks, were highest. Their reputations reached celebrated status, and they earned the respect of their rivals. The alliance of French traders with First Nations was backed by the goodwill of the French Crown and the colonial administration at Quebec. Far from being a laissez-faire, free-trade arrangement, it was actually a well-regulated and systematically developed scheme of commerce beneficial to all participants, not least the First Nations, who were the key to its strength and their prosperity. They also, understandably, had been central to French resistance to the British Empire in North America.

When the British took Canada, they did not act as revolutionaries.

They tended to leave well enough alone, granting the conquered people their essential liberties. But in one way the new colonial administration differed from its French predecessor. Amherst was the new Caesar. He did not share the altruistic and paternalistic position of some of his officers, or indeed of statesmen at home, who saw the Native tribes as trusted allies. He did not understand the ancient system of exchange of goods and services that tied the centre to the periphery and crossed many cultural divides. From experience in the field commanding, he had always regarded the Native peoples of North America as a menace and allies of uncertain value, and this had a profound impact on the immediate post-war settlement. He thought like an accountant, too. Against all warnings, including those of Sir William Johnson, he put in place what he regarded as reforms in the administration of Native peoples, which though driven by imperial policies of budget tightening, fiscal economy, and retrenchment, represented his understanding that conquerors had full powers over the tribes who had backed the failed French war cause.[1] So began implementation of a fateful policy.

Amherst decided to eliminate the use of presents, which had always served as tokens of friendship and an invitation to exchange. Native–European alliances, we now know, were not predicated merely on trade goods and gift exchange but on the ceremony and ritual that always preceded such exchanges. One familiar example is provided by *wampum*, the discoidal and later cylindrical beads fashioned from white and purple shells of coastal waters. A Native wampum industry arose at Long Island, and by the mid-seventeenth century valuable wampum and wampum belts, or collars, became not only the means of peace and exchange between and among tribes but also the magnet that drew furs from the forest. The beads and belts carried symbolic meaning and acquired historic value, and in Native hands the ritual handling of wampum strings developed into an art form. All who treated with the Native peoples and advanced proposals with wampum belts had to be conversant with the protocols of presentation.[2] The belts were central to "the covenant chain," the grand alliance between participating Native nations and the King of Great Britain. However, the proffered wampum belts that promised good conduct would not suffice everywhere. Those who engaged in trade also needed to bear gifts. Even trifles would do to start a fair exchange.

Thus, when British Indian agents called a great council at Detroit in

1761 to guarantee that the Native peoples could keep their lands, free from settlers' encroachments, they were at a disadvantage. This promise, without the accompanying presents, was not enough to keep the peace and promote the alliance. The absence of presents demonstrated British failure.

There were similar problems when British traders began to press into the old realm of the French western trade even before Canada came under British sovereignty in the Treaty of Paris, 1763. In the fall of 1761 a trader from Montreal, James Stanley Goddard, and another from Albany, known only as McKay, opened British trade at Green Bay, on the distant, western shore of Lake Michigan, about 450 miles from Michilimackinac. They arrived with Lieutenant James Gorrell of the British army, sent to be commander of the Green Bay post, the newly named Fort Edward Augustus. Already, British Indian agents had worked hard to build up a trade based on friendship with the tribes. But to the disappointment of their Native trading partners, the traders arrived empty handed, without the presents, the necessary overture to trade and even friendship, the tribes had so eagerly expected. Amherst's policy was misguided, and for the moment the fur trade suffered. As Alexander Henry, the famous trader from New Jersey (whom we meet more thoroughly later), noted at Chequamegon Bay, in 1765 the people were destitute, "almost naked," for lack of the accustomed supplies.[3] Pontiac, the Ottawa chief, led a rebellion at Detroit in 1763, in part because of Amherst's policy, and he has survived in history and legend.

Once the disaffection caused by Pontiac's rebellion ended, in 1765, the Native alliance had to be rebuilt, old French posts reoccupied, the British military presence increased, and trade gifts ("the milk" of British imperial policy) and goods (guns, ammunition, knives, rum, and tobacco) made more available. Amherst's policy was abandoned and a new surge of commerce occurred.

Even during this fluid state of affairs, the importance of the fur trade is clearly indicated by trade statistics of the United Kingdom, which show the rapid increase in furs imported into Britain after the fall of New France. Imports for the year 1761 were double those of 1760, and those of 1762 showed an even greater increase in volume over those of 1761. Most of the furs came from the Province of Quebec: of the 173,586 beaver pelts imported in 1762, 93,630 came from Quebec, compared with 50,499 from Hudson Bay and 14,912 from New York.[4] The conquest of Canada gave Britain complete control of the fur trade; this constituted one of the chief commercial consequences of the war (another was the addition to the British Empire of more of the sugar-producing islands in the Caribbean). The Board of Trade, which regulated all trade and commerce of the empire, and the British government of the day were keen to include the newly conquered territory in the commercial policies of the British Empire. Accordingly, in 1761, the Board of Trade recommended that Canada be placed within such regulation, and the King, speaking in Parliament on 9 March 1761, acknowledged this policy when he noted that the conquest was "of the utmost importance to the security of our colonies in North America, and to the extension of commerce and navigation of my subjects." The government, under pressure from the Hudson's Bay Company to maximize its interest in the fur trade, wiggled out of difficulty by making the fur trade of Canada an administrative appendage of the Province of Quebec, in effect extending the old system of New France. The Board of Trade further recommended the proclaiming of an Indian territory, an area reserved for aboriginal people, but in which any trader who possessed a licence issued by the Crown could trade.

All of this formed the background to the now famous Proclamation of 7 October 1763, which defined the enlarged boundaries of the Province of Quebec and made the Indian Territory administratively attendant to it (the latter a radical measure repugnant to the Thirteen Colonies). Some First Nations came to regard this proclamation as their Magna Carta; they saw it as recognition of their existence and affirmation of their title to land. From this, all sorts of difficulties would develop with the old American colonies as it hampered their ability to extend their westward boundaries. But also of great difficulty for the future was the cost of administering the interior, for the British government determined to garrison the key posts of the fur trade—Detroit, St. Joseph, Michilimackinac, and Ouiatanon on the Wabash River. In 1761, Major Robert Rogers, who we also meet again later in this narrative, was sent with two hundred Rangers to these posts to accept the surrender of the French garrisons there. This was a challenging assignment. The object of British policy was to maintain "quiet possession" of the whole interior, and to this end General Amherst planned to repair the various posts as anchors of empire and to build small vessels for communication over the Great Lakes. In 1762 he further ordered the establishment of outposts at Sault Ste. Marie and Kaministiquia on Lake Superior "to entirely secure that Frontier." By the time the Treaty of Paris was signed, Amherst had nine thousand troops on garrison duty, extending from Newfoundland and Nova Scotia to Michigan and Wisconsin, altogether an expensive establishment.

British officials soon instituted those elements of the Proclamation that related to the *pays d'en haut*, that is the interior or far country. They undertook the military occupation of the key posts; they declared "the Indian Territory," a reserve in which settlement was not allowed; and, in repetition of the French of yesteryear, they put in place a system to regulate the trade by licensing traders and supervising them using the same military organization they had dispatched to the western posts.[5]

In order to effect this tight trinity, the British pressed forward with a policy of administration, one based in existing, pre-war policy and enacted through the offices of the Superintendent of Indian Affairs for the Northern Department, Colonel Sir William Johnson. To retain the interest and friendship of the western tribes was the fervent hope and policy of the Board of Trade and its chief agent, Johnson, and of the Military Department that ran the agency. Under proper regulations and restrictions, a free and open trade—that is, one without a corporate monopoly—was to be carried on with the tribes of the interior. Johnson who had previously, in 1761, been at Detroit at the great council, now had more extensive powers designed to please disgruntled chiefs. He took it upon himself to issue injunctions to those in command of the western garrisons, including Lieutenant Gorrell at Green Bay, to see that civilian traders adhered to the new regulations. No person was allowed to trade unless he had a licence from Johnson or his deputy.

Some traders objected to what they saw as a high-handed measure, but by and large the system was implemented without difficulty. Here was the origin of what Lord Egremont, Secretary of State for the American colonies, said was a measure to protect the tribes from unscrupulous traders who would trick them. Principles of humanity and proper indulgence lay at the root of the government's intentions,[6] and it was under these general considerations that Pond was later to go to the interior as an emissary of the commandant of Michilimackinac (see below). However, the policy was not totally benevolent; it was also driven by commercial self-interest, and British policy-makers encouraged the Quebec and northern trade, reducing mercantile duties through Montreal and other Canadian ports at the expense of Boston, Philadelphia, and New York. Duties on spirituous liquors were preferential in the Province of Quebec, far lower than elsewhere, and in consequence of a rising demand in the interior, a steady flow of supplies came from Montreal. These were years of burgeoning trade.

Geographical inquiry went hand in hand with business expansion. The English mercantile class had been pursuing the dream of a northwest passage since Elizabethan times, albeit without success. Martin Frobisher had found fool's gold rather than a seaway to Cathay. Captain Thomas Button passed the winter of 1612–13 at the mouth of the Nelson River on Hudson Bay and claimed the vast watershed for King James I. Optimistically, he carried letters from his sovereign for the Emperor of Cathay. Another century followed with equally slim results, and the northern lands and waters of the Canadian Arctic were soon festooned with geographical place names attesting to the cold labours of Davis, Fox, James, and Baffin. In 1742, Captain Christopher Middleton declared wryly that they could never discover what was not there. Meanwhile, the Governor and Company of Adventurers of England Trading into Hudson's Bay, founded in 1670, had been granted a bullish charter giving it a monopoly over all English trade in lands drained by the waters flowing into Hudson Bay—a cardinal consideration in the unfolding fur trade drama that would be acted out as far as Athabasca and even beyond. Young Henry Kelsey was sent to the Churchill River and to the Saskatchewan drainage basin in 1689–91 to explore the fur possibilities of the interior. Already there was an indication (as yet only a glimmering) of the rivalry that the French west of Lake Superior would face from the traders coming overland from Hudson Bay. Louis de la Corne would have to come to grips with Anthony Henday, but as yet there was room for all.

Immediately after the cession of Canada, Montreal-based traders (now numbering among their kind British and colonial Americans) took up the dream of commercial empire that the French under Frontenac, La Salle, Cadillac, La Vérendrye, and others had advanced. La Salle had opened the region south of the Great Lakes. He had also explored the Mississippi River, and in this valley he lay the foundations of a new

French empire based on New Orleans but connected to Quebec by more than imaginary links. These French imperialists going back to Samuel de Champlain also advanced the still vague concept of an "Adventure to China."

During the British era, as in the waning French one, the colonial administration in Quebec kept an eye on the prospects of a northwest passage. In the absence of a military means of making such discoveries, the governor saw British traders as agents of exploration. Sir Guy Carleton, governor of Quebec, in 1768 advised Lord Shelburne, the president of the Board of Trade in London, that British traders should be induced to proceed across the continent to Pacific Ocean shores. There, the governor suggested, they should select "a good port, take its latitude, longitude, and describe it so accurately as to enable our ships from the East Indies to find it out with ease, and then return the year following."[7] Governor Carleton, short on geographical details, wildly imagined a voyage to the western shore in a single year and a return the year following, with much work to be done when at the destination—an impossible task, surely, but one with a prescient understanding of what would be required in the future. Here was the basis of a geopolitical strategy based on the commercial possibilities of the fur trade and shipping on the far ocean, with ties to China and India.

Carleton was not alone in holding hopes of a western design. His ideas probably owed much to Robert Rogers, already mentioned, and they also reflected what London wanted to see in the way of discoveries in North America, tired as the government was of wishful thinking and bleary-eyed visions of a sea lane through the continent with imagined commercial capabilities. As early as 1765, Rogers expressed "moral certainty," as he put it, of the existence of a northwest passage. He had emerged from the Seven Years' War as one of the outstanding American colonial figures, popular in the American provinces and well known in the United Kingdom.[8] He had written books about North America and his experiences there as a successful frontier warrior and scout, and he had pressed for a command (for he was no stranger to self-promotion) that would allow his capabilities to do their next great work for the betterment of the British Empire. He had reason to be hopeful.

Successful in lobbying key members of the British government, he took command at Michilimackinac in August 1766. Rogers was loaded with debt, and his new appointment as governor, even if it was in what he called the "least known part of North America," offered a chance to advance his fortunes and win him even more fame. Michilimackinac, he reasoned, could be used as a base for the discovery of the Northwest Passage. Western travels might yield geographical fruit. A trading factory might be erected on the far Pacific shore near the outlet of the fabled Strait of Anian. A settlement could be planted there, one of great imperial advantage. Coastal and trans-Pacific trade would doubtless flourish. China and East India business would benefit. Further exploration and discovery would ensue. British coffers would grow. That year, gathering all his thoughts together, he submitted a plan to the Board of Trade. The Board was interested but not enough to give such a project official support.[9]

Meanwhile, Rogers had shared the 1765 plans with Jonathan Carver. Born in Massachusetts, Carver, a war-scarred former Ranger with the rank of captain, may best be described as a surveyor and self-taught cartographer with an itch for exploration, though rich in imagination.[10] Rogers liked what he saw in Carver and made him advance agent and draftsman. The plans developing for 1766 and 1767 called for an attempt to find the "Oregan River" (usually spelled nowadays "Oregon") and a waterway to the Pacific Ocean. With Carver was another ex-soldier from Massachusetts, Captain James Tute, who had commanded one of Rogers' Ranger companies in the late war. Tute was the real leader of this expedition of discovery. The second-in-command was Goddard, previously mentioned, who in 1761 had opened British trade at Green Bay. "Rogers had grandiose plans for himself and his

A curious character who has received more attention than his due, Jonathan Carver claimed to have explored the Northwest and gave a teasing description of the River "Oregan," now the Columbia River. The memoir of his travels, popular in its time, is now known to include many fabrications.
COURTESY OF THE LIBRARY OF CONGRESS, LC-USZ62-38490

Michilimackinac post, plans that brought Carver and Tute west," writes Alan Briceland, an authority on British exploration of the continental interior. "He not only hoped to steal the fur trade away from Spanish and French fur traders operating out of New Orleans by way of Saint Louis but also had revived the two-century-old British dream of finding a water route to the Pacific."[11] Rogers also hoped to gain the handsome, still unclaimed prize money that the British government had offered in 1744 for finding a northwest passage, and Carver, Tute, and Goddard, as well as a fur trader named William Bruce, one of the first British traders to enter Wisconsin, were to be the tools of his western destiny. But it was Carver who claimed all the glory.

In 1767, in a well-equipped armada of canoes, Carver set out from Michilimackinac. With him was Bruce, one of the company of English and French traders on whose supplies Carver depended (by a credit arrangement that Rogers had fixed up for him). Carver also carried instructions inviting Natives he met along the way to send representatives to a great council of peace scheduled to be held at Michilimackinac the following summer. Crossing Lake Michigan, he approached Green Bay, termed by the French the Bay of Puants (Stinking Bay), where the Natives fired a frightening fusillade of welcome. The post, Fort La Baye, was dishevelled. Heading west, Carver made a leisurely fall journey to the St. Peter's River (now the Minnesota River).

En route he arrived at Prairie du Chien. It was already mid-October, the forests a riot of colour, with a whiff of advancing winter in the wind. The settlement, on the upper Mississippi River not far above where the Wisconsin River joins it, was delightful in comparison to the shabby places Carver had seen in the course of his wilderness rambles. A Fox village of some three hundred families, their dwellings built well "after the Indian manner," was situated in a broad, handsome field, fronting the east bank of the Mississippi, that measured about six miles long and three wide. This was likewise a place of seasonal attraction to other tribes. Carver made no mention of French persons in the settlement or nearby. He did note many horses of a good size and shape, indicating the Fox probably had contact with Plains tribes and their trade, which ranged far south (possibly to Santa Fe), or more likely with the Spanish directly by way of the river.

Prairie du Chien was significant in another way: it marked what was then the gateway to Sioux country, and the Sioux were moving westward out of the forest, through the parklands, and onto the plains. British traders intended to follow in their influential track. Carver wintered among the Sioux in Minnesota. But lack of supplies prevented the exploring parties from pressing their inquires out to where the French had put up posts on the Saskatchewan, and the disappointing news was relayed to Rogers.

Meanwhile, the latter's political credit with the Indian Department had come under close examination, and with a black cloud hanging over him on account of expenses and debts, he was removed as governor at Michilimackinac and placed under house arrest by order of General Thomas Graves. Then he was falsely accused of treasonably plotting with the Spanish and was court-martialled in Montreal, though the case was not proved and he was released. He fought again on the British side during the War of the American Revolution, but his flaming arc in the sky faded quickly. To the end he talked of a River Oregan in the far west leading to Pacific tidewater, and, although the origin of the place name was never recorded or explained, its advertised existence had a powerful influence on the course of American exploration history. At Michilimackinac he was highly regarded, particularly among the Native peoples, as he had treated them with respect and was not miserly with his presents.[12]

Carver, on his return to Boston, could not find a publisher, and his account of his travels did not see print until 1778. The work was hugely popular—three editions had been published by the time Carver died in 1780. However, latter-day scholars have pointed out the falsehoods contained in Carver's boastful narrative. Reading between the lines, Peter Pond must have known of Carver's rambles by word of mouth, before the book was published. When he entered the same region in 1773, he knew that Carver had preceded him and noted what he thought was Carver's winter cabin. Later, when Carver's account was published, Pond must have been puzzled by the literary production of what one writer called a "traveler and a travel liar."[13]

Carver's enduring legacy was not the description of the waters of the upper Mississippi River but his ability to fire the imagination with a claim that the "river Oregan, or the river of the West, that falls into the Pacific Ocean at the Strait of Anian" was one of the great rivers of

North America. This became the great river of American western destiny, pursued and advanced by Thomas Jefferson and explored by Captains Lewis and Clark between 1804 and 1806. Many schemes were then afoot to find the Strait of Anian; Juan de Fuca's Strait; Admiral de Fonte's entrance to a river at 47° North latitude; the Western Sea, as shown by French cartographers Delisle and Buache; and the River of the West.[14] As we will later see, Pond had his own idea about finding the Northwest Passage.

Before his fall from grace, Rogers had instructed Tute to command a party to search for and discover this great river, thought to fall into the Pacific at about 50° North latitude. Rogers' instructions spoke of a great mountain, gold, an inhabited country, and a great town whose people travelled two thousand miles to trade with the Japanese. Tute was to open trade across the North American continent, drawing bills on Rogers as necessary. Tute was given much excellent advice by Rogers: members of the party were not to molest Native women, were to pay punctually for all their requirements, and were to observe proper places for locating posts. Tute was to report to Rogers or, failing that, to the Lords of Trade and Plantations in London. But Tute fared no better than Carver or, for that matter, Rogers, and the whole western discoveries project died. Carleton's idea, and Rogers' too, would have to await firmer plans and better financial backing.[15]

It was at the time of Rogers' appointment at Michilimackinac and Carver's expedition into the interior that Pond entered the fringes of this same territory. Although his purpose was entirely commercial, his visions of geographical discoveries still minuscule, he was nonetheless attracted to the geostrategic advantages of waterways as vectors of trade and routes to fur-bearing wealth and trade with various tribes. His connections with the British military authorities during the late war, his standing as a former colonial officer, and his knowledge of Native ways all counted as attributes. Because British administration of Indian affairs and key forts of the Great Lakes area came under the purview of the British military, Pond was well fixed to undertake imperial missions of diplomacy and trade. He never proclaimed himself to be an agent of empire, but we read from his record of his experiences that he was one such (and, indeed, one of many). As long as the British military regulated the trade and sought peace among the tribes for the purpose of profit and order, Pond served to benefit from the system. And in the future he would come to play his own role as diplomat to the tribes. All of this lay ahead.

4

Trader and Emissary to the Sioux

We retrace our steps momentarily. We know from what Pond wrote that his father had traded from Detroit in 1761 with a number of others. Pond, deciding to follow his father and enter the fur trade, left Milford for Detroit, likely in 1765. Some of his brothers may have taken the same path, but at other times. For six years he carried on a fur-gathering business in that western vastness of well-watered lakes, forests, and marshlands that now comprises the states of Michigan, Wisconsin, and Minnesota. He worked in a world of cross-cultural interaction, social dysfunction, alcohol abuse, conflict and violence, and intertribal war, among hard-driving and mercenary traders, unpacified tribes, and competing influences—a seemingly uncontrolled world in which brandy and rum ruled the trade and debauched the Natives. This was "the middle ground," as described by Richard White, and it remained so until the American "long knives" came to demand peace in the face of war. Many "Wounded Knees" lay ahead. In Pond's time, and right through to the end of the War of 1812 (when they shamefully abandoned their Native allies to their fate), the British government and King's representatives in North America, principally the Governors in Quebec and the

Superintendent of Indian Affairs, kept to their obligations of friendship with the Ojibwa, Saulteaux, Nipissing, and other nations of the St. Lawrence and the Great Lakes. Their aim was to have peace for the purpose of trade and profit, and to keep rivals, including the Americans on the southern frontier, out of the area that was regarded as the western lands of the Province of Quebec.

Jealousy among traders necessitated caution and watchfulness; at the same time it instilled suspicion. Familiarity might breed contempt. Political differences and national antipathies could be exposed. Flare-ups could and did occur. In Pond's case, it happened that another trader abused him "in a Shamefull manner" (Pond gives no further details). Knowing that if he resisted, the man would "Shake me in Peaceis," Pond concluded that he must challenge the antagonist to a duel. This challenge was accepted, and, as Pond writes, "We met the next morning eairley and "Discharged Pistels in which the Pore fellow was unfortennt."[1]

Pond then came down out of the country and, when others surely would have let the matter drop, freely declared the results of the duel to an authority. The matter went unattended to: he claims he was not prosecuted.[2] Pond was aware of his own responsibility in this case, and many another would not have bothered to report such a deed. This was the last indication that Pond had any kind of guilty conscience about his actions.

Like all the traders, Pond was probably under the close watch of Sir William Johnson, Superintendent of Indian Affairs. With those other traders at Detroit, Pond signed a petition dated 26 November 1767, asking Johnson to restrict the annual amount of rum brought by traders into the interior: the volume specified was fifty gallons in each three-handed bateau load of dry goods. The same petition asked permission to trade beyond the fort of Detroit, since otherwise the trade would be lost to small unscrupulous traders who were swamping the southwest area with spirituous liquors.[3] Pond and others saw enlargement of the area of legitimate trade as a way to curtail the interlopers, and control of rum seems to have been the way to control the market.

In 1771 Pond came down from Detroit to Milford. The next year, 1772, he braved another cruise to the West Indies. The details, perhaps commonplace, are lost to history. However, on his return home a letter greeted him. It was from a man in New York, Felix Graham, asking Pond to call on him there, for he was seeking to go into partnership with him.

Pond describes Graham as a gentleman, and we may infer from this that the older Graham was well fixed and of a secure mercantile class. Graham had been an Albany-based trader as early as 1767 and had probably traded at Michilimackinac for several years. Alexander Henry the Elder did the same thing. Pond does not state how Graham heard of him. But Graham, whom we suspect perhaps knew Henry, had come searching for Pond. What we can deduce is that Graham was mighty important to Pond's commercial rise. Graham doubtless had the greater capital, though Pond had accumulated wealth from his years in the trade by Green Bay to the Mississippi. He was master of the Albany–New York-based fur trade to the interior, sometimes called the Anglo-American trade, which was active in the Old Northwest toward Minnesota and Ohio, even as far as the Mississippi River. Pond, who became the active or in-the-field partner, took up Graham's invitation. His apprenticeship in the Detroit trade had ended.[4] Together Pond and Graham laid in a cargo of 4,600 pounds. Pond left Milford in April 1773, and it would be as many as twelve years before he returned. He was thirty-three years old.

Dating back to the era of the Dutch colonists, the New York fur trade was based on Albany, and its success depended on the cooperation and energies of the Iroquois nations, through whose woodlands and waterways the trade flowed, in both directions. Pond, in his narrative, explains the route by which inbound goods passed to the most remote parts of the interior country for that trading season or year. The Erie Canal, the engineering marvel completed in 1825, was in Pond's time but a dream, and for the moment the route was complex, tedious, and slow, for the passage of freight from Albany on the Hudson River to Buffalo on Lake Erie ran something like this: first the trading goods were shipped at New York for Albany. From there they were taken fourteen miles by land to Schenectady in wagons. Then they were loaded on board bateaux and taken up the Mohawk River to Fort Stanwix, carried a mile by land with the boats and put in to Wood Creek, from thence through Oneida Lake and downriver to Lake Ontario, then coasted along the south side of that lake to Fort Niagara. From the landing place a few miles south of that fort they were, with the bateaux, transported across the carrying place, about nine miles, and then put into waters that come out of Lake Erie into Lake Ontario at a place called Fort Schlosser. They were then conveyed in boats to Fort Erie on Lake Erie. The second part of the journey saw the goods travelling from Fort Erie to Michilimackinac: coasted along the north side of Lake Erie until they came to the Detroit River, and then moved up those waters to Lake St. Clair. Skirting the west shore of Lake Huron for about five hundred miles, the boats came to their destination, Michilimackinac, the fortified garrison and trading rendezvous of all the traders.

Pond did not accompany the goods from Albany, leaving his partner to attend to that matter. He had something more specific on his mind: he wanted some small articles in demand by the Natives to complete his assortment of trade goods. These special items were not to be had in New York. Pond had his own trading vessel, and from soldiering days he knew the track north of the waterways. He therefore took his boat through Lake George and Lake Champlain to Montreal, where he found all he wanted.

In that spring of 1773, a number of canoes were fitting out for Michilimackinac. At Montreal he arranged with Isaac Todd and James McGill, merchant-traders he had known at Detroit, to have these items shipped inland. When the forwarding arrangements were complete, Pond set out with Todd and McGill from Lachine by the Ottawa River route for Michilimackinac. Pond was in good company, for Todd, McGill, and those connected with them were the key financiers of the trade to the northwest, a position they held well into the War of 1812. It was the beginning of a powerful business connection.

This was Pond's second visit to Montreal. He had been there previously with Amherst's army, but it was perhaps on this occasion that he took note of the lading of the canoes at Lachine and, new to him as a New Englander and a Protestant, the social and religious character of that special breed of men, the Canadian voyageurs and canoe men. Gaiety and vitality marked the scene, the jabber and clamour of men making ready for a tour into the vast world of water, forest, cascades, and portages that began only a day's travel west. The canoe route to the interior began eight miles upstream at Lachine on Montreal Island. This tidy if sprawling village, lying on the north side of a canal, was a collection of traders' houses, warehouses, outfitting establishments, and taverns.

On the day of departure the river's foreshore was a blaze of colour, a scene of unimaginable urgency. But still there was a need to appeal to the Almighty for protection against all dangers. A small distance upriver, and within two miles of the western extremity of Montreal Island, lay the church of Ste. Anne,[5] where appeals were made to the titular saint of all voyageurs. Here they prayed for help and protection against the perils of the voyage that lay immediately ahead. Pond, ever the observant one, notes that there was a small box with a hole in the top for the reception of a little money for the Holy Father to say a small mass. Few voyageurs did not stop and put some small amount in the box. By that means, Pond contends, the voyageurs all supposed they were protected. After the ceremony of crossing themselves and repeating a short prayer, they were ready to depart on the great adventure. Superstition and fatalism were in ample supply. "Even Protestant clerks and *bourgeois* traveling with the brigade put coins in the box," writes Grace Lee Nute, historian of the voyageur.[6] Indulgences had not gone out of fashion: all of these workers in the fur trade desired insurance against whatever hazards lay ahead upriver and on into the great interior.

In our mind's eye we can see this remarkable birchbark flotilla setting out, a long line of slender canoes with eight or ten men in each vessel plus baggage, trade goods, provisions, oilcloths for shelter, a sail and pole, a kettle, a sponge for bailing, and gum, bark, and watape (spruce tree roots) for canoe repairs. "A European on seeing one of these slender vessels thus laden, heaped up, and sunk with her gunwale within six inches of the water, would think his fate inevitable in such a boat, when he reflected on the nature of her voyage; but the Canadians are so expert that few accidents happen,"[7] writes Sir Alexander Mackenzie, who made many such a canoe voyage and was arguably the greatest canoeist in North American history. A few years earlier, a Hudson's Bay trader, Anthony Henday, wrote that "thin Birch rind Canoes will carry as much as an India Ships Long boat and draws little water; and so light that two men can carry one several miles with ease; they are made in the same form and slight materials as the small ones; only a thin board runs along their bottom and they can sail them before the wind, but not else."[8]

Goodbyes, if said at all, had been made. The wilderness now beckoned irresistibly, with all its physical exertions as well as risks and the promise of sexual freedoms and liaisons in the custom of the country. A day's paddling upstream into the continental interior took those in the canoe another twenty-four hours from the parish influences of Catholicism. At the end of the first night's voyaging was the *régal*, the

The freight of the fur trade floated in canoes: inbound supplies of food, drink, arms, and other essentials, and outbound skins of the mammals of North America. The freight canoe remained necessary as long as fashion kept up the demand for the felt hat made from the pelt of the noble waterways master, the beaver. Portaging took time, energy, and much care in moving the canoe. LIBRARY AND ARCHIVES CANADA, ACC. NO. 1934-380-1

treat.[9] Each canoe had been given eight gallons of rum as its ration for the voyage, but each of the voyageurs knew that, by custom and by tradition, the first night's debauch was guaranteed to put a dint in the supply. They also knew that when the keg of rum was opened that first night, they would give voice to blasphemous lewdness. Year after year, ever since the first expeditions into the interior, the trading ethos had gradually taken on its own customs. To the trysts with the keg were added songs and stories describing not so much the loneliness but the happiness of the work. The metres of the lyrics echoed that of the paddle in the endless cycle of plunge, thrust, and lift.

The hard-driving voyageurs, to a man brightly arrayed, profligate, and apparently carefree (but devoutly Catholic nonetheless), were a society unto themselves in the *pays d'en haut*, and their story is the stuff of song and legend. They were the muscle and the brawn of the Canadian fur trade, forming a distinct working class that invited the envy of the Bay traders. An officer of the Hudson's Bay Company at York Factory, after seeing the feats of a brigade of Canadians on a portage, reported to his superiors in London, "The Canadians are chosen Men inured to hardship

& fatigue, under which your Present Servants would sink. A Man of the Canadian service who cannot carry two packs of eighty lbs each, one and a half leagues, loses his Trip that is his Wages."[10] In the far interior, where more manpower was needed, Métis and Iroquois served as boatmen alongside the voyageurs. They were illiterate, brazen, and fearless.

The Canadians lived for the moment. The wilderness drew them far from their families, who lived in towns and on farms, and gave them financial incentives to live out their prodigal ways. And when, eventually, they returned to hearth, home, and family as veritable cocks of the walk, flamboyant in dress and prodigious in the spending of hard-earned wealth, they were seen by clergy as a wanton and destabilizing (and thus unwelcome) force on the stable, sedentary communities and parishes of the St. Lawrence lowlands. In the interior, the company of the Canadians could drive a well-educated New England trader to distraction. As one Nor'Wester, Daniel Harmon, derisively writes, "What conversation would an illiterate ignorant Canadian be able to keep up[?] All their chat is about Horses, Dogs, Canoes and Women, and strong Men who can fight a good battle."[11]

Daniel Harmon kept an excellent account of his sixteen years in the interior as a trader for the North West Company. Though it reflects the prejudices of the day, his journal is an excellent treatise on the company's trading relations with various tribes and nations at many posts, mainly on the Saskatchewan River and up to the ramparts of the Rocky Mountains. REPRINTED FROM DANIEL HARMON, *A JOURNAL OF VOYAGES AND TRAVELS IN THE INTERIOR OF NORTH AMERICA*, ALLERTON BOOK CO. (NEW YORK, 1905)

Pond, who was not a gossipy sort, would have given none of these things much consideration when he took the mainline fur trade route west in 1773, though he was interested (as we have noted) in the voyageurs' religious traits. From Montreal and Lachine, Pond travelled via the Ottawa and French Rivers, and then the North Channel of Lake Huron to rendezvous with his partner Graham at Michilimackinac, where all trade canoes seemed to converge. The place, his contemporary Alexander Henry writes, had taken on the double role as "the place of deposit, and the point of departure, between the upper countries and the lower."[12] Another trader and traveller, John Long, regarded Michilimackinac as of the greatest importance to the commerce of England, "as it intercepts all the trade of the Indians of the upper country from Hudson Bay to Lake Superior, and affords protection to various tribes of Savages, who constantly resort to it to receive presents from the commanding officer, and from whence the traders, who go to the northwest, take their departure for the grand portage, or grand carrying place, which is nine miles in length, before they enter on the waters communicating with the north-west."[13] He was referring to Grand Portage, at the western end of Lake Superior.

Pond noted that Michilimackinac was kept up by a captain's command of British soldiers, lodged in good barracks. Within the stockades there were some old French buildings of yesteryear and a commodious Roman Catholic church, where the French inhabitants and *engagés* went to mass.[14] Most importantly, he reported that the majority of the French wives there were white. There was, besides, a large floating population, and in the spring the inhabitants headed out with the men, women, and children on trade expeditions. Large amounts of maple syrup were made at that time too. The country nearby he thought barren, a mere sandbank. However, with the use of manure the garrison garden grew potatoes and some vegetables. Trout and whitefish could be caught there, and Indian corn, beans, and other commodities grown and harvested. The Native men were great hunters and shots, and from far and near they brought partridges, venison, hares, raccoons, and wild pigeons. From a great distance every summer, they also brought dried venison and bear grease and other supplies; this formed a considerable part of the trade, according to Pond.[15]

The traders' canoes arrived at Michilimackinac from Sault Ste. Marie, carrying European goods via the Ottawa River–Lake Nipissing–French River route, or by way of the longer, less difficult passage via the St. Lawrence River and lower Great Lakes. The latter route had reinforced Detroit's influence in the southwestern fur trade and made it an important shipbuilding and repair yard. And while Detroit was the key to the southwest, as Quebec official La Galissonière remarked in 1748, Michilimackinac was the entrepôt for the north and west. "At Mackinac," writes Grace Lee Nute, "a long halt was made, for *commis* [clerk] and *bourgeois* [proprietor] must conduct negotiations with other traders, attend to supplies for their men in the big warehouses along the water front, and determine the destination and route of each of the canoes. It was here that the supply of Indian corn was shipped, to take the place of the peas eaten on the route thither from Montreal. From this point many routes diverged."[16] Here and again at Sault Ste. Marie the voyageurs rested while their masters attended to business matters. The same authority describes the scene: "Gay were the sashes and plumes that were donned to win the favors of dusky maidens, and many the *piastres* spent for high wines, candles, and food. Carnival was the order both of day and of night, and he was an alert *commis* who could keep his men within bounds and round them up on the day of departure in condition to paddle his canoes."[17]

Michilimackinac owed its origins to a mix of religious and commercial motives. Then situated on the mainland—the fort was moved to nearby Mackinac Island in 1779—it had been built by order of the Jesuits, not the Governor of Canada, in 1670. The explorer Father Marquette had been there in the 1670s en route to the Mississippi, on reconnaissance with the trader Louis Jolliet, and in the following years itinerant Jesuit priests had called there. In 1715, Captain de Lingnery built the first European outpost of the French. The church, Ste. Anne de Michilimackinac, though in a dilapidated condition by the time Pond got there in the 1770s, was a last remnant of Roman Catholicism dating from the French regime. There was no resident priest, only an itinerant who called there on his circuit. The bell rang for the angelus morning and evening.

War with France had given Michilimackinac a new and different form of strategic value. The British administration had swept in here in the aftermath of the conquest of Canada. Two companies of British redcoats manned the garrison, this westernmost post of the British Empire in America. It was here in 1763 that the Ojibwa had turned on the British, murdering many and enslaving others, and after the British regained control, Michilimackinac was the scene for negotiations with the western tribes. Now, in the 1770s, all trade canoes converged on the Straits of Mackinac, whether destined for the Wisconsin or Minnesota country, the Missouri River to the southwest, or Lake Winnipeg and the far northwest. Alice E. Smith, historian of Wisconsin, describes the activities there each fall and spring, when canoes arrived from Montreal and the interior, piled with trade goods and furs respectively. She notes that "for some traders, the great rendezvous of Mackinac was only a stopping place... between Montreal and the interior, but for many winterers in the distant regions, it was often for years their only contact with the outside world." While they were at the post, traders "turned in their packs, watched the furs being sorted and weighed, paid off their creditors, then attended to laying in goods and supplies for the coming season, perhaps hiring new canoe men and clerks." (This last was particularly vital to any future fur enterprise, for the Canadians who manned the oars and packed heavy loads over the many portages were the backbone and muscle of the trade.) Traders also "learned the news of the world and of their colleagues and rivals and enjoyed the brief taste of what was for them metropolitan life" before loading their canoes again and setting off for the interior.[18]

At Michilimackinac, Pond rearranged the goods that he had brought from Montreal so that they could be apportioned when the time came to outfit his several canoes destined for various locations. Also at that post he bought the necessary canoes and additional supplies, including Indian corn and maple sugar. He engaged men for the work ahead, and he arranged for the loading of the bales that would be shipped in the canoes. Everything had to be checked and double-checked. Altogether he had a dozen canoes, "my small fleat," he calls it, loaded with 4,600 pounds of goods valued at more than £1,200—a rich, precious cargo. Each canoe was made of birchbark and white cedar; such a canoe, fully loaded, could carry 700 weight (7,000 pounds).

The summer's preparations and pleasures had ended. In September 1773 Pond, guided by those with him who had been on this type of venture before, set out with his brigade for the Wisconsin and Minnesota country. He was about to follow the age-old route of canoes in this part of the world, but we are left wondering about the particulars of his route and the distance he travelled. Could it have been into South Dakota, where the La Vérendryes had been thirty or so years before? Did he cross the plains on horseback? He does not say. He is silent about so many of the details of this trading adventure. But we can speculate based on the usual route traders followed south and west of the Great Lakes, exhibiting the American progression across the lakes, woodlands, and plains.

Crossing the Straits of Mackinac formed his first task, the course almost due north from Michilimackinac on a line to the old Jesuit mission of St. Ignace, from whence, almost exactly a century before, Jolliet and Marquette had started on their expedition to discover the upper Mississippi.[19] Then his canoes, again in tidy procession, coasted the rocky shore of Lake Michigan. His guides took a course that, wherever possible, gave shelter in the lee of islands as they made their way to the safety of Green Bay, that ancient vestibule of the upper Mississippi and Wisconsin River trade.

In the summer months, Green Bay took on a delightful appearance as a seemingly verdant paradise wedged between vast rocky escarpments. The French in the old regime had long been interested in it as a gateway west, and Champlain sent Jean Nicollet in the summer of 1634 to follow the traditional Ottawa River route west from Montreal, then head for Michilimackinac, enter Lake Michigan, and steer for the land of the nations they called *Gens de Mer* (the Puants, Ounipigons, or Winnebagoes). These people were surrounded by Algonquin tribes with whom they had a cool relationship. Nicollet was sent as peacemaker. In the course of his diplomatic round he hoped to find the China Sea, which according to information gathered from the Natives was near Green Bay. Thus he had in his possession a robe of Chinese damask, liberally strewn with embroidered flowers and multi-coloured birds. He was, or so he thought, resplendently and suitably dressed for an appearance at the court of Kublai Khan. Many tribes welcomed him at Green Bay, but no oriental court could be found there or at the Mississippi, to which he crossed. Nicollet's dream faded quickly when he learned the "great sea" reported by Native informants was not the South Sea but the Mississippi. Later the explorer La Salle would pursue these same objectives. More often than not, despair and disaffection would accompany these brave if not rash schemes when the instigators discovered the waters flowed south to the Gulf of Mexico rather than west to the Vermilion Sea or the Gulf of California.

In Pond's time, dreams of a northwest passage in this region had dissipated, so the fur trader's work was more prosaic. At the head of Green Bay, as was customary, Pond would have called at Fort Edward Augustus, the British military post, to declare himself in possession of the required licence to trade. He visited a Menominee village on the north side of the long bay. These people, he says, were hunters, who also lived on wild rice gathered each year in September.

Next he travelled for two days to the Puant or Winnebago village at the east end of "Peuans Lake" (Lake Winnebago in present-day Wisconsin). He recounts how the women raised corn, beans, and pumpkins to accompany the rabbits, partridge, and venison that made up their diet. Pond thought their language particularly peculiar, so much so that it was probably impossible to learn. He recounts amusingly that when the Puants went to Michilimackinac, the officer in charge, Captain George Turnbull, could not understand them. What to do? Turnbull thought that he might get an interpreter in the form of a Highland soldier "that spoke little but the harsh langwege—perhaps he mite understand for it sounded much like it." Pond describes the Puants as a tightknit and unsociable people, and he seems to imply that they deserved their neighbours, the Fox nation, which had been evicted from Detroit by the military authorities because of their mischievous, cheating, and thieving ways.

Now the time had come to penetrate inland. On the Fox River he paddled to where he came to a high piece of sacred ground, the Grand Butte des Morts. This is where the Fox nation interred its dead. Pond and his men stopped here for a while, finding some members of the tribe who had come to pay their respects to one of their departed friends. They had a small keg of rum, he says, and sat around the grave. They filled their calumet pipe and began their ceremony by pointing the stem of the pipe upward, then turning it toward the head of the grave, then east and west, north and south, after which they smoked the pipe, filled it again, and set it aside. Then they drained some rum out of the keg into a small bark vessel and poured it on the head of the grave. This was their way of giving it to their departed brother. Then they all drank themselves, lit the pipe, smoked, and "seamed to enjoi themselves verey well." They repeated these steps until the rum began to take effect and "thare harts began to soffen," at which point they started to sing. When the keg had been bled, they began to reminisce about the departed, "how fond he was of his frends while he could git a cag of rum and how thay youst to injoy it togather." Soon they "all fell a craying and a woful nois they made"—until they "thought wisely" that they could not bring him back from the dead and it would not do to grieve too much, but perhaps "an application to the cag was the best way to dround sorrow and wash away greefe." The motion was soon put into execution and "all began to be marey as a party could bee."[20]

This continued until near nightfall, and as the men became "more than half drunk," they began to approach the females and chat freely "and apearantley friendly," then began to lean on each other, kiss, and appear very amorous. Pond observed clearly that "this bisiness was first pusht on by the women who made thare visit to the dead a verey pleasing one in thare way." One of the women, who was quite drunk, approached Pond, who was sitting by himself, "observing thare saremones [ceremonies]," and asked him to "take a share in her bountey." Pond decided it was time to leave and went about half a mile up the river to where his men were encamped.[21]

Bruce Greenfield, who studied Pond's recounting of this episode, makes these important observations:

> Pond does not present himself as a participant in this occasion, but he is very close by, and his description of what occurs is matter-of-fact and not overtly judgmental. There is no obvious ethnographic framing, although one may sense in the background the attention to funerary practices that was commonly a feature of the ethnographies...Pond's vocabulary is not technical; the dead are referred to as "Departed frend" and "Departed brother," rather than "ancestors" or some such term; in Pond's account the loss is personal rather than typical, and the behavior is not in any way mysterious. Pond seems to position himself on the edge of this group, but within their circle of feeling. His presence does not seem to affect the actions of the mourners, suggesting that his presence was on some level a normal thing, and that he was regarded, to some extent, as a participant. At the same time, however, Pond does not recount any interaction between himself and the mourners until the end of the episode, and it is, in fact, his being approached by the woman that seems to prompt his retiring and thus the end of the scene. Pond does not portray himself sharing in the event in such a manner. Yet he tells us that some of his men did—that "the Women had bin at the Camp In the Night." Pond is not aloof or critical in his recounting these particulars, and though an observer is not a direct participant

> except in passing, and he does not describe customs with condemnation or classification.

I like what Greenfield says: "Physically, economically, socially, sexually, Pond's life was meshed with what he describes here; at the same time, the act of describing for [intended] print draws him in the direction of his readers. The subject of Pond's story is his life in the middle ground."[22]

Then Pond portaged to the Wisconsin River—he thought it a gentle, gliding stream—which formed part of the Mississippi drainage system. Toward the end of September, the autumn now well advanced and a hint of winter in the air, he reached the Sauk village on the north side of the Wisconsin River. In his narrative he records cultural traits of that tribe: they were less inclined to tricks and bad manners than their neighbours, and "Thay are Not Verey Gellas of thare women." Some of their huts were sixty feet long and contained several families. The women raised great crops of corn, beans, pumpkins, and potatoes.

The canoe is a venerable symbol of voyaging through the Canadian landscape. It also represents a triumph of Native technology, for the canoe is both light and strong, and ably adapted to lake and river travel. Here humanity is in harmony with nature, though danger lurks at the next rapids. LIBRARY AND ARCHIVES CANADA, ACC. NO. 1989-510-1

He descended the river some fifty miles and came to a village of Foxes. These were, he says, a different sort of people who were "bred"—that is, they were the "home Indians"—at Detroit under the French administration and clergy. Later they had become difficult, Pond writes, and the French had been obliged to go to war against them. Now they lived in "Sad Sarkamstanis." They had recently been infected by an epidemic, and Pond remained among them only one day, managing to do a little trading before continuing downstream to the Mississippi.

Pond then came, as had Carver before, to Prairie du Chien, the "Planes of the Dogs," he calls it. Next to Michilimackinac, this ranked as the most important post in the interior south of the Great Lakes and stood at a crossroads of trade. It controlled the entrance to the Sioux county, and therein lay its essential value. British Indian agents had justifiably paid special attention to it, encouraging trade and forging an alliance with the Native peoples, and agents such as John Long had arrived there laden with presents. When Pond arrived, he found a cluster of French traders and Natives engaged in the annual preparations for the next winter hunt. He stayed ten days, during which time he dispatched nine clerks to various tributaries of the Wisconsin and Mississippi for trade. He also learned that every year, in the springtime, a great gathering of the tribes occurred at Prairie du Chien. Taking note of this, he made his plans for the interim. He could spend the intervening months in winter quarters somewhere, where trade could be profitable and some new frontier of influence gained.

Prairie du Chien was also a place where "the merchants' plenty," or stores, were kept in packs in a log house guarded by a British army captain and some home guard. There was always the worry that Spanish traders from St. Louis and the Mississippi would make a raid there, and if not these rascals, then some Americans coming out of the Ohio country.[23]

In October, in the company of two other traders, he set out from Prairie du Chien for St. Peter's River, now the Minnesota River. This forms a powerful tributary of the Mississippi, then little known, but the three traders must have seen its promise from the point of view of gaining business and new trading connections. They travelled with a strange leisureliness, odd for fur traders in canoes, who were invariably in a hurry. The reason was that they did not wish to overtake the Sioux, who had set out before them and who would pester them for goods on credit; as

Pond notes, the Sioux did not always honour their debts. Pond and his associates ate well, living off the bounty of the country: geese and ducks, venison and bear. There was plenty of flour, tea, coffee, sugar, and butter, also spirits and wine, so that, as he says, they fared as well as voyageurs. Crab apples were available on the shore, particularly tasty when frost had touched them at a suitable time.

On the banks of the river, some fourteen miles upstream from its mouth, Pond found a log house which he supposed to be that of Carver, where the explorer had wintered in 1766–67. Pond may have been in error, for other evidence indicates that Carver wintered not here but at nearby Swan Lake, an ancient Dakota village site.[24] In any event, Pond gradually came to think of Carver as a shadowy figure, and he was correct in this appreciation. Later he wrote that he thought little of Carver and bragged that he could have completed the explorer's whole tour in six weeks. This was no idle boast. Knowing Pond's drive and endurance, this well might have been possible, and the claim is fortified by the fact that Carver was not a speedy traveller. Yet it must be said, in defence of Carver, that he was hindered by lack of supplies and uncertain arrangements for the same.

Now the three traders decided it was time to build a place for the winter. They encamped on a high bank of the river so they would not be flooded out at spring breakup, built themselves a comfortable house for the winter's trade, and got their goods safely under cover.[25] In December an advance party of young Native men from the plains arrived. They had been searching along the river for traders and found Pond and his companions. After staying for a few days' rest, they departed to take the joyous news to their people. In January the main party duly arrived, bringing dried and fresh meat, along with beaver, otter, deer, fox, wolf, raccoon, and other skins to trade. They were welcome, Pond writes, and the traders conducted their business to advantage.[26]

Pond had entered a promising trading realm, one hardly known to the outside world. He passed that 1773–74 winter west of St. Peter's River at a place called Coteau des Prairies, an adjacent wooded plateau named by early French traders. Looked at on a map, this locale resembles a flatiron, with the point directed to the north. Nearly thirty years later, Lewis and Clark identified its conspicuous features and placed them on one of their maps, as well as the Sioux and James Rivers that flow south to the Missouri along the plateau's western flank. This elevated and forested hump, containing many lakes, lies on the borderlands of present-day Minnesota, South Dakota, and Iowa. Pond included his post here on his Map of North America (the one copied in 1785 by St. John de Crevecoeur in New York), naming it Fort Pond.

French traders were no strangers in these parts; they had visited the location for three decades or more and had pursued a vigorous trade. Some French and Spanish had ventured north from Louisiana and Illinois. Others had come west and south from Quebec and the upper Great Lakes. In the era after the surrender of Canada to British arms, the French still held great sway in the upper Mississippi Valley. Canadian governor Sir Guy Carleton had no qualms about encouraging the Montreal-based traders licensed by the Crown in the peltry business, regarding it as a multi-beneficial tool of empire making. He saw these traders as a tool for promoting peace with the western tribes, removing the discontents of the Native peoples, ending scurrilous misrepresentations by the French about the British, underselling the Mississippi traders, and, in short, keeping the French rivals at bay.[27] British manufactures and other goods would supply the necessary wants of these tribes and encourage their loyalty. That was the Carleton schema, a form of soft power, and one so different from that proposed by General Thomas Gage, Amherst's successor as commander-in-chief, who had suggested a show of power by a thousand soldiers and new, strong posts to be built at vital points on the rivers of the west.[28]

Pond did not see himself in the guise of a pathfinder of empire. In any case, he found himself now in lands where the Sioux, or Nottawase (his spelling, but more correctly *Nadouessioux* or *Nadowisiweg*—that is, Snakes—as their Ojibwa enemies called them), were predominant.[29] In Pond's day these were still people of the forest; they had not yet moved west onto the parklands of Minnesota and westward again to the plains, where they took to the horse. At that post, several different bands came to trade. (We return to Pond's discussion of them presently.)

That winter Pond lived in easy association with a French trader, one of the *hivernants* or winterers, who marked the history of these western lands in those years. They were a unique breed, fiercely independent and suspicious of outsiders. They lived easily among the Natives and often served as interpreters for the English. Pond does not give the name of this one, which is sadly lost to history, but the fellow was obviously an old hand in conducting business with the Natives. With palpable anguish, Pond saw that his rival seemed to be receiving preferential treatment from those who came to trade, and profited accordingly. The two became good friends, and on one occasion when they were talking, Pond noted that the other got more than his share of trade, adding that this was not to be wondered at as he had been so long acquainted with the local peoples. In reply, the French trader told Pond that he "had not hit on ye rite eidea... the Indians of that quorter was given to stealing and aspachely (especially) the women. In order to draw custom he left a few brass things for the finger on the counter, sum needles and awls," small knives and bells, which cost "but a trifel." For the sake of stealing these trifles, he said, they came to see him, and he got what they had to trade. Pond believed what his companion said and tried the experiment. It proved effective.[30]

Pond had learned a nifty business trick: that a small item, a trifle, could be an inducement to trade, a prelude. Although the trader might think of the "exchange" as theft, on the Native side it might well be conceived as a gift. At any rate, Pond and those with him proceeded eastward with ease and profit until spring. It was now 1774.

Spring came and at last the ice broke. The water rose twenty-six feet and washed away large parts of the riverbank. Then, when the floodwaters mercifully receded, Pond and his party passed down the Mississippi River to Prairie du Chien. There, as anticipated, the annual rendezvous of tribes was in full gaiety. He remarks on the fact that they had gathered from every part of the Mississippi, even from New Orleans, which was 800 leagues (about 2,400 miles) "belowe us." Their encampments extended a mile and a half in length and presented a fabulous, colourful sight. Here, he wrote, was "Sport of All Sorts," by which he meant gambling, games, music, dancing, and sexual activity.

Trade competition was naturally stiff at this great mart, and Pond bargained hard and successfully. He collected pelts from various tribes, doing so against keen trade from New Orleans, the Illinois, and Michilimackinac. The French traders were very numerous here. No fewer than 130 canoes had come from Michilimackinac under licences and permits issued by the British commandant there, each canoe carrying trade goods of sixty to eighty hundredweight apiece. From New Orleans and Illinois and other parts had come numerous flat-bottomed river barges, and stout trading galleys from the Mississippi delta had pressed upriver, powered by thirty-six men rowing as many oars. A single boat, deep in the water in consequence of its cargo and crew, would bring in sixty hogsheads of wine plus ham and cheese, all to trade with the Natives and the French. And although Pond would not speculate as to the number of Natives, it is clear from the trade returns that they had come in great number. He estimated that 1,500 packs of furs, a hundredweight each, had gone out to Michilimackinac. Then he turned to his own success. "All my Outfits had Dun well," he wrote. "I had a grate Share for my Part a[s] I furnish Much the Largest Cargo on the River. After all the Bisness Was Dun and People Began to Groe tirde of Sprot, they Began to draw of for thate Different Departments and Prepare for Insweing winter."[31] This statement suggests that Pond was relying heavily on bulk imports and that he had a good source of supply.

When the rendezvous at Prairie du Chien came to an end, it was time to head east, and by July 1774 Pond was back at Michilimackinac. Here, as he expected, he found his partner, Graham, from New York, with a large cargo of trade items, the makings of the "outfit" for the next season. Pond had done so well on the St. Peter's that he proposed to buy Graham out and take on the whole venture himself. Graham accepted, and the partnership was brought to an end.[32] Pond paid him for the previous year's cargo and, perhaps more importantly, was also able to make a substantial down payment on the goods Graham had brought him for the next year. This was a decisive moment in Pond's rise to commercial fame, and Graham had been important in his ascent. Pond's first venture had ended in triumph; he had learned the trade; mastered the art of getting along with traders of convenience, out-trading others when necessary; and made himself familiar with wilderness travel and survival. But more important to his individual autonomy, he had emerged a successful capitalist, a self-made man. He now entered into partnership with another merchant, Thomas Williams, an arrangement that would last for three years.[33]

Pond gives no hints that anything unusual occurred during the outfitting of his next expedition to the interior. He recounts how he applied himself to fitting out a cargo for the same part of the country he had just left. He also describes the "grate concors of people from all quorters" who were at Michilimackinac. Some were preparing to take their furs to Canada, others to Albany and New York, or to their intended wintering ground. Still others were trading locally with tribes who had come from different parts with their furs, skins, maple sugar, grease, "taller" (small trifles for trading), and other products. Then there were the ones who amused themselves in good company at billiards, drinking fresh punch or wine, while the more vulgar were fighting each other. "Feasting was much atended to," and "dancing at nite with respectabel parsons. Notwithstanding the feateages of the industress [industrious]," he says in his own curious syntax, "the time past of agreabley for two months."[34] By then, most of the traders were ready to leave for their different wintering grounds.

He hired men as required, probably having no difficulty in doing so, and he recounts the experience of one of them, young Baptiste. The fellow felt great guilt for a theft he had committed the previous winter. A visiting priest was hearing confessions at Michilimackinac, and

> the young man heard from his comrads who had bin to confess [that the priest] was doing wonders among the people. His consans smit him and he seat of to confess but could not get absolution. He went a seacond time without sucksess but was informed by his bennadict that something was wanting. He came to me desireing me to leat him have two otter skins promising that he would be beatter in future and sarve well. I leat him have them. He went of. In a few minets after or a short time he returned. I askt him what sucksess. O sade he the father sais my case is a bad one but if I bring two otter more he will take my case on himself and discharge me. I let him have them and in a short time he returned as full of thanks as he could expres and sarved me well after.

We can sense Pond's glee in recounting this anecdote. Baptiste's confession had led to absolution. He was satisfied and relieved. The priest had reason to be pleased, too, as four otter skins were a handsome benefit of his labours for Christ in the wilderness.[35]

Pond was ready to go—"I had now a Large & Rich Cargo," he says—but a trader from Lake Superior arrived around 1 August 1774, warning that trade from Michilimackinac to the Mississippi was threatened by war between the Ojibwa (also known as Chippewa) and Sioux. His report seemed credible, setting off alarms among the traders who were intending to venture to that territory and those peoples with the next consignments of trade goods.

The commandant of Michilimackinac, Major Arent Schuyler de Peyster of New York, an aristocratic Dutchman and a person of resolute and cool bearing, gathered Pond and the other traders together to take a sounding of their opinions. Then de Peyster told them he intended to send messengers of peace. Ancient forest diplomacy was to be carried out. Beginning in the French era, Michilimackinac had been the place for the forging and renewing of peace. It was the centre of the middle ground. De Peyster's plan was that King George's couriers would carry gifts of friendship and exchange. They would also take, and deliver when appropriate, the commandant's specifically written speech calling for an end to war. De Peyster had ordered six large wampum belts made, three for each of the warring nations.[36] He selected Pond as emissary to the Sioux, for he above all others knew these people and, more to the point, was known to them. Other traders would take the other three wampum belts to Lake Superior posts for delivery to the Ojibwa. Not least in de Peyster's great plan was the idea that Pond and the other agents would bring the chiefs of the opposing sides to a grand council to he held at Michilimackinac in the spring of 1775. This was to be the winter's work, and all the while the individual traders would carry on as before.

Thus it was that, in keeping with de Peyster's instructions, Pond, bearing the three precious wampum belts, returned to Prairie du Chien on the upper Mississippi River. He was prepared to take a decisive role in the diplomacy that was required of him. Likely he was dressed in his regimental attire. However, and contrary to expectation, he found upon investigation that the Sioux there were quite unengaged in the fighting.

He continued to St. Peter's River to trade. On the thirteenth day out from Michilimackinac he reached his old house, Fort Pond, in good time to make arrangements for the winter. Here he knew the country and the people, but he was, as always, looking for new customers. An opportunity presented itself nicely when he learned of a large band two hundred miles upriver "which wanted to see a trader"—another example of Native consumers demanding trade and facilitating exchange. Pond answered the demand. He immediately put a small stock of goods into a single canoe and went up to them. Pond notes that this was an enterprise never before attempted, even by the oldest and most seasoned traders, on account of the rudeness of those people who were "Nottawaseas [Snakes] by nation but the band was called Yantonoes [Yankton]."

This encounter had remarkable consequences for Pond as it brought him among the Yankton Sioux. From his memoir we learn much about these remarkable people, one of the most powerful tribes of the Great Plains. At this particular juncture the Sioux were in the ascendant, their power growing through war and trade, more often than not at the expense of other tribes.[37] On the plains the chief always led them, Pond remarks, in clear reference to their war parties. He also comments that the Sioux were formerly one nation. In fact, they called themselves the *Oceti Sakowin*, or Seven Council Fires. On account of internal disputes, the Seven Council Fires had broken up. How recently he does not say. Now they were six different bands, according to Pond, each led by chiefs of their own choice and all speaking the same language. He listed the bands as Yankton, Band of Leaves (Wahpeton), Band of the West (probably the Wahpekuta), Band of the Stone House (the Sisseton division of the Dakota); and two bands to the north—the Assiniboine and Dog Rib.[38]

The Yankton Sioux had never met whites before, and Pond left a useful account—perhaps the first—of their life and customs at that time. The Yankton, he says, were ferocious and rude in their manners. He thought that perhaps this was in some way related to their living an obscure life on the plains. They were not conversant with every tribe and seldom saw their neighbours. They led a wandering life on that extensive plain between the Missouri and the Mississippi, which Pond estimated to be about four hundred miles broad east and west, and three hundred north and south. "They dwell in leather tents," he recounts,

> cut sumthing in [the] form of a Spanish cloke and spread out... in the shape of a bell—the poles meet at the top but the base is forten [fourteen feet] in dimerter—they go into it by a hole cut in the side and a skin hung befour it by way of a dore—they bild thare fire in the middel and do all thare cookery over it—at night thay lie down all around the lodg with thare feat to the fire—They make youse of Buffeloes dung for fuel as there is but little or no wood upon the planes.[39]

The Sioux, Pond reports, had a great number of horses and dogs that carried their baggage whenever they moved. When marching or riding over the plains, they donned a garment like an outside vest, with sleeves that came down to their elbows. These were made of soft skins, several layers thick, and would deflect an arrow shot from a distance. A shield of the same material and thickness, two and a half feet in diameter, hung over their shoulders to guard their backs. When there were a number of men so dressed, massed together in front of their band, Pond says, they made a warlike appearance. They were continually on watch for fear of being surprised by their enemies, who were all around them. Their war implements were firearms, bows and arrows, and spears, which they had continually in their hands. When on the march at night, they kept advance parties on the lookout.[40]

Pond also had a chance to observe their hunting capabilities. The Sioux, he says, ran down the buffalo with their horses and killed as much meat as they pleased. In order to have their horses "longwinded," they slit their noses up to the gristle of their head, which made them breathe freely. He recounts that he had seen them run with those modified nostrils and arrive back apparently not the least out of breath.[41]

At the close of the winter at his post on the St. Peter's, Pond arranged an assembly of eleven Sioux chiefs. He presented the wampum belts, the gifts of peace he bore from the British commandant at Michilimackinac, and explained their purpose, reading the greetings from de Peyster that set out the Crown's position and promises. The British wanted peace, peace for the purpose of profit, and the chiefs were in agreement. Pond puts it this way: "The Spring is now advancing fast. The chefes cuming with a number of the natives to go with me to Mackenac to sea and hear what thare farther had to say...By the intarpretar I had the speach explaind and intenshun of the belts—and after we had got ready for saleing we all imbarkt and went down the River to its mouth."[42]

Where the St. Peter's joins the Mississippi, they found some traders who had come from near the head of the Mississippi with Chippewa chiefs. The Chippewa mixed easily with the Sioux, much to Pond's surprise, "for the blod was scairs cold—the wound was yet fresh." Pond provides a unique detail: "While we stade thare a young smart looking chef continued singing the death song, as if he dispised thare threats or torments." After a brief stay, Pond and the Sioux chiefs embarked for Prairie du Chien, where they joined a vast number of people of all descriptions, he says, who had been waiting for him to come out of the interior and go to Michilimackinac, to the council. These people had never been there nor had they been out of their territory except on a war party. According to Pond, the meeting at Michilimackinac excited the curiosity of every nation south of the Lake of the Woods, which he estimated, a little wildly, was two thousand miles away. "Indead the matter was intresting all parties...for the following reason—each of these nations are as much larger than eney of thare nighbering nations as the Inhabitans of a sittey are to a villeag and when thay are at varans [variance] property is not safe even traveling threw thare countrey."[43] In other words, the safety of the trade in the interior demanded that the differences should be settled. And we learn from Pond that the various tribes were in search of the same goal of peace and prosperity through trade and exchange. In expectation, the whole procession headed eastward—first downstream on the Mississippi and then, where the Wisconsin joins it, heading up that tributary and portaging to the Fox River as soon as possible.

The expedition descended the Fox to the bottom of Green Bay and then joined the rest of the canoes bound for Michilimackinac. The way was fair and pleasant, he says, and they proceeded together across Lake Michigan. Two days later, and about five miles from Michilimackinac, they all came together in what must have been a vast armada of canoes. What happened next appealed to Pond's sense of military order. They "aproacht in order," he says. "We had flags on the masts of our canoes—eavery chefe his flock. My canoes beaing the largest in that part of the cuntrey and haveing a large Youon [Union] flage I histed it and when within a mile and a half I took ye lead and the Indans followed close behind."[44]

On shore, the approach of such a canoe procession was duly noted, and a grand welcome prepared. The flag in the fort was hoisted. The cannons of the garrison "began to play smartley." Along the shore, people lined up and set up such a cry and whoop that it got the tribes in the fleet "a going to that degrea that you could not hear a parson speak." At length they reached the shore and the cannon ceased. Pond then took his party of chiefs to de Peyster, who treated them all "verey well." Pond sat with them an hour and related what he calls "the affair"—that is, the embassy to the Sioux—and what he had done during the winter. After introducing the chief, Pond went to his own house, where he found a number of old friends. He passed the remainder of the day with them. After so long on such a great expedition, with the mission completed, he found rest and repose in his home at Michilimackinac. How pleasant to have his friends with him to share the stories and recount the anecdotes. Pond does not enlarge on his own grand voyage; he had done his job.

However, the final steps of the business still lay ahead. Pond says that the people from Lake Superior, the Ojibwa, had arrived at the council before he and the Sioux did. That day and the next the grand council was held in front of the commandant and a "vast number" of spectators in the great chamber. Here the articles of peace were concluded. Promises were made on both sides to abide by the articles so as to prevent further bloodshed. The gist of the agreement was that the Sioux would not cross the Mississippi to the Chippewa territory on the east side, either to hunt nor, tellingly, to cause any disturbance on the Chippewa ground. Rather, they "should live by the side of each other as frinds and nighbers." The Chippewa likewise promised to observe the same regulations toward the Sioux—they would not cross the river to hunt or cause disturbance on the west side. After all the articles were drawn up, everyone present signed them.

The commandant then made a present of a keg of rum to each nation. Each left the fort and went to their own camps, where they sat around and enjoyed their present, sang a few songs, and went to rest in a very civil manner. The next day a large fat ox was killed and roasted by the soldiers. All of the Indians were bidden to the feast. They dined together in harmony and finished the day by drinking moderately, smoking together, singing, and "britening the chane of frindship in a veray deasant way. This was kept up for four days when the offeser mad them each a present and thay all imbark for thare one part of thare cuntrey."

All had gone according to plan. The grand design had been effected; peace had been brokered and established; promises for the future given. Boundaries had been set and agreed to, and the rules and regulations set down by the commandant on behalf of the Indian Department, representing the Crown. De Peyster was a central figure, not only by asking the traders their opinions but also in sending them out as emissaries, complete with wampum belts and other gifts, plus pronouncements of his requirements and an invitation to attend, with others, at Michilimackinac. His grand council of 1775 restored peace and secured the interests of the warring parties.[45]

A student of the history of imperialism might note with interest that the First Nations were involved in the business of peacemaking at every stage. They desired trade, as Pond's example so clearly shows. They were perhaps more accommodating to the British than they were to other nations, their rivals. Thus, on the indigenous side of the imperial equation, their peace was being brokered by the British as middlemen, neutral partners who took no favourites in the process. It is undeniably true that European commodities of trade and consumption were in heavy demand in the interior and that the traders were responding to these needs. It is not correct, in this historian's opinion, to say that such goods were thrust upon the Native peoples. In the history of commerce it is demand that is of fundamental importance.[46]

Pond had demonstrated an unusual ability to travel and live among the tribes, and he had shown a clear capability in diplomacy with Native peoples. He seems to have been fearless and quite prepared to put himself in positions hazardous to his personal safety. As a soldier he must have been cool under fire, and this capacity he translated to wilderness travels and trade. All the more remarkable is the fact that he seems to have done this on his own. Solitary action is his motif.

After this venture, Pond said goodbye to the upper Mississippi, deciding instead to pursue trade in the northwest via Grand Portage, the lakeside emporium of traders near the west end of Lake Superior. He was now a partner in the firm of Pond and Graves, with Englishman Booty Graves. At the same time, and taking all sorts of complicated arrangements in his stride, he was also connected to Pond and Williams (that was Thomas Williams, with whom he had gone into partnership in 1774). News of business prospects and reverses travelled quickly among fur traders, and Pond always had his ear to the ground for word of new developments and opportunities. At Michilimackinac or, less probably, Prairie du Chien, Pond had learned of the rich possibilities farther north, where better furs were to be had, and greater profits. The Thirteen Colonies were now in revolt against King George III. This interested Pond not at all; he had been a soldier of the King in days gone by but not now. Instead he was being drawn into the most vital conduit in the history of the fur trade, and he was soon to become its master—the most prominent trader. North and west lay the course of empire. He was the fist in the wilderness.

5

Among the Canadians on the Saskatchewan, and the Rivals from Hudson Bay

From the days of Champlain, Frontenac, and La Salle, the lifeblood of Canada was the fur trade. The northern economy, based on the St. Lawrence River, linked the hinterland to the ports of France. Tax revenues from the trade enriched the colonial coffers. The defence of the Canadian realm came from European waters. All the while, in Hudson Bay and Britain's American colonies, forces of subversion threatened the empire of the St. Lawrence. Then came the catastrophe of 1759 and its aftermath in 1760, when Montreal fell. The great fur realm collapsed. The settlements came under the control of British soldiers.

For a few years after the conquest of Canada, the interior trade did not pass into British hands. Trade goods were lacking and export links spoiled. The French posts began to decay; the portages became choked with forest debris. The friendship of the British Crown and First Nations west of Detroit was uncertain, and no garrisons were established anywhere west of Grand Portage, where only a small guard was kept. The episode

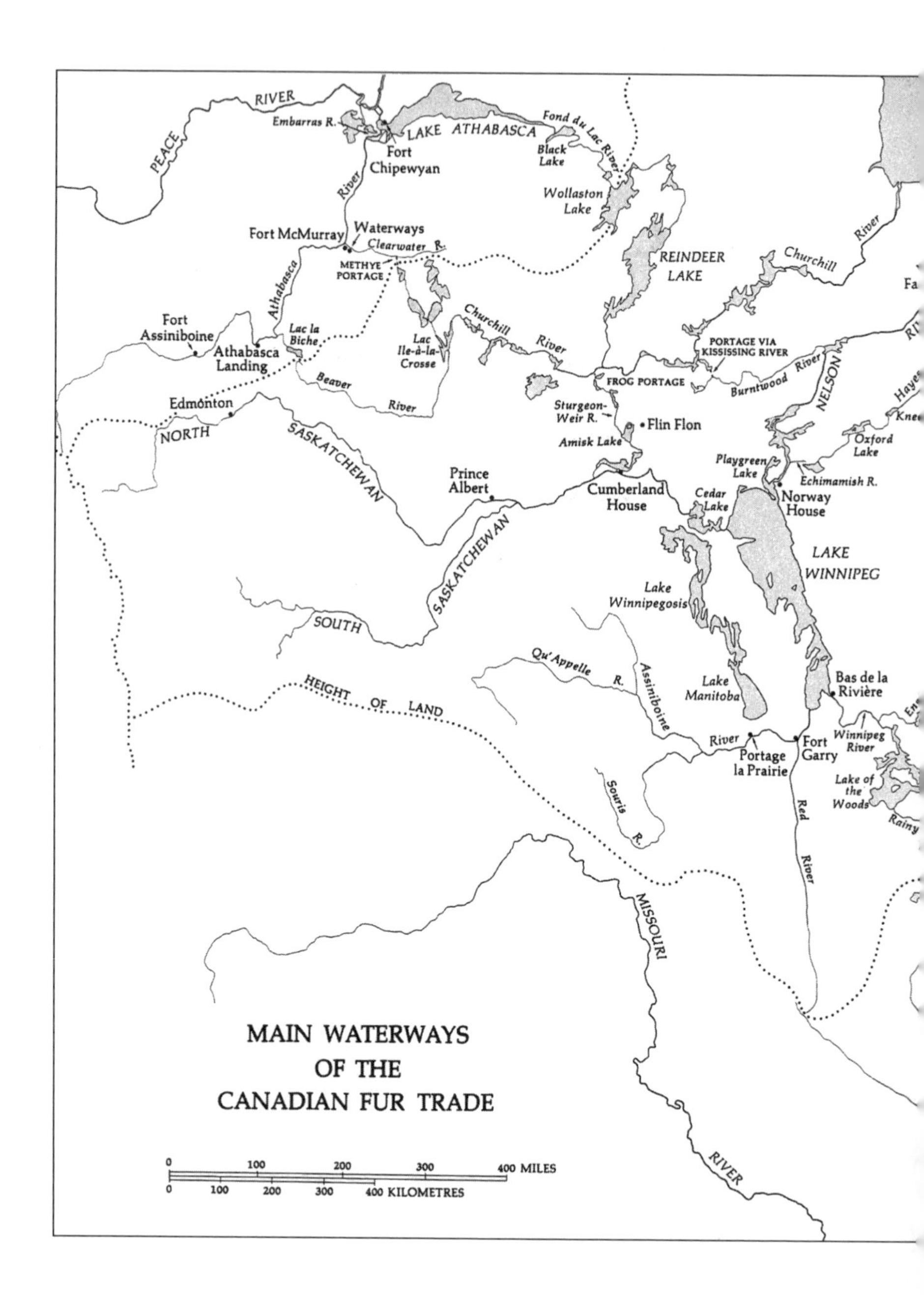
PEACE
RIVER
Embarras R.
LAKE ATHABASCA
Fond du Lac River
Black Lake
Fort Chipewyan
River
Wollaston Lake
Fort McMurray
Waterways
Clearwater R.
METHYE PORTAGE
REINDEER LAKE
Churchill
River
Athabasca
Fort Assiniboine
Athabasca Landing
Lac la Biche
Lac Ile-à-la-Crosse
Churchill
River
PORTAGE VIA KISSISSING RIVER
FROG PORTAGE
Burntwood
River
NELSON
Beaver
River
Edmonton
NORTH
SASKATCHEWAN
Sturgeon-Weir R.
Flin Flon
Amisk Lake
Playgreen Lake
Oxford Lake
Echimamish R.
Prince Albert
Cumberland House
Cedar Lake
Norway House
LAKE WINNIPEG
SASKATCHEWAN
SOUTH
Lake Winnipegosis
Qu'Appelle R.
Assiniboine
Lake Manitoba
Bas de la Rivière
HEIGHT OF LAND
River
Portage la Prairie
Fort Garry
Winnipeg River
Lake of the Woods
Souris R.
Red River
MISSOURI
RIVER
MAIN WATERWAYS OF THE CANADIAN FUR TRADE
0 100 200 300 400 MILES
0 100 200 300 400 KILOMETRES

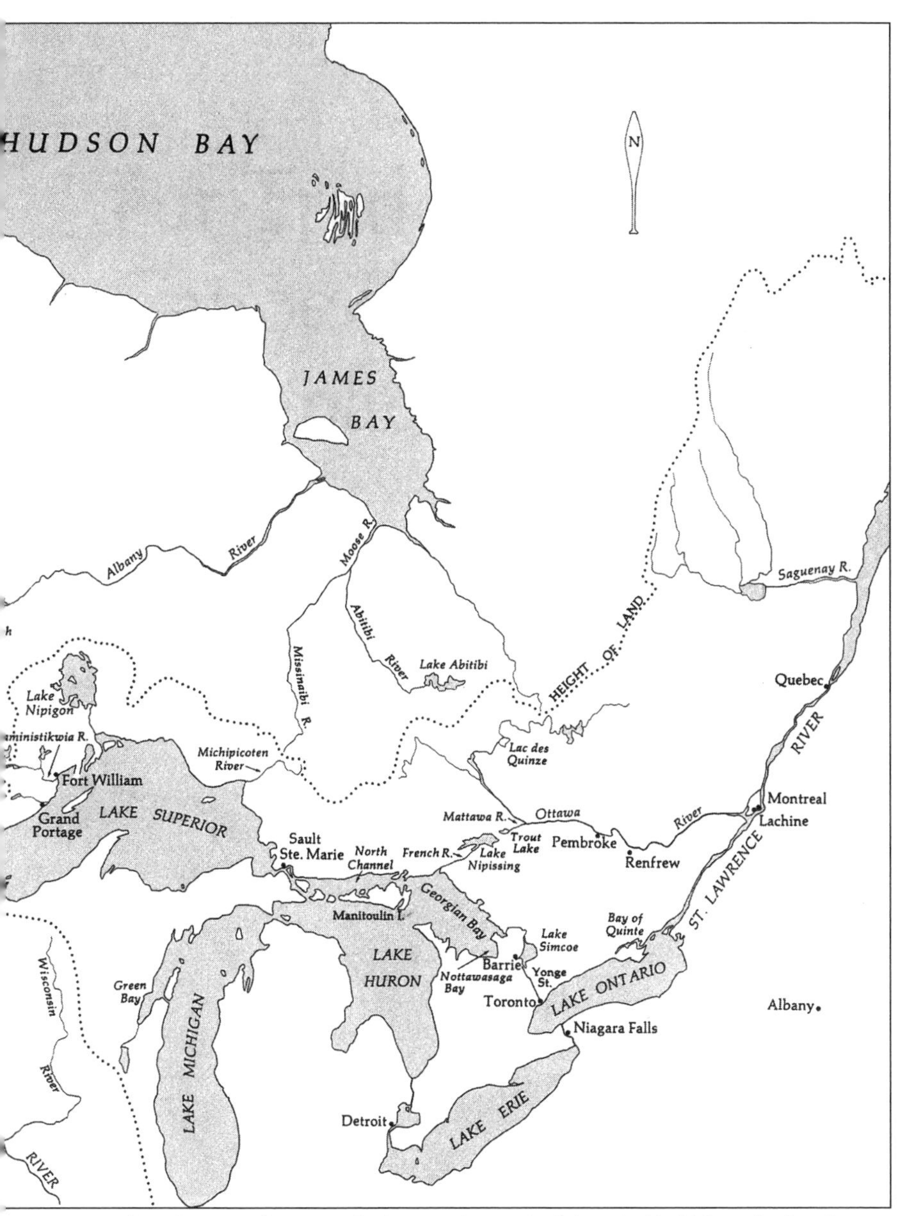

French traders were drawn ever farther west in search of the valuable, high-quality furs that provided the economic lifeblood of the colony. Along with this expansion came considerable problems, however, as transportation grew difficult and costly. MAP DERIVED FROM ERIC W. MORSE, *FUR TRADE CANOE ROUTES OF CANADA/THEN AND NOW*, WITH MAPS BY ROBERT MANN, OF MORTON BASLAW AND CO. LTD., OTTAWA, 1968 known as Pontiac's war was not ended until 1765. But shipping was easily available, and inexpensive English manufactures sought new avenues of commerce. British merchant enthusiasm was unbounded. High risks could be taken. The traders, when they returned, moved into the waters that led to the Red and Assiniboine Rivers, fanning out as required to establish tributary posts. That first phase was the easiest; more demanding was to move into the Saskatchewan River valley, to and beyond where the French had been. This was the new field of endeavour.

The Saskatchewan, a short but powerful river system, drains a vast area of prairie and parkland stretching eastward from the ramparts of the Rocky Mountains, taking in its north and south branches, and eventually reaching salt water at York Factory on Hudson Bay. The Saskatchewan's northern flanks lie hard by the boreal or northern forest. Here, for the fur traders and the business interests of Montreal, lay the new opportunities, for here were fine furs in abundant quantity. Here, too, were trading allies, the Cree.

The southern flanks of that river were of inestimable value to the burgeoning economy. The Saskatchewan drained lands adjacent to the northern Great Plains that were teeming with buffalo. From the buffalo, wholesome and portable pemmican and other dried provisions could be produced, making that river the larder of the fur trade. Pemmican was the food of western expansion. Native and Métis labour and talents combined to make possible its production. Credit for the organization of the pemmican trade as a necessary adjunct to the fur business—and its westward expansion—is accorded, by at least one authority, to Pond.[1] He had ample opportunity to use his knowledge of logistics and the handling of supplies, learned from his years of military service, in the distant fur trade then developing, where the voyageur depended on food supplies readily available and the Native partners demanded goods in trade for the furs gathered.

Traders from Montreal had begun their advance into the Saskatchewan valley a decade before Pond. As they did, they spotted along the way the old French posts, now abandoned and crumbling or even burnt, remnants of another era. The first adventurer from Montreal went from Michilimackinac in 1765. His name is lost to history, but we do know something of his experiences. The tribes at Rainy Lake (Lac la Pluie, the French had called it), "having been long destitute of

Goods, stop't and plundered his Canoes, and would not suffer him to proceed hither. He attempted it again the following year, and met with the same bad Fortune." So wrote Benjamin and Joseph Frobisher about twenty years after the fact. Mackenzie says that in 1766 the inland trade commenced from Michilimackinac along the Kaministiquia River, which is upstream and west from present-day Thunder Bay, Ontario.[2] "Their success induced them to renew their journey, and incited others to follow their example," he writes elegantly.[3] Some of the traders remained at Kaministiquia while others proceeded to Grand Portage, which soon became the principal depot of the trade and the route to the interior rivers and lakes.[4] "After passing the usual season there, they went back to Michilimackinac as before, and encouraged by the trade, returned in increasing numbers."[5]

Mackenzie identifies Thomas Curry as a noteworthy pioneer. Curry exhibited a spirit of enterprise superior to his contemporaries. He determined to penetrate to the farthest limits of the French discoveries and hired guides and interpreters who were acquainted with the country. With four canoes he arrived at Fort Bourbon, one of the old French posts, on Cedar Lake, part of the Saskatchewan River system. This is likely the same expedition referred to by the Frobishers when they say that another attempt was made in 1767. On this occasion, the traders left goods at Rainy Lake post, and the Natives there permitted them to proceed with the remainder. From this time the Rainy Lake post grew as an important depot and larder (especially so, we might note here, when the Athabasca trade began and a separate sub-depot was designated there). Curry continued on his way, penetrating beyond Lake Winnipeg for the first time. He was well compensated for his risk and toil. The following spring he came out with his canoes heavily laden with fine furs, which he took to Montreal. He had had his fill of the business, "and was satisfied never again to return to the Indian country." He then disappeared from history.[6]

Persons such as James Finlay, the first to follow Curry's example, came into that country and traded with varying success. But because of what traders regarded as the rapacious and ungovernable character of the tribes of Rainy Lake, who plundered their canoes and "would not suffer any part of our Goods to be sent further," the trade faltered. That season, 1769, may have been ruinous to the investors; it seems that some of the firms and alliances were on the verge of breaking up, and the whole scheme might have been abandoned, except that goods for the next season, 1770, were already ordered for delivery to Grand Portage. In the circumstances, they had no option but to proceed. The breakthrough came that year: the traders got through to Lake Bourbon, where the French had been years earlier. "Thenceforth we were determined to persevere," the Frobishers wrote in their pleading memoir to government for help and protection, adding, "Taught however by experience that separate Interests were the Bane of that Trade we lost no time to form with those Gentlemen, and some others, a Company, and having men of Conduct and Ability to conduct it in the Interior Country, the Indians were soon abundantly supplied and being at the same time well treated."[7]

After 1774 the traders to the northwest went beyond where the French had previously been, and they put up new posts, binding themselves together in defence. But rivals to these partners—independent actors in the larger game—were now coming on to perplex them and threatening to upset the financial stability of those allied in trade. These were precarious days, ones of high risk. In these circumstances, and to enhance their security, promote their commerce, and keep the rivals at bay, the northwestern traders sought the protection of government. However, the upstarts had little chance of getting the attention of the British government. The reason is clear.

By the 1770s the Hudson's Bay Company had been trading for a century in the northern wilds of Canada. Throughout this domain, called Rupert's Land in the charter given by Charles II on 2 May 1670, the Bay traders were lords and proprietors of a world of water, forest, and swamp that has been estimated at 2.75-million square miles. The Company came under the purview of a board of directors, or committee, and ultimately the surveillance of parliament and the Crown. Here was empire within empire. The Company's strongholds remained several posts on the shores of Hudson Bay and James Bay, at the mouths of rivers that drained the seemingly limitless continental interior. The various tribes customarily came to them for trade; it was easier that way, and the profits continued.

On the distant margins of Rupert's Land, the company had watched for interlopers, some of whom might come by sea (as the French did on occasion) or overland from New France while that regime still existed. After the fall of New France, the challenge was not soon felt, though news had reached London headquarters that "Pedlars" out of Montreal were penetrating the southern margins of the Company's territory. For the present there seemed little to fear. In fact, as of 1767, Bay traders were of the opinion that the petty traders from Quebec and "such a pitiful game" were hardly worth their attention.[8]

Soon the Company learned that it had under-represented the threat and that it had reason to be worried. In 1768, the abrasive William Tomison, an Orkneyman who had risen from labourer to officer rank, reported "a vast Number of Pedlars" in the interior.[9] This set the alarm bells ringing at York Factory and in London. The initial Hudson's Bay Company response, quite understandable in the circumstances, was to send for Cree and Assiniboine leaders who might guide their people from the interior to the Company's posts. But this allurement did not answer, for these nations naturally preferred to deal with the Canadian traders, who brought their wares to them, on the spot. Why should they serve as tour guides? Why should they bother to take the three-month summer voyage in their small canoes from the Saskatchewan all the way to posts on Hudson Bay?

That same year, 1768, the Company trader Ferdinand Jacobs concluded that the only way out of the problem was to match the rivals by building establishments inland, where they could cultivate trade with the tribes' headmen and leaders, especially the influential White Bird. Company servants from Hudson Bay explored the possibilities, but these expeditions produced only incoherent and unintelligible written accounts. These were of no use to those determining trade policies.[10] A change came in 1772, when the diligent and articulate Yorkshire man Matthew Cocking, of rising importance in the push inland, made a pioneering reconnaissance. Cocking travelled by canoe on the Hayes, Fox, and Minago Rivers to the South Saskatchewan. At the site of an old French post, he and his companions "threw away" their canoes and proceeded across the South Saskatchewan to the Eagle Hills. In his report, he detailed the buffalo country and the customs of the people, notably the Siksikas, or Blackfeet. He described the prairies and parkland, their wildlife and vegetation, and the route that connected them with Hudson Bay. The posts, procedures, and trade standards of the Canadian peddlers who were intercepting the York Factory trade were of prime concern to him. Like Jacobs a few years earlier, Cocking suggested the solution was for the Company to push trading operations inland. He also identified the obstacles to be overcome, not least the company's lack of canoes and experienced men. Another trader, Isaac Batt, after a visit to the plains, made a representation to London headquarters to this same effect in May 1773. The London Committee, already alarmed by the slumping fur returns from York Factory, decided to establish a post inland, near "Basquiau."[11] The Company's years of slumbering by the shores of the Bay were over.

But imperial motives were also driven by consumer needs. The Company answered the call of the Western Woods Cree to establish a post in the heart of their territory. The Cree, great travellers who had visited Hudson Bay and Michilimackinac on trading and diplomatic missions, were skilled at entangling English and French in their trading web. Their central position in the Saskatchewan River watershed made them a force to be reckoned with. They were tough traders and kept up a steady demand for trade items. As masters of their own destiny, in the early 1770s they abandoned their middlemen status by which they carried trade items to posts on Hudson Bay. But they held to their position in the trade. "The European traders held no power over the Cree," writes historian Paul Thistle, "and even the influence attached to trade goods was minimal since the Indians could easily have traded with the competition, or simply done without it."[12] As Edward Umfreville, sometime trader with the North West Company and HBC, remarked at the time, with insight, "It is no more in the power of the trader to hinder them from going to war than it is of the Governor of Michilimacina, who does all in his power annually to prevent it."[13]

Marriages in the custom of the country now began to anchor the trade to the Cree heartland and made that nation richer. Those women directly connected with fur traders, and their children, were borne on the establishment's books. Food and shelter were their benefits. All these arrangements, and the benefits, devolved from Cree demands that the traders come to the interior, and this suited the HBC because it would allow them to compete directly with the Canadians. Once again we see the essential value of the Native alliance in trade. The Cree connection was central to HBC progress. By the same token, it brought the HBC into territories where other tribes and nations had influence. The traders' security in their posts, in their trading expeditions, and in their transit along the waterways depended on good relations with the Native peoples. The traders were there on sufferance.[14]

It was just after the Hudson's Bay Company made its decisive move to go to the interior that Pond came to the same location. In 1775 he had become connected with the outfitter Simon McTavish, a Scot who had immigrated to New York at age thirteen, then engaged in business at Albany.[15] McTavish began a remarkable rise to wealth by outfitting Peter Pond, his intention being to compete against various Montreal interests such as the Frobishers, who hailed from Yorkshire, and the McGill brothers from Glasgow. In 1775, McTavish shifted his base to Montreal, which gave him the protection of British trade laws designed to advance the interests of the Canadian fur trade.

On 18 August 1775, Pond joined Alexander Henry while coasting along the east side of Lake Winnipeg near the Cree village at the mouth of the Winnipeg River. The shores of the lake were rocky and lofty, the wood there was pine and fir, and there were good-sized catfish for the catching. A few days later, on the 20th, they crossed the lake to Oak Point, where scrub oak provided diversification from pine and fir. "The pelicans, which we every where saw, appeared to be impatient of the long stay we made in fishing," Henry mused. On the west side of Lake Winnipeg they spied a great rock, Roche Rouge, composed of a stone, calumet, used for making tobacco-pipe bowls. They escaped from the dangers of a severe gale, finding safety on Buffalo Head, an island. Not so fortunate were a canoe and four men, lost in the raging waters.

Born in colonial New Jersey, Alexander Henry (the Elder) was prominent in the American-based fur trade that came into the northwest via Albany, New York. As a dominant partner in the North West Company, he knew Pond and remarked that he was a celebrity of some renown. Henry is famous for his book of travels that describes Pontiac's rebellion and life at Michilimackinac. LIBRARY AND ARCHIVES CANADA, ACC. NO. 1977-34-2

Henry (of whom more presently) refers to his new companion in his memoir, *Travels and Adventures in Canada and the Indian Territories*, as "Mr. Pond, a trader of some celebrity in the northwest."[16] Henry, invariably circumspect and prudent, does not give any particulars as to why Pond had so soon gained celebrity status. We are left guessing. It may be that Pond's reputation as a hard-hitting, violent trader in the First Nations country had given him unique status. It could be that his diplomacy with Native peoples was revered. Or it may be that Pond had a reputation as a uniquely successful trader. If the last of these possibilities is correct, it would have earned him the respect, if not the envy, of rival traders. In any event, Pond's reputation had preceded him and he was known as a force to be reckoned with, an independent spirit. The Montreal traders needed him on their side, not in opposition to them.

Henry, born in New Jersey, had ventured north via Albany, a place with easy connections to Montreal and its warehouses and shipping links. Pond, Henry, and other New Englanders would make arrangements in Albany for the western trade and then go west to Detroit, Michilimackinac, and Grand Portage before heading farther west to their intended place of winter trade. Henry himself had spent the winter of 1774–75 at Chequamegon and he had sent a clerk with two canoes to Fond du Lac, at the southwest end of Lake Superior, near present-day Duluth. The initial returns from Fond du Lac were fabulous—150 packs of beaver and twenty-five of otter and martin skins. Before connecting with Pond at Lake Winnipeg, Henry had left from the Sault with Jean-Baptiste Cadotte, or Cadot, a seasoned trader from Sault Ste. Marie. Henry chose his partner well: Cadotte and his two sons, Michel and Jean-Baptiste, had become allied with the Ojibwa, and for two generations they made the name Cadotte synonymous with successful business on Lake Superior's south shore.[17]

After surviving the hazards of Lake Winnipeg, Pond, Cadotte, and Henry came to the Winnipeg River, the mainline of east–west canoe travel. There Joseph and Thomas Frobisher and Charles Paterson overtook them. All together they formed a very large brigade, a birchbark armada, perhaps one of the biggest of its times. The whole, consisting of thirty canoes and 130 men, reached the mouth of the Saskatchewan River on 1 October. They pressed upstream, and sixty miles beyond The Pas they came upon the HBC's newly built Cumberland House on Cumberland Lake. They doubtless regarded this as an intrusion into a realm they had taken for granted as theirs and theirs alone. There flew the HBC flag, symbol of chartered authority—and of the Crown's complicit backing of an imperial venture of trade and commerce. Though historians treat the founding of Cumberland House as just another event, when seen from Pond's perspective, and Henry's too (indeed, all who came out of the Montreal nexus), a challenge had been set before them. Who knew where it might end? But for the moment, winter was in the air, and the men were hungry.

The distress of the Company's resident manager, Cocking, can be imagined. Here were unwelcome guests in large numbers—far too many to feed and, more importantly, unwanted by virtue of the competition they posed to the HBC's intentions of interior trade, which the Company had announced by planting its new fort on the Saskatchewan River. In the circumstances, Cocking greeted them with cool civility.

Only the year before, Samuel Hearne, sailor turned fur trader, had come inland from Hudson Bay with Cocking to establish a post above The Pas.[18] That place had connections, via the Saskatchewan River, to both Lake Winnipeg and the Rocky Mountains; it became an important supply depot for fur traders working upriver. From this junction the Montrealers headed toward Athabasca. However, this confident first step of the HBC's expansion into the interior was not easily followed on, for manpower was at a premium and the inland trade arrangements were as novel as they were experimental. The tyranny of distance, so often a feature in historical developments, or lack thereof, had always to be contended with in the communications networks of the North American fur trade. Having adequate food supplies was another prime consideration, as were good Native relations. The Company depended on Cree friendship, and the headman, Mameek Athinnee, could prove insolent and difficult. At the same time, new recruits like Robert Longmoor and Malcolm Ross carried out the necessary winter work of diplomacy among the plains Assiniboine at the Eagle Hills. In the next few years the Company built posts upriver—sometimes called the middle settlements, or the "Forts des Prairies"—from which the bison could conveniently be hunted. Upriver again, when opportunity allowed, the Hudson's Bay Company expanded to counter the peddlers on the North Saskatchewan River.

The rivalry with the Montrealers has been described as ruthless, but this was only one issue challenging the Bay traders. Some have said the Canadians' expansion was arrogant in its approach to the Indians.[19] Violence on the frontier would hit Hudson's Bay Company coffers. It was, in all, a cutthroat business—of that there can be no denial. It also took on all forms. Ruthless competition also existed between the Canadian peddlers themselves, and as to arrogance toward the Indians, this may be taken to mean that the peddlers had a take it or leave it attitude when dealing with their trading partners—a view that flies in the face of the customary argument and, indeed, the historical evidence that Native peoples demanded traders give them full measure in their transactions with Europeans.

There is a darker side to this rivalry between the Montrealers and the Bay traders, and it does not always get the attention it deserves in the historical literature, perhaps because Native-induced violence has little currency among readers who wish to blame whites as agents of brutality and murder. It is true that Natives killed three Canadians on the Saskatchewan in 1776–77, but whether this is related to traders' arrogance, a response to disease, or some other factor is not known. The tribes could and did play one set of traders against another, and historical sources tend to confirm that the Canadian traders continued to face violent positions on the frontier, and that the Hudson's Bay Company enjoyed more genial relations on the plains. The same authority states that in 1779, Cree on the North Saskatchewan River, "resentful of the callous, fraudulent, and abusive treatment they received at the hands of Canadian traders, attacked Canadians at Eagle Hills, killing two men, including New Englander John Cole. As a result the Canadians fled their Eagle Hills establishment."[20] We know, as stated, that in 1776–77, Indians killed three Montrealers on the Saskatchewan. This affected trade expansion: no attempt was made by the Canadians to travel above Cumberland House the following year.[21]

Taking stock of developments on the Saskatchewan in the mid- and late 1770s, we can see that the Montrealers' drive for dominance, which began in the 1760s, was being challenged by the Hudson's Bay Company; that the tribes were countering with sporadic acts of violence that would interrupt traders' plans for the future; and that the Bay traders were mindful of the tempestuous circumstances in which they now found themselves. As for Peter Pond, in all of this his role is of critical significance. His knowledge of logistics, forward planning, and Native diplomacy, and his capacity to forge alliances with other like-minded traders, coalesced at this time into the prominent role he is credited with having. It might be speculated that this had less to do with the rivalry from the HBC than it did with the Native challenges above Cumberland House. Once again it was these latter considerations that compelled the Euro-American response, whether from the Canadian or Bay traders. The traders were on sufferance, no matter how strong or well-armed they were. Their lives could be snuffed out in a minute should an uprising occur.

The Hudson's Bay Company was driven by the actions of its rivals. Throughout its history, the pre-emptive impulse prevailed. On the margins of the trade, its employees always took firm action, even at great expense to themselves. In 1775, Hearne, a helpless onlooker at Cumberland House, reported to London startling news that was bound to be worrisome to the Company of Adventurers of England Trading into Hudson's Bay: more than sixty canoes had come inland from Grand Portage that summer, Pond's and Henry's included, conveying their goods all the way from distant Montreal—powder, shot, muskets, small trade items in metal and glass, Brazilian tobacco, and West Indian rum. This was distressing information, but more alarming news was soon to be sent to London. Cocking learned that these various traders from Montreal—hitherto working for themselves, though some were backed by Montreal merchants—had tired of the ruinous rivalry among themselves or, more likely, had found that they could better trade in a sort of combination, sharing the costs, the risks, and whatever rewards the trade would allow. This indeed was alarming. For here was the genesis of the North West Company, unproclaimed as such. That company was born in the field, in the *pays d'en haut*, not in the corporate boardrooms or the later rendezvous of inland and Montreal partners.

Pond and Henry worked well together, though such harmony was not always exhibited between and among traders. Cocking scribbled, in his Cumberland journal of 1776, words which gave him personal satisfaction: "The Master Pedlars up above are at present at Variance, and some of them parted stocks."[22] In other words, there had been a difference of opinion about ways and means, and perhaps personal difficulties too. Being in an arrangement of shares was bound to lead to the pointing of fingers as to who had done least to benefit the concern. By the same token, he who had done the most might claim a larger share of profit than the partners could release. We return to this point shortly.

On 8 October 1775, Pond, Étienne Cadotte, Joseph and Thomas Frobisher, and Alexander Henry, all veterans of western commercial enterprise, and others besides—as mentioned above, the brigade totalled 130 men—were waylaid at Basquiau, a Cree encampment at the mouth of the Pasquia River, by Chatique, the Pelican. Thirty followers, all armed with bows and arrows and spears, attended Chatique, the headman of about thirty families of Cree. Chatique, of striking appearance and tall and corpulent bearing, summoned the traders into his tent. He desired to trade but also demanded tribute. As Henry reported, in describing Chatique's demands, the headman hinted

> that we must be well aware of his power to prevent our going further; that if we passed now, he could put us all to death on our return; and that under these circumstances, he expected us to be exceedingly liberal in our presents: adding, that to avoid misunderstanding, he would inform us of what it was that he must have [gunpowder, shot and ball, tobacco, rum, guns, knives, flints and smaller articles]...He went on to say that he had before now been acquainted with white men, and knew that they promised more than they performed; that with the number of men which he had, he could take the whole of our property, without our consent; and that therefore his demands ought to be regarded as very reasonable; that he was a peaceable man, and one that contented himself with moderate views, in order to avoid quarrels,—finally, that he desired us to signify our assent to his proposition, before we quitted our places.[23]

The traders were hopelessly outnumbered. There was no alternative but to give in to the demands, which they must have thought extortionate but had to be attended to as a necessary prelude to trade. The traders brought forth the tribute, then left. But with two miles behind them they saw Chatique approach in a canoe. He boarded one of the canoes and demanded another keg of rum. "We saw," wrote Henry, "that the only alternative was to kill this daring robber or submit to his exaction. The former part would have been attended by very mischievous consequences; and we therefore curbed our indignation, and chose the latter." Chatique got his rum, saluted the traders with a cry, and departed.[24]

From here, Pond and his brigade of canoes separated from the others. Cadotte, we know, went to Fort des Prairies,[25] which later became the key post of the Nor'Westers on the Saskatchewan River, located near the forks where the south branch of the Saskatchewan joins the main, northern stream. Henry, combining with the Frobishers, headed northwest to distant Churchill River, also known as English River. Others unnamed, perhaps including Peter Pangman, pressed out in other directions. Invariably they located themselves cleverly on the waterways south, west, and north of Cumberland House, their intention being to intercept Indians bearing furs before they reached the HBC's establishment.[26]

For his part, Pond, with two canoes, went up Mossy River to winter at his Fort Dauphin.[27] He gives the location of this post as at the northwest corner of Dauphin Lake itself.[28] Unless an agreement to cooperate had been undertaken, Pond would have been in opposition to John Cole at Peter Pangman's Fort Dauphin.[29] Pond was not trading with the "common concern" of Henry, Pangman, Paterson, Jean-Baptiste Cadotte, and James Finlay. At Dauphin Lake he was favoured in two ways. First, there was plenty of buffalo meat available, and, second, he was in a position to divert the furs bound for Cumberland House.

In the spring of 1776, Pond went out to Michilimackinac and arranged to have the next season's goods brought to Grand Portage. He had realized the necessity of keeping his supply base as far forward as possible. In so doing he assisted the process by which Grand Portage, and later Fort William (now Thunder Bay, Ontario), supplanted Michilimackinac as the western supply depot of the northwest fur trade.[30]

It was in that year, 1776, that the North West Company first emerged as an entity, an organic association of like-minded traders. Still in its infancy, it would reformulate itself several times, but it always had the same purpose. Its founders had seen the presence and threat of the rivals on the Saskatchewan. They had witnessed at first hand the resistance and demands of the Cree on that same river. The far distant trading necessitated new measures and greater planning and coordination, for costs and risks had risen with these threats. The coalition had rid itself of dissidents and was now more powerful than the original formation of "The Master Pedlars," as Cocking called them.

Three years later, a nineteen-share organization burst into existence. Nine groups of traders dominated it: Isaac Todd, James McGill, Benjamin and Joseph Frobisher, Simon McTavish, Robert Grant, Lawrence Ermatinger, and others, including the nonpareil Peter Pond. Of these, Simon McTavish was the corporate fixer to be watched out for, and we return to him presently. Yorkshire men Benjamin and Joseph Frobisher, and their young brother Thomas, were a rising force in the trade: Benjamin was the administrative genius of the three; Joseph, the active trader; and Thomas, the far traveller. This trio seems to have worked parallel to Pond and his several business connections. It was from Thomas that Pond seems to have learned about the prospects of the Churchill River and what lay west of it, though we infer that from the progression of discoveries and advances, not from any testimonial document to the same effect. And it was the Frobisher trio that brought Pond in to sign, as spokesmen, a memorandum to government calling for support for the Nor'Westers in the face of compelling dangers. That lay ahead, though the circumstances that led to the memorandum were quickly developing in the North Saskatchewan area.

North West Company trading tokens such as these manufactured in the United Kingdom in 1820 are now exceedingly rare. One side shows the prince regent (George IV) and the other, the venerable Canadian symbol, the beaver. COURTESY: NATIONAL CURRENCY COLLECTION, BANK OF CANADA, OTTAWA

Pond wintered for the next two years, 1776–77 and 1777–78, at the junction of the Sturgeon-weir River and the North Saskatchewan River, a short distance downstream from the place where HBC employee Robert Longmoor would soon challenge the peddlers' hold on trade. We have only a glimpse of Pond's explorations in those years upstream on the Saskatchewan: a site on his map that was given to Congress states that in the western mountains he had seen flints, or *pierres à fusil*, containing veins of white metal that looked like silver.[31] No other details are given, and we have no corroborating evidence. Perhaps Pond made a journey of examination, an overland trek on horseback, as fur traders were fond of doing as a form of relief from day-to-day bartering. We do know from scant documentary materials that he collected geological samples, and so the record is not altogether devoid of meaning.

On 17 April 1777, Pond entered into a partnership with yet another trader, George McBeath, who, in turn, was associated with that rising power among all Northwest traders, Simon McTavish, "the Marquis," as they called him, who was also known to Pond. McBeath and Pond were the field generals of the new enterprise. As the fur trade tentacles reached ever to the interior, so did the logistical lines increase. As a result, McBeath looked after the Montreal to Grand Portage section of the enterprise, the eastern half if you will; Pond looked after the interior or western half. It was a powerful, potent combination. The firm was referred to as McTavish and Company, and Pond was its front man, leader in the field.

All indicators pointed to the conclusion that a trade strategy ought to be prosecuted beyond the plains, with all its dogged rivalry, and into the rich and untapped northern forest zone. There lay the prime beaver and the eagerly awaiting Native traders. Thomas Frobisher's success in 1777 at Lac Île-à-la-Crosse, on the southern side of the ridge of the Athabasca watershed, led others to push forward in that direction. And there was another factor at work. Harry Duckworth has explained that the number of traders on the Saskatchewan River at that time, and the corresponding quantity of goods, were surplus to requirements of the trade.[32] In other words, the market was oversaturated from the supply side. Current customers could be satisfied, so were there others who could be brought into the web of the Nor'Westers?[33]

Pond was about to enter one of the world's great back doors. On the eve of his arrival at the doorway, no one knew if the source of its waters would turn out to be Hudson Bay, the Arctic Ocean, or the Pacific Ocean. The vast and dark quarter of the North American continent that was about to open to him had geographical riddles and secrets that were sure to surprise, its dimensions so stupendous that no single traveller could trace its watercourses or transcend its western mountain ramparts. The dogged fur trading explorer would take it one season at a time, with long-range thoughts of empires and destinies of nations a shallow substitute for workaday lives in pursuit of the rich beaver pelt upon which the immediate future depended.

6

Athabasca Odyssey

In the spring of 1778 a handful of traders, chiefly representing the powerful houses of Benjamin and Joseph Frobisher on the one hand and McTavish and Company on the other, put into a common stock their goods remaining at Pine Island, Cumberland Lake. This joint concern, building on the earlier association of traders, was probably the direct forerunner of the North West Company. Its future prospects depended on commercial expansion—and on new long-distance trade to fresh Native partners. They entrusted the management of the enterprise to the strongest partner, Pond.[1]

Ahead lay travels through distant lakes, rivers, and portages known only by reports from the aboriginal people who lived among them. At the end of his journey, in high, cold latitudes, and with daylight shortening, Pond would have to put up winter quarters before the ground froze. His destination was a land known as *Athabasca*—"where there are reeds" in the Cree language, a reference to marshy land in the heart of a rocky, timbered region. More than in any previous trading season, it was especially important for Pond to get an early start that year.

As early as the season would allow, Pond set out from Cumberland Lake with five canoes, passing the Hudson's Bay Company's Cumberland House on 26 May.[2] On its lower reaches, as far as Cumberland House, the Saskatchewan River was relatively featureless, as Eric Morse, canoeist and expert on fur trader routes, tells us.[3] But this changed upstream when they approached the spot where the Sturgeon-weir River flowed into it. The voyageurs called the Sturgeon-weir the *Rivière Maligne*, for going up it was tortuous and tiring (going down was sheer white-water joy). Alexander Mackenzie thought the whole river almost one continuous rapid, and so it is—the river drops four feet to a mile. Pond went upstream on the Sturgeon-weir and then crossed Frog Portage to the main stream of the Churchill River.

The Cree name for the Churchill was *Missinipi*, or Big River, which is found in the York Factory journal for 1714. But the Nor'Westers called it the English River, a name given to it by Benjamin Frobisher when he reached its upper waters and niftily intercepted Crees and others bound for the English post at the river mouth on Hudson Bay.[4] That post, Fort Prince of Wales, was a stout stone establishment and one of the most remarkable bastions of defence put up in the New World (though it was soon to be destroyed by the French officer La Pérouse in 1782, a story that lies outside the Pond saga).

Pond's instructions called for him to enter the English River—that is, the upper Churchill—follow Thomas Frobisher's pioneering route, and, if possible, cross into the Athabasca region.[5] Pond was able to reach farther north only because the Frobishers gave him additional food from their winter supplies so that he would not have to make the usual return to Grand Portage.[6] In the future he would have to figure out a system that would allow him to be locally self-sufficient without drawing on fellow traders' supplies. This was the challenge faced by all who came with him or followed him in subsequent years.

He was now five hundred miles west of Cumberland House, working through a chain of attractive lakes mostly in rugged rock country. In time, the water highway provided by the Churchill River brought Pond's brigade of canoes to Île-à-la-Crosse Post. From here the canoe route for Athabasca skirted the south shore of Churchill Lake, passed Buffalo Narrows, and crossed a lake (now called Peter Pond Lake). All of these waters and others soon to be met—Methye or La Loche River and Lac La Loche (also known as Methye Lake)—were Pond's discoveries. Much back-breaking work lay ahead. Late in the season, when water was low, rocks and sunken logs posed additional hazards, and damage to canoes could occur. Over the years not a few canoemen died in these difficult channels. There were many portages, some on soggy ground and marshland. They worked upriver, fighting the swift current of Methye River, wading and poling as required, until they reached its source, Lac La Loche. It was named for the loach (or luch or loache), a fish taken at the nearby lake in abundance.

Now they had to cross the lake, at the head of which lay a little shoal and a zigzagging muddy stream that a canoe or boat could navigate. At the end of the stream was a one-mile portage that brought the travellers to an encampment. Eric Morse writes: "Now the voyageur was approaching a portage that he would be telling his grandson about."[7] In later days it became customary for the bourgeois or partner, on his first visit to this portage, to treat the men to an extra dram—if he neglected to do this, he

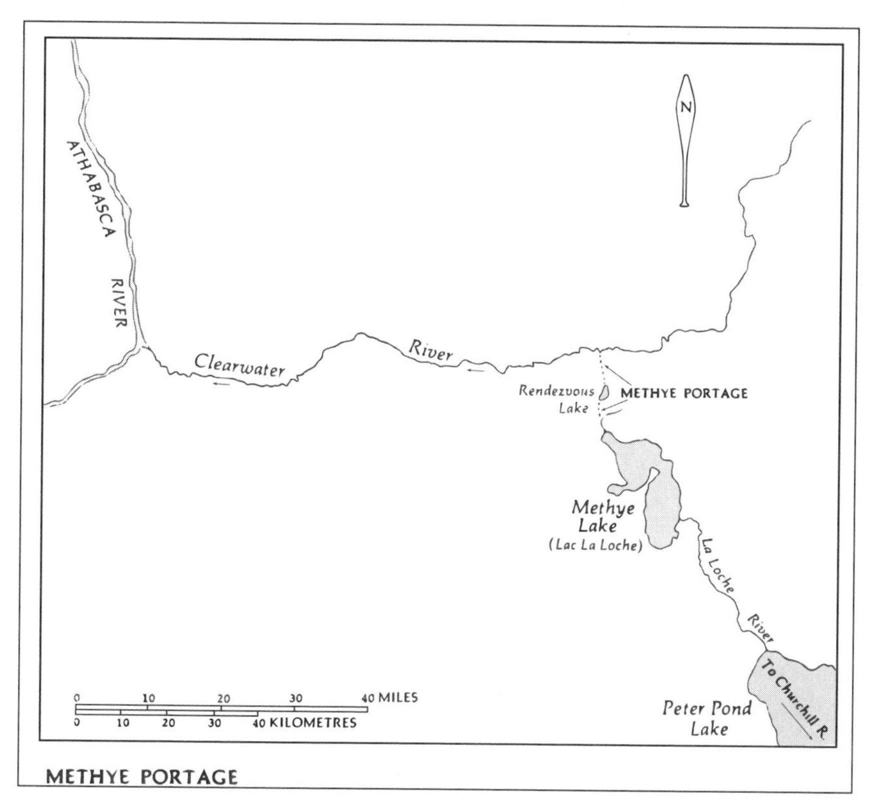

As is shown in this map the Methye Portage or Portage La Loche leads to the Clearwater and then to the Athabasca Rivers, which are the upper reaches of the Mackenzie River watershed. A native track that became a route of the traders, the Portage was the gateway to the western Arctic and also to the Peace and Parsnip Rivers. Methye Portage marks one of the crowns of the North American continent. MAP DERIVED FROM ERIC W. MORSE, *FUR TRADE CANOE ROUTES OF CANADA/THEN AND NOW*, WITH MAPS BY ROBERT MANN, OF MORTON BASLAW AND CO. LTD., OTTAWA, 1968 would be subject to the unpleasant process of shaving, as was practised on board ships crossing the line. The ancient voyaging custom had to be respected. Perhaps it even began in Pond's time.

To any human contemplating its transit, in either direction, Methye Portage (also known as Portage La Loche) posed a challenge to personal strength and determination, no matter how great the rewards at trail's end. Like the nine-mile Grand Portage from Lake Superior to the Pigeon River, it was a land bridge to a different watershed. The portage extended from Lac La Loche to the Clearwater, straddling two watersheds and crossing the height of land that divides waters flowing eastward to Hudson Bay at Churchill Factory from those that flow northward to the Arctic after passing through Athabasca, Great Slave, and other lakes. It thus became the route for supplies to the posts of the Mackenzie, Peace, and Lower Athabasca valleys, and all furs brought out to Hudson Bay or Montreal passed over this historic portage. "The Portage is full twelve Miles over," recounted Daniel Harmon, "and across which the People are obliged to carry both Canoe & Ladings—however the road is excellent, as it is over a level Country but thinly Timbered."[8] The scene was glorious beyond imagining according to travellers who crossed the watershed. Alexander Mackenzie described it as follows: "Within a mile of the termination of the Portage is a very steep precipice...rises upwards of a thousand feet above the plains beneath it, [and] commands a most extensive, romantic, and ravishing prospect."[9]

At the northwest end of the portage, Chipewyan peoples—now known as Dene—who had come down from the north might be waiting for the traders. They were ready to supply provisions or provide additional labour. The provisions often came at a good time, when stocks were running low. "Just at this end of the Portage, we have from a high hill an extensive & beautiful prospect of the level Country that lies before us as well as of the different windings of a small River that we are to Descend." This was Harmon again, and when his editor touched up the text for publication it read: "About a mile from the end of the portage is a hill, which towers majestically, to the height of a thousand feet, above the plain below; and which commands a most extensive and delightful prospect. Two lofty and extensive ridges enclose a valley, about three miles in width, which stretches, far as the eye can reach. The Little River, which is also by different persons denominated Swan, Clear water, or Pelican River, winds, in a most delightful manner, along this charming valley. The majestick forests, which wave upon these ridges, the delightful verdure of the intervening lawn, and the beautiful stream, which wanders along through it, giving a pleasing variety to the scene, until these objects become blended with the horizon, form, on the whole, the most delightful, natural scenery, that I ever beheld." Harmon and his editor may be forgiven excesses in descriptive details.[10]

Pond's discovery marked the first known use of the Methye Portage by a trader,[11] though doubtless Native traders and warriors had used it before. Beyond, a new world awaited the fur trader—new sources of furs, new markets for goods, and new trading partners. Here the beaver were of finer quality than anywhere else in North America, streams were frequent, and poplar (so suitable for the beaver's plans and labour) in abundance.

Pond passed downstream on the Clearwater, which here runs virtually west, an oddity for Canadian rivers in these parts. This is magnificent country even nowadays, hardly changed from Pond's era, with splendid views of rock and trees. The Clearwater is a national heritage river, the delight of today's northern voyageurs. Pond was the first of them, their crusader. There were the customary portages where the river violently fell in stages, but there were salt deposits along the way too, and hot or sulphur springs. In its lower reaches the Clearwater, also known as the Little Athabasca in the days of the fur traders, becomes a powerful run of water.

Before long he was on an entirely more powerful stream, one we now call the Athabasca River. Here the geography is complicated, with powerful rivers flowing from distant mountains and converging in tight places. The mighty Athabasca River originates from a point on the compass that is almost opposite the source of the Clearwater; it flows out of the high glaciers of Mount Brown in the Rockies and from a lower height called the Miette, which is close to Yellowhead Pass. It ventures through the foothills, passing dark pine and spruce forest and occasional lighter patches of aspen, and in doing so crosses what is now the Province of Alberta, falling into Lake Athabasca after a course of nearly a thousand miles. Where Pond joined it, coming in from the Clearwater River, it flowed virtually north. Daniel Harmon referred to it as the Great Athabasca; others called it the Grand River. Pond called it the Athabasca River. According to Mackenzie, the Native peoples called it the Elk River. Mackenzie described it as about three-quarters of a mile wide where the Clearwater joins it, and from there it ran in a steady current, sometimes contracting but never increasing its channel, until, after receiving several small streams, it discharged itself into the "Lake of the Hills"—Lake Athabasca—at 58° 36' North.[12] There were good runs for canoes on this river.

The Athabasca is truly a river to the North, ancient in its formation but long kept a secret from the outside world. Here, the landscape takes on different features from those Pond and his men had seen on their approach to the Methye Portage. Along the high banks of the river they might have observed brown coal in spectacular protrusions twenty to thirty feet high, coal whose thermal heat value would need to be tested by geologists. And at several places oozed tar or pitch in plenty—the great oil sands of Athabasca—fluid bitumen that even in those days had a use. When mixed with gum or spruce resin, it was used for gumming canoes.[13] Pond left no record of the oil sands of the Athabasca, so we turn to Mackenzie for a contemporary—in fact, the first—observation of what was to become the world's greatest single source of oil:

> At about twenty-four miles from the Fork [where the Clearwater joins the Athabasca], are some bituminous fountains, into which a pole of twenty feet long may be inserted without the least resistance. The bitumen is in a fluid state, and when mixed with gum, or the resinous substance collected from the spruce fir, serves to gum the canoes. In its heated state it emits a smell like that of sea-coal. The banks of the river, which are there very elevated, discover [that is, show] veins of the same bituminous quality. At a small distance from the Fork, houses have been erected [after Pond's time—in fact, in 1790—marking the early origins of Fort McMurray] for the convenience of trading with a party of the Knisteneaux [Cree], who visit the adjacent country for the purpose of hunting.[14]

We return to Pond on the inaugural expedition of trade. Downriver once again, and now, on the last hundred miles of the Athabasca, his laden canoes sped steadily through a forested realm, home of the Cree and rich in game. Beaver, wood buffalo, elk, and deer inhabited it, and many fur-bearing animals. It also comprised the northernmost part, or extremity, of the boreal forest. Not far to the north, beyond a comparatively narrow strip of lichen woodland that stretched from the Alaskan arctic all the way to

Labrador's shore, lay another ecological region: tundra.

Throughout this vast area of Athabasca, aboriginal people followed migratory animals and, in doing so, crossed ecological boundaries. In these latitudes, Pond knew he would be dependent on the hunting skills of the Cree and Chipewyan, but he also knew he could use his trade goods to advantage to acquire caribou and moose meat, grease, and, less prominently, fish and foul. The lateness of the season caused anxiety, and Native assistance would be required for survival.

The Chipewyan who guided traders north from Methye Portage were known to the Hudson's Bay Company men indiscriminately as the Northern Indians. As travellers, they had few equals. Their homeland of forest and tundra north of Churchill River had already given them an advantage, for they had become middlemen in the trade between the Bay traders and the interior tribes. To the west of them lay the tribes of the Cordillera and Plateau. To the southwest lay the Beaver, or Dane-Zaa, an Athapaskan-speaking people of the Peace River. To the north—that is, the north shore of Lake Athabasca to Great Slave Lake—were the Dogrib, while to the northeast of them again were the Yellowknife living hard by the Inuit. Northward west beyond Great Slave Lake were the Hare.

Now that Pond and the Montrealers had arrived through the back door, so to speak, the Chipewyans' strategic advantage on the upper Mackenzie River took on new dimensions, and they grew rich with this advantage. Andrew Graham, who had seen the Chipewyan at Fort Churchill, described them as a strong and able people, with three blue strokes on each cheek, and always dressed in deerskin. They drank no spirits, he said, and bartered their furs and pelts only for necessities such as ammunition, iron, and cutlery; they had no demand for cloth, beads, or other superfluous articles. Mackenzie, too, noted the lack of ornaments among the Chipewyan, but added: "The women have a singular custom of cutting off a small piece of the navel-string of the new-born children, and hang it about their neck: they are also curious in the covering they make for it, which they decorate with porcupine's quills and beads."[15] The baby cradles were similarly adorned. Before long, however, the introduction of cloths of various colours, scarlet and green, and of coats and jackets cut to military fashion and ornamented with a profusion of tin or silver trinkets, giving them a noble appearance, changed the customary dress of these people. Pond, as we will see, took pains to adorn his new allies in the

European fashion, to their delight. He knew that the Chipewyan—they were his objects—held the key to the wealth of the northern realm. First, however, he had to set up a post, and this he did among the Cree, who lived in the forested margins south of the limitless emptiness that seemed to be the land of the Chipewyan, the barrens.

Pond and his canoes were about sixty days out of Rainy Lake post. In late September or early October 1778, the days were shortening and the season well advanced, with winter fast approaching in those higher than customary latitudes. We can imagine at least a sharp northern chill in the air, the golden leaves of the aspens and the parched ones of the cottonwoods being blown away by the sharp, cutting winds, and ice forming on the river in mid-October. It was time to prepare for winter.

About forty miles from where the Athabasca empties into Lake Athabasca (or Lake of the Hills as it was called in those days), under the cold autumn sky, Pond selected a site for a post now generally known as Athabasca Fort. Pond did not give it a name, but it survives in the record as the "Old Establishment." Mackenzie called it "Pond's House," which might be the best way to describe it in historical terms. Pond and his clerk, Cuthbert Grant, called it *Arabasca*, and spelled it that way. Pond showed Lake Athabasca as *Great Araubaskska* on his 1790 map. As might be expected, the spelling of the name of both the river and the lake has been a matter of dispute. Peter Fidler and David Thompson (like Pond) called the river *Athabasca*, and that, after a time of uncertainty and even error, is the spelling that has been settled on by the Geographic Board of Canada.[16]

This newest post of the Nor'Westers, Pond's House, stood on the east bank, on a bench thirty feet above the north-flowing, powerful river. The site was upriver from a prominent point, rare on this stream, where the river constricts slightly. The soil in this particular spot was excellent, suitable for growing vegetables, and Pond intended to plant a garden the next spring (necessarily fenced against animal intrusions). Not all locations on the riverbank were so handsome for gardening prospects, for in many places bitumen was not far beneath the spongy top layer of soil.

The site location is known.[17] David Thompson, who passed this way in 1804, fixed its position as 58° 25' North and 111° 23' West. Historian and Dominion land surveyor J.N. Wallace says that Pond's House stood near the place where the river divides into two branches a little south of the 28th surveyed base line; this is a useful tip for someone looking for it nowadays.[18] The elevated site would have been chosen for its commanding view of the stream; there was also drinkable water near at hand, as well as a softwood forest to provide wood for a picket fence and the raising of numerous buildings as required, plus the necessary cordwood to stoke the hearths and stoves for the long winters. The location was about 1,200 feet above sea level.

We have no record of what buildings were put up but we can imagine four or five different squared log buildings with split-wood roofs. A stout storehouse that could be securely locked, the dining hall, and lodgings for all the traders and voyageurs would have been the first to be erected. Pond would have masterminded the construction of his own living quarters, and these would have doubled as an office. Each of the structures intended for habitation would have had a stone fireplace and chimney. At a short distance from the post the men erected an outstation for the tribes who came to trade and to drink and game (Mackenzie knew the location of this). They were not allowed to remain in the fort or to live adjacent to the stockade, fear of fire being the principal reason but also the necessity of securing peace during the feasting bouts that followed trade. We can imagine that a Nor'Wester flag—a red duster with "NWC" on the field—flew from the pole erected outside the post's gate, likely at a spot so as to attract attention from those coming by river.

At this latitude, 58° North plus, the traders were not quite far enough north to see the midnight sun, but winter days were as short as summer days were long, the pale sun making its appearance at the coldest part of day, dawn, which was just before 9 a.m. on the shortest day. Summer could bring intense heat (90 degrees Fahrenheit), and winter, deep cold. Winter weather was also often serene, the stars shining with unimaginable brilliance, and the aurora borealis flashing up above the trees and hills on the northern horizon. The river would have been frozen after 15 December. Violent weather came at the change of season. The rush of spring brought growth to trees and a quickening of vegetation. Here, as at York Fort on Hudson Bay, the factory people were planting gardens by the middle of June, and soon producing a little garden stuff—cress, radish, lettuce, cabbage, and even, with especial care, peas and beans.[19]

On their first expedition to Athabasca, Pond and the men in his company depended, in the first instance, on the pemmican they had brought with them from posts on Lake Winnipeg or the Saskatchewan River. But already the long duration of their gruelling travels to get to the Athabasca River would have cut deeply into their food stocks. Thus, once arrived on the Athabasca River, the hunt for wildlife and wildfowl was a pressing requirement; coupled with this was making arrangements with the Cree in the area, who were great hunters, to provide food supplies of fish and game for immediate use, for the fast-approaching winter, and for the requirements of the following summer. This was wood buffalo country, and that made all the difference, providing the essence of a healthy diet. From the buffalo could be taken the delicious tongue, the rump, and the hump (from which fat, or grease, could be acquired). Pemmican, insurance against starvation, could be made on the spot using trained labour. From distant parts Native hunters brought moose (*orignal* they called it in French), recently killed, to Pond's House. This, too, was a real delicacy. In subsequent years, Pond learned that it was the Beaver nation of the Peace River who were the great suppliers of pemmican. In fact, the Peace River became the larder of the traders who wintered at Lake Athabasca, Great Slave Lake, and the Mackenzie River. One canoe manned by three men could bring two tons of dried provisions out of the Peace River country.[20] This made the Athabasca fur trade possible.

Apart from this source, these northern lands were by and large the world of the fish, especially downriver from Pond's House. Forts later established on Lake Athabasca had an advantage in being close to the great fishery of that lake, but fish was not to everyone's taste. Peter Fidler of the Hudson's Bay Company noted in his diary of 1799 that his men did not want to go to Athabasca nor to any similar place where "the living is mostly fish." Besides, he noted, it was rumoured (incorrectly) that the best furs were not to be found there. Fidler, indeed, would have liked to go to Athabasca from Greenwich House, but he had found "the Canadians are got so greedy of late that they want every skin."[21]

During the first winter of his far northern enterprise, that of 1778–79, Pond saw "a vast concourse" of Crees (or Knisteneaux) and Chipewyans, who went down each year to Fort Prince of Wales or Fort Churchill, on Hudson Bay, via long difficult routes. According to Mackenzie, who was in the Athabasca country himself a few years later, living in close company with Pond, these tribes were pleased to see Pond and others, as well they might be. The Crees and Chipewyans reported that the new arrangement would, in Mackenzie's words, "relieve them from such long, toilsome, and dangerous journeys; and were immediately reconciled to give an advanced price for the articles necessary to their comfort and convenience."[22]

It may be estimated that Pond's collection, that first trading season, was well over 100,000 fine beaver skins, and it has been suggested Pond obtained twice as many furs as his canoes could carry out to the east the next spring. He brought out eighty thousand that spring, stockpiled the remainder in winter huts, and safely recovered them the next season. Our authority for this is Alexander Mackenzie, who writes, "Mr. Pond's reception and success was accordingly beyond his expectation; and he procured twice as many furs as his canoes could carry...Such of the furs as he could not embark, he secured in one of his winter huts."[23] Pond's actions were contrary to the views of partners, who always demanded that the partner bring out his furs with him. The worry was that those left *en cache* could be pirated, an advantage to opponents. Alexander Henry the Younger got his knuckles rapped for doing the same thing, though this occurrence was slightly later, and he was told in no uncertain terms that this was not to happen again.[24]

That same winter, Pond, by prodigious effort, set in place a network of distant trade based on Pond's House. From it, in subsequent trading seasons, he sent his right-hand men out to put up tributary, outlier houses when and where possible. In addition, there were travelling traders (who traded *en dérouine* on credit supplied by Pond) who ventured far and wide in search of Native allies interested in trading.[25]

Mackenzie gives us the impression that Pond was master of all he surveyed, but this is only half the story. Athabasca Post and its tributary stations may have extended Pond's reach, but he could not control the independent Montreal-based traders who entered this same watershed. Pond soon found himself facing all sorts of rivals. They were petty traders by comparison to him but a terrible distraction nonetheless, upsetting trade alliances, fomenting discord against Pond and his associates, and driving up prices in trade. That is why Pond, in addition to setting up his outstations, turned to the business of exalting the principal chiefs of the trading bands by raising their wealth and, above all, prestige among their own people and rival bands.

At every step the Crees and Chipewyans aided his progress. In

Athabasca country that first year, Pond met Matonabbee, the "leading Indian," who seven years before, in 1771–72, had guided the HBC explorer Samuel Hearne west to the Coppermine River. Through Matonabbee, Pond came to meet the famed English Chief—Nestebeck or, more correctly, Ageenaw. The English Chief first attracted the attention of fur traders when he was travelling in company with Matonabbee and Hearne in more northern locations. He next was noticed as the leader of those Chipewyans who trekked overland from English River with their furs to the HBC at Churchill Fort on Hudson Bay. He had, with forty persons, made that long trip, thereby saving the Bay traders the toil of coming to him and his tribe. He was the ultimate traveller in the barrens and boreal forest and was a man of fabulous proportions, strong of body and keen of mind. After Pond came into contact with him, Alexander Mackenzie and David Thompson encountered him in turn. All would sing his praises for he was a friend of the white man's trade; in fact, he opened doors to business, so to speak, and he often guided the traders' travels, thereby making life safe for the interlopers then seeking a permanent foothold in the north country.

Pond gave the English Chief his full due. He clothed him in garments befitting his powerful influence. The English Chief is said to have dressed richly, in a red greatcoat, short breeches, and common stockings, a style that other Native leaders emulated. The English Chief had been raised to the position of a great chief, admired and respected by others who aspired to his high pitch of glory, as one of them said.[26] Much of the benefit of the connection with the English Chief would come in the later years of Pond's trade in Athabasca, and Mackenzie and others profited from this same connection in the future. The English Chief not only acted as the trusted guide for Pond and Mackenzie, with knowledge of many Athapaskan tongues and dialects, but he also became leader of the Yellowknife middlemen operating on the upper Peace River and other locations, not always unopposed by other tribes.

From his post on the Athabasca River, Pond made voyages of reconnaissance. Bit by bit he worked out the details of the upper Mackenzie River country and the sources of that great stream. The details of his discoveries are a matter of speculation. But we may be assured that he followed the Athabasca River down to the great marshy delta where it enters Lake Athabasca. He would have examined the location where the

Athabasca River joins the lake near where the first Fort Chipewyan was later put up by Alexander Mackenzie and Roderick Mackenzie. And he would have known most of the features of that lake, including the spot where Cuthbert Grant, by Pond's direction, had set up his post. Beyond lay a maze of lakes and rivers not yet laid out on a reliable map.

We now know that Lake Athabasca, in turn, drains to Great Slave Lake via the Slave River. And we know that from a northwesterly bay in Great Slave Lake there is an exit. This is the majestic and wild Mackenzie River, a stream possessing its own savage beauty, pointing north a distance of 1,200 miles to Arctic waters and shores. Pond, consumed by curiosity and anxious to unlock these riverine secrets, would have crossed Lake Athabasca or coasted its western rim, then gone north, or downriver, on the dangerous Slave River to Great Slave Lake, en route examining the lower reaches of the Peace River. If he knew where the Peace River enters the Mackenzie, he did not tell the river's namesake about it, for the tough little Scot missed it on his intended expedition west in 1789. Except by Native report, Pond would not have known of the Finlay and the Parsnip Rivers, two of the main sources of the Peace, that drain a wild and spectacular region of what is now north-central British Columbia. The exploration of these rivers would have to wait for further explorers such as John Finlay and Samuel Black.

The key to western travels in these latitudes was the Peace River, the oldest of the rivers hereabouts, one that courses wildly through a steep canyon and drains a great agricultural plain. We know that Pond became familiar with it by degrees. At first he knew little of the real course of the Peace River, for he showed it incorrectly on his 1785 map, flowing north directly into Great Slave Lake. Later, however, on the map compiled by Ezra Stiles (see Chapter 8) he has the details correct. It could be that Pond travelled west from his post on the Athabasca River and in doing so encountered the Peace near Lake Claire, where the course of that river indicates a clear run to the north and an outlet in Great Slave Lake.[27]

Farther to the north, another geographical puzzle presented itself. Slave River, mighty in its intensity, drained the vast eastern flank of the Rockies, and Pond pieced together its geographic logic too, its essential unity. But what he did not know was the confirmed course of the Mackenzie River draining Great Slave Lake. Did it drain to the North

Pacific? The nagging question remained. His discoveries had to be financed by his trading pursuits, and these came first in priority.

Like Radisson and Groseilliers, self-styled "Caesars of the wilderness" who traded north of Lake Superior in the 1650s, Pond found no one to challenge his trade. At the end of that first winter in Athabasca, he and his canoe brigade came out of that country, heavily laden. They came up the Clearwater, then south over Methye Portage, retracing land routes, streams, and portages. Their destination was Grand Portage, there to place his furs in the warehouse preparatory to shipping them east over Lake Superior and ultimately to Montreal.

On 2 July 1779, after narrowly escaping disaster in white water, he arrived at the Hudson's Bay Company's Cumberland House "with three Canoes from the Northward very much distressed for want of food having bad Success on his Journey down his Canoes being broke upon the falls."[28] From the factor or master William Walker, who treated him civilly for previous kindnesses, he acquired tobacco, powder, and meat.

While he was at Cumberland House, Pond told Walker that he had gone far enough north to trade with Matonabbee and the Northward Indians, hitherto trading allies of the Hudson's Bay Company. In consequence of Pond's indiscreet boasting, the Hudson's Bay Company received confirming evidence that the Nor'Westers had gone into that far north. Pond told Walker of Methye Portage. He said that this crossing into the Arctic watershed was about twelve miles in length and, further, it was so steep that it had taken the party eight days to complete it. The Bay traders now had the startling news that their rivals had gone from Lac La Loche, in the Hudson Bay watershed, to the Clearwater River in the Athabasca watershed.[29] The ring of the rivals was making its final turn to the north, toward the mouth of the Mackenzie River and to the Yukon.

Pond may have been boasting of the ease with which he traded, and he recounted that the Indians he encountered were so distressed, as well as eager to trade, that he had exchanged the clothes off his back.[30] During trading, he said, he had made 140 packs of ninety pounds each (the customary bale weight) but had been obliged to leave most of them behind. Since one pack contained about sixty pelts, the whole would have constituted some 8,400 made beaver. This would have been about six tons of furs—an extraordinary load for three canoes, given that the average *canot du nord* had a carrying capacity of a ton and a half.

Pond, we can imagine, reached Grand Portage just in time for the traders' yearly rendezvous. He would have consulted with his partners and told of his success. His reputation was hugely enhanced, for to that time no trader had brought in such a haul as his. At this 1779 rendezvous, in discussion with other traders, the basis of a grand trade strategy for the West was put in place. Pond made arrangements for the coming season and did not remain at Grand Portage but returned directly to Athabasca.

He came out very late in the season the next year—the distances that had to be travelled were immense—and so it was not until 28 November 1780, when it was already winter, that he arrived at Michilimackinac. Once again he had fetched a large cargo of furs from the interior. This time the going had been better and safer for Pond and his men, the navigational hazards avoided. And even in terms of trade returns, Pond's outbound fur cargoes stood in contrast to generally declining returns from the interior. Charles Grant, reporting on 24 April 1780, put it graphically: "The Indian Trade by every communication is carried on at great expense, labour and risk of both men and property; every year furnishes instances of the loss of men and goods by accident or otherwise."[31] Coupled with this were the dislocations of the American Revolutionary war.

Michilimackinac was on a war footing, and the local military administration was in the process of erecting a new fort on Mackinac Island. The British always preferred islands as places to defend from real and imagined enemies, and so it was with Michilimackinac. Pond's arrival there with seven *engagés* in a bateau from Lake Superior is recorded in the logbook of His Majesty's Armed Sloop *Welcome*, by Captain Alexander Harrow.[32] The reference to Pond's bateau is noteworthy, for customarily a trader would have arrived with one or more canoes. We can imagine this bateau to be more than a flat-bottomed boat customarily used in rivers and shallow waters; rather, it may have been suitable for deeper, more open waters, carrying a mast or two, and capable of wearing sail. Pond's experience as a sailor would have come in handy on Lake Superior. Pond may have had a large cargo in his bateau, or perhaps he had found that it was cheaper to ship his goods in such a vessel rather than in canoes. The reference to the seven *engagés* also drips with historical intrigue. It appears as if these persons—engaged in trade with Pond and beholden to him as an authorized licence holder—were acting as a unit or a team. One thing is clear: Pond was not going to stop at Grand Portage with his large cargo of furs. Instead, he superintended the dispatch and delivery of them to Michilimackinac, where they would be transshipped, in canoes, for Montreal.

He passed the winter of 1780–81 at Michilimackinac, remaining there at least until 10 May, when Captain Harrow borrowed a bateau from Pond to use as the *Welcome*'s tender. The navy captain identifies Pond as a merchant. The record is silent as to how long Pond's bateau was used by the captain, but we may imagine that he kept it for the summer, perhaps longer, and that in the interim Pond set out for the north country in a canoe brigade for the trading season. He entered another partnership, this time with McBeath and Booty Graves.

That fall, in October 1781, his associate Alexander Henry, who we know as a man of wide vision and good sense, wrote to Sir Joseph Banks, the noted naturalist and man of science, because he thought the presiding genius of British science ought to be informed that Pond had penetrated to Athabasca. In doing so he had opened to explorers a new and large drainage basin. Henry recounted the results of Pond's travels, and his description suggests that Pond had acquired a fairly accurate conception of the character of the county—although Henry states that Methye Portage is at 60° North latitude and 140° West longitude, a wildly inaccurate location. Pond had no scientific instruments and no scientific training, and his guesses as to longitude and latitude may be understood if not accepted uncritically. But Henry thought his discoveries important enough to report them to Banks, and Henry also, searching for notoriety himself in the business of explorations, helped to follow on Pond's discoveries, even to claim for himself great discoveries beyond Methye Portage.

In 1781, Henry's suggestion was to send a party down the river right to the Arctic coast. That location, he mused, could not be too far distant from Bering Strait. He proposed that the party should return by Hudson Bay, that being the shortest way back. This information indicates that Pond believed at that date that the Mackenzie River drained to the Arctic Ocean.[33] In his letter to Banks, Henry noted the difficulties of northern travel, emphasizing that frost and ice had to be contended with, and that foodstuffs were difficult to obtain in such northern lands, requiring some local food sources such as pemmican. We return to

Henry and to Banks at later times. The point to note here is that at this stage Pond's northern progress was being observed, his geographical breakthrough worthy of comment.

Hereafter Pond's story becomes cloudy and dark. He seems caught in a tenacious web not entirely of his own making. It was, nonetheless, a web from which he could not extricate himself. These were particularly crowded years. Events swirled rapidly around him.

As the number of traders increased, so, too, had competition heightened and the introduction of spirituous liquors increased. The beaver trade floated on rum and brandy, "high wines." The demand from the interior was incessant. British mercantile regulation encouraged the Province of Quebec's role in the fur trade, purposely disadvantaging American traders to the Old Northwest. Rum from the West Indies saved the fur trade from American competition after British authorities lifted all duties on imports into the North American colonies, making it cheaper than illegal, cut-priced rum from the United States. London won out in this trade war, and the fur trade remained an important feature of the Canadian economy, in fact the only real source of value in terms of exports other than fish and, later, naval stores.[34]

Hostilities between traders were heightened by rivalry among the tribes who formulated plans to get back for infractions of protocol, bad booze, and laudanum in rum (used to put a begging Native person to sleep). In the spring of 1780 on the Saskatchewan, a drinking bout ended in the death of one trader and several white *engagés*. Mackenzie relates that two trade establishments on the Assiniboine were also attacked about this time. There were deaths on both sides. Mackenzie comments: "In short, it appeared, that the natives had formed a resolution to extirpate the traders." He adds, "Without entering into any further reasoning on the subject, it appears to be incontrovertible that the irregularity pursued in carrying on the fur trade had brought it into its present forlorn situation; and nothing but the greatest calamity that could have befallen the natives saved the traders from destruction."[35] We can speculate as to what sort of uprising might have taken place, perhaps a diminutive precursor of the great Saskatchewan rising of 1885.

But we do know that the smallpox epidemic, "the greatest calamity" to which Mackenzie refers, ended anything the tribes had in mind. Trader Ross Cox, of a much later generation than Mackenzie, writing in 1831, tells harrowing stories of the legacies of the dread peril—of devastated and deserted villages, of deaths when individuals in the grip of a fever jumped into cold rivers to seek relief, of suicides by hanging. Some survivors of the Cree nation believed that the "Great Master of Life had delivered them over to the Evil Spirit for their wicked courses," and subsequently sought new moral codes.[36]

The early 1780s witnessed terrible tragedies among Native peoples, for the dreaded smallpox made its lethal visitation in October 1781. Mackenzie wrote that the disease "spread its destructive power and desolating power, as the fire consumes the dry grass of the field."[37] This smallpox was a particularly virulent type, with a twelve-day incubation period. It was generally believed that it had been brought to the Assiniboine from the Missouri River by a war party. New discoveries by medical historians, including Jody F. Decker and Elizabeth A. Fenn, in Hudson's Bay Company post journals spell out the specifics.[38] William Tomison at Cumberland House contended that the disease originated with the Spanish. David Thompson said the Dakota Sioux picked it up at the Missouri River trading villages, then brought it north. In any event, the arrival of smallpox at Cumberland Post can be dated to 11 December 1781, carried there by a Native woman. From there it spread east and north, reached Churchill River, Athabasca and Great Slave Lake, then crossed the Rocky Mountains at the sources of the Missouri, and passed westward to Pacific shores. "The fatal infection spread around with baneful rapidity which no flight could escape, and with a fatal effect that nothing could resist. It destroyed with its pestilential breath whole families and tribes; and the horrid scene presented to those who had the melancholy and afflicting opportunity of beholding it, a combination of the dead, the dying, and such as to avoid the horrid fate of their friends around them, prepared to disappoint the plague of its prey, by terminating their own existence." So recounts Mackenzie, who adds: "The habits and lives of these devoted people, which provided not to-day for the wants of to-morrow, must have heightened the pains of such an affliction, by leaving them not only without remedy, but even without alleviation. Nought was left them but to submit in agony and despair."[39]

The furs obtained from the interior fell in number. From the Churchill River in 1781 a small party brought out only seven packs. The Montreal merchants took heavy losses. The Nor'Westers were forced by circumstances to reposition themselves for future trade, and to cut back on their excessive exploitation of the northwest's furs. The more irresponsible traders were eased aside by the corporate mergers and alliances within the larger North West Company. A possible war had been averted, but smallpox had taken a savage toll, the effects stretching from the northwest to the heart of empire, in London.

In 1782 the Hudson's Bay Company paid a dividend of 8 percent, but in 1783, for the first time since 1717, no dividend payment was made, and 1784 and 1785 followed suit. Gloom set in. Only in 1786 did the managing directors issue a small dividend of 5 percent, much to the relief of expectant investors.

It was in the midst of this turmoil of interracial strife, Native hostilities, smallpox decimation, and hitherto unimagined challenges to trade that Pond returned west. In late 1781 he arrived to winter with another trader, Jean-Étienne Waden, at Lac la Ronge in northern Saskatchewan.

Waden, or Wadens, Waddens, Vuadens, or Wadins, was sometimes known as the Dutchman.[40] He was baptized in the canton of Vaud, Switzerland, son of Adam Samuel Vuadens and Marie-Bernadine Ormond. He had lived in Switzerland until at least 1755 and then came to New France with the colonial regular troops. In 1757 he renounced "the Calvinist heresy," and after the capitulation of Montreal in 1760, he stayed on in Canada. Though technically a deserter, he felt secure enough to marry Marie-Josephte Deguire at Saint-Laurent late in 1761. A property owner in Montreal, he went into the fur trade as a small independent trader and did well in the business. The number of canoes licensed to him increased and so did his profits. As early as 1772 he was at Grand Portage with a group of eight traders. He had good backing from Montreal financial interests and was bankrolled by Richard Dobie and John McKindlay of that city. He expanded west with the fur trade of the era to the Saskatchewan Valley. In 1779, to offset "the Separate Interests...the Bane of that Trade," firms trading into the far northwest set forth the formal agreement for the North West Company, with Waden as one of its members.

Waden had been at Lac la Ronge in 1779, on the southern margin of the Athabasca country, and was poised to strike north and west to enhance his interests. We know that, at Lac la Ronge, he carried on a lucrative trade with "the Northward Indians" from Lake Athabasca. Now, in 1781, Pond was there too.

Consider the circumstances of this strange conjuncture. Both Pond and Waden, as traders, had been at Lac la Ronge as of 1779 and perhaps on later occasions, likely 1780–81. They were thus well known to each other, though they represented rival interests in the North West Company. Corporate machinations and deals they might not have been privy to or in agreement with had thrown them together in a circumstance not of their choosing or, indeed, of their liking. They were near contemporaries. Waden was two years Pond's senior. Pond was a Protestant; Waden, a former Protestant turned Roman Catholic. They were ex-colonial soldiers and had fought for different kings at the battle of Fort Niagara. At Lac la Ronge that long winter, Pond and Waden lived in close proximity, in houses side by side (what the English would call semi-detached). Such a cozy arrangement was not unusual. For a time Pond and Waden worked in combination; in fact, it was common for such traders, even if nominal rivals, to pool resources, travel together, and erect or shift posts as required. Economy of time and motion had to be observed. But it would be safe to say that they were allies of convenience, nothing more—and reluctant ones at that.

Of the two concerns, Pond's was the larger and was built around the more sizeable Montreal houses, such as those of the Frobishers and Simon McTavish. Waden, by contrast—and here he resembled Alexander Mackenzie in later years—acted for an association of smaller houses, such as those of Forrest Oakes and John Ross. The two groups were affiliated in some way, and in 1779 it had been intended that Waden should replace Pond in trading with the tribes of Athabasca. However, rivalry between the two sets of interests remained unresolved, perhaps a festering sore, and in a compromise arrangement the men had been instructed to trade side by side at Lac la Ronge for the outfit of 1781–82.

In such confined circumstances, the role of personality could not be overstated. Alexander Mackenzie, who knew both men, was unequivocal in his description: "Two men, of more opposite characters, could not be found." Waden was a Swiss gentleman, says Mackenzie, "of strict probity and known sobriety." By implication, Mackenzie draws a damning picture of Pond—a North American of questionable business ethics and practice, and of a drinking persuasion. "In short from various causes, their situations became very uncomfortable to each other, and mutual ill-will was the natural consequence." Mackenzie does not spell out the particulars nor provide "a minute history of these transactions." In the absence of details we are left to imagine the many sources of the bother. Perhaps there were many flare-ups, many points of dispute. All we know is what was later reported.

One day in early March 1782, when northern Saskatchewan was still in the grip of deepest winter, Waden was shot through the lower part of the thigh and bled to death. He was buried, despite the frozen ground, the next morning.[41] Waden was shot by his clerk, Toussaint Lesieur, or by Peter Pond.

Word of the incident quickly travelled eastward. Eventually Waden's widow, Marie-Josephte, learned the sad particulars from a voyageur named Joseph Fagniant (sometimes spelled Fagnant and even misspelled as Sagnant). Understandably aggrieved and doubtless facing destitution, Mme. Waden pressed charges against Pond and Lesieur. Her petition, supported by an affidavit sworn by Fagniant and dated 19 May 1783, fully fourteen months after the event, reads: "That from the affidavit here annexed your petitioner hath a great cause to believe that the said murder was committed by one Peter Pond and one Toussaint le Sieur the deceased's clerk."[42] The widow based her claim on the following affidavit:

> The examination and report of Joseph Fagniant of Berthier, voyageur in the upper country, who having sworn on the bible, declared that having wintered in the upper country at the Lake de la Rivière aux Rapides in the English River, he was, in the month of March 1782 in a small post with Peter Pond and Jean Etienne Waden traders. On a day early in March about 9 o'clock in the evening he retired to his house, which was at the side and touched the house of Sieur Waden, which he had just left, and after taking off his shoes or about ten minutes after his return, having left Waden on his bed, he heard two gun shots, one after the other, suddenly, in Waden's house on which he sent a man to see what it was. The man went and returned saying that Mons. Waden was on the ground having received a gun shot, at which he got up and ran immediately to Waden and found him on the ground beside his bed on which he had

> left him a short time before, with his left leg shattered from the knee down. On approaching Waden the latter said to him *Ah mon ami je suis mort*, at which he attempted to tear his trousers to examine the leg and found the mark of powder on his knee and holes where two balls had entered and the leg shattered below the knee where the two balls had left from behind, having found them [the balls] on the spot. Sieur Waden asked him to find the Turlington Balsam and stop the blood. Having asked him who had done this to him he replied I will tell you but having lost very much blood by that time he was not able to say more. On entering Waden's house on this occasion, he saw Peter Pond and Toussaint Sieur leaving it, and entered their own. He found an empty gun and another broken in the house and saw that the one that was empty had been recently fired but that the other had been carried away. On entering Waden's house after the shots he saw Peter Pond and Toussaint Sieur at the door. Sieur asked Waden if it was he Sieur who had killed him Waden replied *Go away both of you that I may not see you.* Thereupon two men led Toussaint Sieur to bed and Peter Pond entered his own house. About a month before Peter Pond and Waden had fought and again on the evening that Waden was killed. About an hour before supper Peter Pond quarreled and argued with Waden. That he has good reason to believe that it was Peter Pond and Toussaint Sieur or one of them who killed Sieur Waden and for the present has nothing more to say.[43]

The clerk, who was in Waden's employ, and the voyageur, who was similarly situated, doubtless had their own reasons to point the finger at Pond. Even if Pond and Waden's clerk were examined at a preliminary hearing, a clear motive might not have emerged from the details. But it is clear that the voyageur lacked credibility as a witness—he came upon the scene after the fact. His account was thin evidence on which to hang a case of murder or manslaughter. He laid the details before the widow, who had a notarized statement made in Montreal; her son-in-law, Alan Morrison, brought forth the petition and above-quoted deposition. In the absence of a live witness who was not involved in some sort of collusion, a preliminary hearing would have thrown the case out or not allowed it to proceed to trial.

That there had been an argument is beyond question. That Waden was angry at both Pond and his own clerk there also can be no doubt. But was this premeditated murder, manslaughter, or an accident? Waden's last gasp robbed history and the law of the possibility of concrete determination. I have encountered many persons who believe Pond was guilty. Legends have more staying power than facts, and they take on a life of their own. But the facts do not prove the case, and in English law you are still innocent until proved guilty.

Historians disagree as to whether or not Pond stood trial. No court record survives. Against that we have formidable testimony. Mackenzie, who knew Pond personally, writes that the two were tried and acquitted in Montreal. But could it be that Mackenzie had forgotten or embellished the details? His book was published a full nineteen years after the event, and Pond had long since left Canada and the Montreal circle of traders. Errors stated in print have often been repeated. Relying, no doubt, on the above-mentioned remark by Mackenzie, Innis claims that "it may be assumed" Pond was tried and acquitted in Montreal during the winter of 1784–85. The only documentation located, however, is the deposition by Waden's voyageur already cited. And if a trial did take place, both of the accused were acquitted, in part because of the unconvincing evidence supplied in the deposition made by Joseph Fagniant.[44]

The historian Arthur Silver Morton maintains that the absence of any record of a trial indicates Pond was merely examined; he suggests that the case was not taken to court because the murder had occurred in a region beyond the jurisdiction of Quebec's legal system.[45] I believe a trial did not occur, but the reason was that the evidence was too slim. As for Toussaint Lesieur, he, too, survived the legal tangles and continued his prominent role as a trader as late as 1796. Mackenzie referred to him as "the famous Lisseur," and like Mackenzie he was often working the margins of the partnership of the North West Company—that is to say, he was a driving force in opposition, a troublesome pest to the centrality of the partnership.[46]

Pond wintered at Lac Île-à-la-Crosse in 1782–83, which was the most advanced post at that time. The years between 1776 and 1783 had seen a growing tendency of fur trade interests to coalesce, to pool their resources and share their risks. This is demonstrated in a series of agreements,

One of the interior posts of the North West Company in the *pays d'en haut*, Île-à-la-Crosse Post lay in the northern reaches of the boreal forest at a critically important location for trading with various tribes. Traders wintered in frozen isolation, their fires kept lit as the nearby forests were laid low for firewood. LIBRARY AND ARCHIVES CANADA, ACC. NO. 1994-254-1.40R ACQUIRED WITH THE ASSISTANCE OF HOECHST AND CELANESE CANADA AND WITH A GRANT FROM THE DEPARTMENT OF CANADIAN HERITAGE UNDER THE CULTURAL PROPERTY EXPORT AND IMPORT ACT

usually annual, that eventually produced the first declared North West Company, formed in 1783–84. That agreement was intended to last for five years. Pond seems to have had one of the sixteen shares in the 1779 company, but he was not always at the annual rendezvous to consult with other trading partners and to protect his own interests. Certainly he felt that he deserved more than the upstarts who were benefiting from his Athabasca profits were willing to give him. Thus, when this association reorganized in 1783 and he was offered only one share, he was distraught and probably angry. Feeling that he deserved more than that one share, Pond had at first refused it and considered joining with John Ross and Peter Pangman instead. Ultimately, however, in 1785 he accepted the one allotted share.[47]

In late fall 1785, Pond was back at his old post in Athabasca. A journal kept there by Cuthbert Grant, his second-in-command, a young Scot and brother of one of the original North West Company partners, survives, with dates 1 April to 31 May 1786. This significant record of early Athabasca trade recounts an odd assortment of particulars which, when taken as a whole, provide an interesting amalgam of what life was like at that place at that time. Pond was a good shot, and he kept his fowling piece at hand, bringing down a grouse flying over the fort.

Swans flying north heralded warmer weather. Hunters brought in ducks and geese. Cree arrived with a trainload of caribou meat. A moose was brought by others and traded for. Certain Native groupings were eagerly awaited, and emissaries brought news of their whereabouts, as well as of the English Chief, who eventually arrived with forty men. Pond was waiting for him. "Mr. Pond Clothed the English Chiefe," who was deserving of special attention. In fact, Pond had sent tobacco and ammunition to bring him in, worried that he might go over to the Hudson's Bay Company's ally, the Big Chief.

Warm weather came on rapidly, and before long the ice was breaking up on the river. Downstream and below the fort, a small point narrowed the course of the river, and it was at this choke point that an ice dam formed that spring during breakup. Before long the river was rising quickly below, alarmingly. Soon the frigid waters overflowed the banks. The men in the post found themselves scrambling for the rafters. We can see them there now, absolutely helpless and fearfully awaiting the most horrible washing away down the river. However, the crisis passed in the nick of time for them.

There was much rebuilding to be done. Canoes had to be fabricated. Pond was busy squaring timber for a new house. There were rapid changes in weather, the temperatures rising quickly. Eventually it was time, as soon as the navigation was safe, for the departure of the traders. Meanwhile, the summer's trading arrangements in Athabasca had to be put in place, with clerks and traders being sent to various parts of the river basin, to Lake Athabasca, Great Slave Lake, and the Peace River. But we learn, too, of Pond's toughness and his single-mindedness. An irate Beaver man, who had traded his robe when he was drunk ("in liquor"), wanted it back and determined to get it by force. This frightened the traders. They went to get Pond, knowing that he would deal summarily with the fellow. Pond "came and Cutt the Beaver Indian on the head with his Poignard, oupon which they told him it was the last time they Should ever see the fort, But he afterwards gave him a Blanket & some Amunition to appease him." And the next day there was a similar instance of forthright conduct by Pond. A fellow trader, Boyer, wanted to get in on some particular fur trading action but "Mr Pond told him that the Countery and Indians belonged to him & that he would do with them as he pleased & no other Person Should muddle with them."[48]

The Canadian voyageurs, the Métis, and the Natives who travelled with Pond on this expedition and wintered with him in Athabasca became the stuff of legend. They contended, too, that they deserved special attention and credit. After all, they had made the greatest of inland voyages, with the most portages and against the greatest of privations. Others lived in their shadow. Well into the 1820s they were regarded as without equal. Today, although it is correct to acknowledge Pond's successful quest and achievement, we recall that he did it on the back of human labour and with Native guidance and guile. They deserve nothing less than an immortal place in Canada's story.

7

Maps, Dreams, and Empire

When in 1784 Pond came out from the *pays d'en haut* to Grand Portage and then to Montreal, his position in the North West Company was unassailable, and though doubtless he had his critics, as a trader he was unrivalled. He had opened to his partners an entire new realm of opportunity. He had outflanked the Hudson's Bay Company, stolen from them precious Native trading partners, and increased the value of the trading shares of all the partners. He was the Nor'Wester par excellence, respected but unloved. The profits that he had gained for his fellow partners had enriched them all, to no special advantage for Pond. But he carried the curse of the champion. Jealousy and rivalry followed in his footsteps. Montreal was the scene of his triumphal entry. He would, in all probability, have arrived there in November. There, in February of the next year, 1785, he took his place as a charter member of the now historically famous Beaver Club.

Peter Pond's prized Beaver Club medal, passed from him to his heirs and owned at one time by Mr. Winthrop Pond of New Rochelle, New York, carried the customary tribute after his name, "Peter Pond Fortitude in Distress 1769," on one side and, on the reverse, "Beaver Club instituted Montreal, Industry and Perseverance 1785." The date 1769 is significant, for it sustains the view that he first went to, or was west of, Michilimackinac in 1769, and also that he wintered there. The Beaver Club minutes, however, note that he went west in 1770; yet this is not contradictory. It may be that the year 1770 marked the end of his first season, 1769–70, in the British fur trade based on Montreal.[1] Or perhaps it is a mistake. In any event, a member elected to the Beaver Club had to be a successful winterer. As we have seen, Pond was first in the trade in 1765 and then into Wisconsin and Minnesota and even beyond. The Beaver Club apparently discounted such early trading and dates his entry into the Canadian trade as 1769; understandably, and not illogically, that club put a purely Canadian stamp on itself. It is not known when or how often he attended the meetings and lavish dinners. I suspect that social striation was at work, keeping him on the margins, as it were, and certainly eventually forcing his exit. If and when he attended the club dinners, his presence was likely greeted with mild regret.

Of that legendary club, much has been written. Its membership included many persons who had braved the frontier life, excelled in business to the admiration of their peers, and returned to tell the tale. That Pond was elected a member at the date of its inception, in the first draft, speaks to his status among the powerful, picaresque men who dominated the commercial affairs of Canada in those days. (Or perhaps he could not be excluded from membership.) Merchants then carrying on the interior trade instituted the Beaver Club in Montreal. There were fifteen original members, all of whom had wintered in the northwest, a qualification. The object of club meetings was "to bring together, at stated periods, during the winter season, a set of men highly respectable in society, who had passed their best days in a savage country and had encountered the difficulties and dangers incident to a pursuit of the fur trade of Canada." In later days the membership rose to fifty-five, with ten honorary members. Early historians of the club recount that one of the customary activities was that attending members recounted the perils they had survived, and after circulating the Native emblem of peace, the calumet, the officer appointed for the purpose made a harangue suitable to the occasion. Legendary are the long tallies for wine and spirits consumed of an evening, and legendary, too, is the story of Sir Alexander Mackenzie, as fine a fellow to enjoy the company of his wintering partners as well as his resident business partners of Montreal, outlasting them all in the drinking contests that concluded these long evenings. These were evenings to bring out the tall tales and to sing lustily the Highland and Lowland epics and ballads and the boisterous songs of the voyageurs.

But it is hard for us to imagine Pond consumed by jocularity and mirth. More probably he possessed little appetite for enjoyment in such a club, instead preferring solitude to the banter and roistering of the fun-loving Scots and their English confreres at table. No, he was probably an outsider by choice and, moreover, by the determination of others.

With Pond in the initial intake of members were a weather-beaten trio who had gone to the high country before the fall of New France—Charles Chaboilez (in 1751), Maurice Blondeau (1752), and Hippolyte Desrivières (1753)—all of whom went west on the tail of Sieur de la Vérendrye. Then there was the new blood that had come in on the coat-tails of the British army: Alexander Henry (1760), Benjamin Frobisher (1765), and James McGill (1766), whose fortune established McGill University. Also among the first to be admitted were Pond's occasional partner George McBeath (1766) and Joseph Frobisher (1768), both known to Pond and, like McBeath, partners in incipient firms that coalesced or cooperated in the fur business as circumstances required. How often Pond attended the dinner when "in town" is not known, though rules specified that members be present in the winter season of December to April. Pond has left no remembrance of his connection with the Beaver Club—a pity, but, then, few if any members made note of it in their memoirs or correspondence, leaving us to think that the association has more heritage and sentimental value nowadays than it perhaps did at that distant time.

Nor do we have much information about Pond's doings in Montreal. He may have been in contact with Sir John Johnson, the powerful Superintendent of Indian Affairs, well known to Pond, who had served under Sir William Johnson at the battle of Fort Niagara in 1759 and who had been employed on Indian agency work. More research than this biographer has done in Indian agency files may show Pond's continuing connection with this line of work. We do know that Pond arrived in Montreal armed with his papers and his new, fascinating piece of cartography. In the next few weeks a number of persons cast their eyes over this curious map, and we learn all the details of this secondhand—through some very curious sources and snippets of information.

At this moment a strange and wonderful conjuncture occurred: not only was Pond piecing together in graphic form his own understanding of the far waters of the Saskatchewan and Churchill Rivers and the upper Mackenzie and its tributaries—to the degree that he knew them—but Captain James Cook's voyage to the North Pacific, and especially to Nootka Sound on Vancouver Island and the southeastern coast of Alaska, had also been disclosed by the (unauthorized) publication of books written by William Ellis, John Rickman, Henri Zimmerman, and John Ledyard. The official, authorized publication did not appear until 1784. Meanwhile, this quartet of tantalizing accounts sufficed to quench the thirst of those who sat reading at hearthside and speculated on the still unrevealed particulars of that vast area of space we might call Northwest America. The sea otter traders were soon on the hunt with their voyages from India, Macao, London, and elsewhere, and at the same time the Russians and Americans were exhibiting imperial and commercial interest in that long coast lying north of Spanish-held California and Russian-held Alaska.

Doubtless Pond found inspiration in these accounts of Cook's third voyage, including William Ellis's presumably authentic preview of Cook's reconnaissance, published in 1782, or possibly that of his fellow Connecticut colonial John Ledyard, or even that of John Rickman, both published in 1784. All of them talked about Bering's discoveries in the North Pacific and of Arctic seas; all talked about the fabulous fortunes to be made in the sea otter trade, taking Northwest Coast furs to China, and opening other new markets between West and East.

The same year that Cook explored the Northwest Coast, 1778, Pond had crossed the Methye Portage and opened the Athabasca country to the Canadian fur trade. The long-distance tentacles of British exploration and commerce were closing in on this remote quarter of the world. By sea and land the far western dimensions of what would become Canada were being set in place.

Although he was unqualified as a surveyor and cartographer, Pond nonetheless decided to reach for the geographic and cartographic—that is, to show spatially the lay of the land as he saw it. He wanted to show how his discoveries had come ever so close to a link to Pacific tidewater and to places where the Russians and Americans were known to be gathering pelts. After all, he had pioneered trade into distant Athabasca and saw it as a gateway to the north and perhaps the west. He had unlocked an essential secret of western waters and drainage basins. He had revealed a vast interior space, one with doors to the Arctic in the north, the Coppermine River in the northeast, the Churchill River system in the east-northeast, and possibly some form of communication west. From Ledyard and the others he had learned about Russian progress in the Pacific and that they were now trading in Alaskan waters. The link between Athabasca and Alaska was suggestive and alluring. Probably no one thought more about this than Pond.

During the winter of 1784–85, with notes, observations, and journals (now lost) at hand, Pond drew his famed map, sketching out the details on a large sheet. This was a retrospective of his travels and labours, a crude spatial representation of his years in the *pays d'en haut*. On it he placed the rivers and lakes from the Great Lakes and Hudson Bay westward to the Rocky Mountains and even northward to the Arctic. The map contains the earliest depiction of what is now called the Mackenzie Basin. He traced the course of a large river flowing from Lake Athabasca to Slave (Great Slave) Lake and thence to the Arctic Ocean, which he called "Supposed, the Ice Sea." He shows Prince William Sound and Cook's River (Cook Inlet) on his map, indicating that he was conversant with the place names applied in consequence of Cook's final voyage. He found the Russian prospects in trade alluring. Thus he set to work to show on paper how his travels linked with those of Hearne, Cook, and the Russians. But it also seems likely that he was responding to the demands of his ambitious partners, who wished to have a map to accompany the memorandum that they intended to submit to government for support and protection.

In that same year, on 1 March 1785, Pond's map came into possibly rival hands, for a copy was submitted to the United States Congress.[2] And another—strangely, perhaps the earliest—version of a Pond map bears on the question of the Canadian boundary with the United States. At this stage the details are fuzzy. The historical geographer Henry Raup Wagner, in seeking out all versions of Pond's map, received news of a theory from a Mr. Richardson of the Public Archives of Canada (now Library and Archives Canada) who suggested that Pond had prepared a fourth basic map before all the others. Richardson based his proposition on a remark by Thompson: "Shortly after my departure (from London) some maps

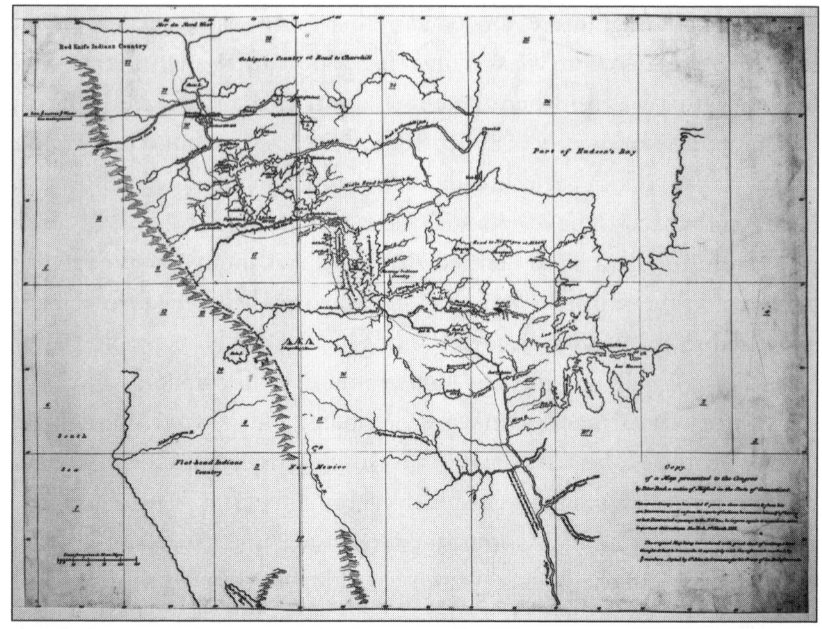

This map by Peter Pond was presented to the United States Congress in 1785, five years before he sold his share in the North West Company and retired from the trade. There is no conclusive evidence that any of Pond's maps were part of a secret scheme to extend or secure a northern boundary with Canada beyond what was specified by the treaty of 1783. GLENBOW ARCHIVES NA-2837-1

drawn by the fur traders of Canada had been seen by Mr [Alexander] Dalrymple [the hydrographer, of whom much more presently] which showed the rivers and lakes for many hundred miles to the westward of Hudson's Bay."[3] "If such a map was made by Pond," opines Wagner, "it could have been used by [Benjamin] Franklin for his negotiations of the Treaty of Paris of 1783, but I am unable to agree with Mr. Richardson's assumption as Thompson's allusion is vague, Thompson's statements are notoriously inaccurate, and I find no other record of [the fourth map]."[4] This monumental slur against Thompson will not go unnoticed by those aware of the general veracity of Thompson's narrative, but in this instance Wagner is right; I think the pre-1783 map would be a premature delineation of the west, including Athabasca. Joseph Tyrrell, first to edit Thompson's narrative, also thought Thompson had the details wrong.[5] Wild goose chases in search of maps are sometimes successful but, sad to say, no such early state of Pond's has seen the recent light of day. Thompson in later years tended to exaggerate and was of the opinion that Pond had led the American commissioners to adopt a boundary that he recommended. It makes a good story but is unsubstantiated. It would be a wild conclusion to make Pond the scapegoat for the international boundary that was set when the United States was recognized by Great Britain in the peace treaty of 1783. Thompson has his chronology wrong.

Now we pick up the threads of an earlier theme and bring them into Pond's theorizing about waters west. On 18 April 1785, almost ten years from the date Pond entered the trade that the Nor'Westers were pursuing on the Saskatchewan and into Athabasca, he signed a memorial addressed to the lieutenant governor of Quebec, the Honourable Henry Hamilton.[6] Pond's was the lead signature on the document, which was sent on behalf of the North West Company and may well have been written by the Frobishers. Pond, a pre-eminent trader and discoverer in the far northwest, was their choice of instrument, a suitable and well-deserved recognition. No doubt exists as to this document's intent; it asked the governor and the British Crown to back a scheme for discoveries at the northwestern reaches of North America under Pond's leadership. The purpose was commercial: to support the North West Company traders, the British government should lend assistance in establishing posts as far west as the Pacific Coast. The intention was to stop the trade from falling into Russian and American hands. The Russians, coming eastward from Siberia and Kamchatka, were known to have places of trade in the Gulf of Alaska and to have their eyes on coastal trade to the south, possibly as far as California. The Americans—that is, Bostonians—were about to enter the maritime, or sea otter, trade to the Northwest Coast of America, with vital connections to China. The sea otter was the means of opening Canton's trade with the West in tea, nankeen, silk stockings, porcelain, carved ivory pieces, cloisonné, and more.

It may be imagined that the partners worked up this memorial during that same winter in Montreal when Pond and others had been inducted as founding members of the Beaver Club. There was pride in their achievement of the past two decades, for these lords of the *pays d'en haut* had developed a self-conscious identity as a group to be reckoned with in the formation of British commercial policy. They wanted even more influence, and Pond, their most senior if not the most commercially successful, was their champion, their instrument, their spokesman. His fame and celebrity in the wilderness trade, as Alexander Henry had said before, made him well qualified to speak the fur trading line, linked as it was to imperial expansion and, not unimportant for the day, geographical science and cartography.

Enclosed with the Nor'Westers' memorial was a map by Pond, or, more correctly, another state of Pond's map.[7] The most notable features of it were "Lake Araubaska" and the Polar Sea—that is, the Arctic Ocean. This map revealed Pond's scientific shortcomings, for his locations were wildly off mark: Lake Athabasca, shown only slightly north of its actual latitude is far too far west—in fact in the longitude of Nootka Sound. Samuel Hearne noted that Pond showed the Polar Sea seven degrees south of its actual position. Historian Glyndwr Williams comments: "Although Pond knew the region better than any other white man, in the construction of maps he was handicapped by his complete lack of training. There is no indication that he could make an astronomical observation, and his reliance on dead reckoning led to absurdly inaccurate maps. Pond was one of the last of the old explorers, men tough in body and mind, but who often returned from the wilderness unable to represent accurately in map form where they had been or what they had seen. The maps they did produce distracted as much as they assisted."[8] Yet another map was prepared, this one showing that in the interval he had become aware of Captain James Cook's discoveries, which indicated that Cook Inlet, as it is now called, was a river and drained from Athabasca.

Anxious to assist Pond and prevent him from aiding the United States or another country, Lieutenant Governor Hamilton urged the British government, unsuccessfully, to help him and the Nor'Westers. It was at this stage that Pond found himself drawn into the imperial vortex—not personally but by association with the Nor'Westers—as, once again, the influence of the Hudson's Bay Company and its friends at the centre of power and empire posed an obstacle.

In London, Alexander Dalrymple cut a formidable figure in British geography. An angular, meddlesome fellow and a bit of a busybody, he liked to see himself at the focal point of scientific advances in geography. In terms of the old conflicting imperial purposes, he stood with the traders not the settlers. He favoured markets in preference to colonies and was an architect of the changes that brought about the Second British Empire. Hydrographer to the East India Company since 1779 (he became Hydrographer to the Admiralty in 1795), he was fully conversant with the special influence that chartered companies possessed, mainly having authority to keep out trading and shipping rivals. When the aforementioned North West Company propositions arrived in London, Dalrymple took notice, for he was a keen proponent of finding a northwest passage, expanding trade in the China Seas, and making discoveries in the Pacific Ocean. The Nor'Westers wanted an exclusive privilege for ten years. But they had forgotten, Dalrymple wrote, that the Hudson's Bay Company already possessed that exclusive privilege. (Dalrymple did not understand the southern limits of the Bay traders' charter, the lands drained by waters flowing to Hudson Bay. The Nor'Westers were prosecuting their trade in lands that lay beyond the HBC's limits. In fact, in 1749 the Company had come under fire in Parliament for failing to prosecute a search for the Northwest Passage. On account of fiery accusations from Arthur Dobbs, a House of Commons investigation was commenced. The Company was vindicated on grounds that until such time as the French could be dislodged from the Great Lakes—and that was not practicable as long as Canada was in their possession—little penetration could be made inland in search of a waterway.[9])

Then he turned to discoveries. "They offered to explore and deliver maps of the country to the west of Hudson's Bay, from 55° to 65° North latitude: but the Hudson's Bay Company had, before their offer was made, communicated Mr. Hearne's map of those parts, and although Mr. Hearne has left much yet to be done, this is more likely to be effected by the Hudson's Bay Company, than by the Canadian Traders, who seem to be scarcely less savage than the most savage of the Indians." Dalrymple contended, wrongly, that the Canadian traders could not successfully compete: "The Canadians having so great a distance to traverse, and so many carrying-places and rapids to impede their way, cannot convey to the Indians our staple manufactures, such as coarse woollens and iron-ware, but their exports must be chiefly in ammunition, and proof-spirits, to the destruction of the Indians." Dalrymple wanted to see examined any obstructions that might exist to navigation beyond what he called Lake Athabasca, actually Great Slave Lake. "It appears, from the Indian maps, that the Arathapescow Lake communicates with Hudson's Bay." These views Dalrymple published in *Plan for Promoting the Fur-Trade* (London, 1789), a pamphlet with myriad imperial implications bearing on international rivalries; elsewhere he advanced a scheme for a union of the East India and Hudson's Bay Companies, the whole designed to

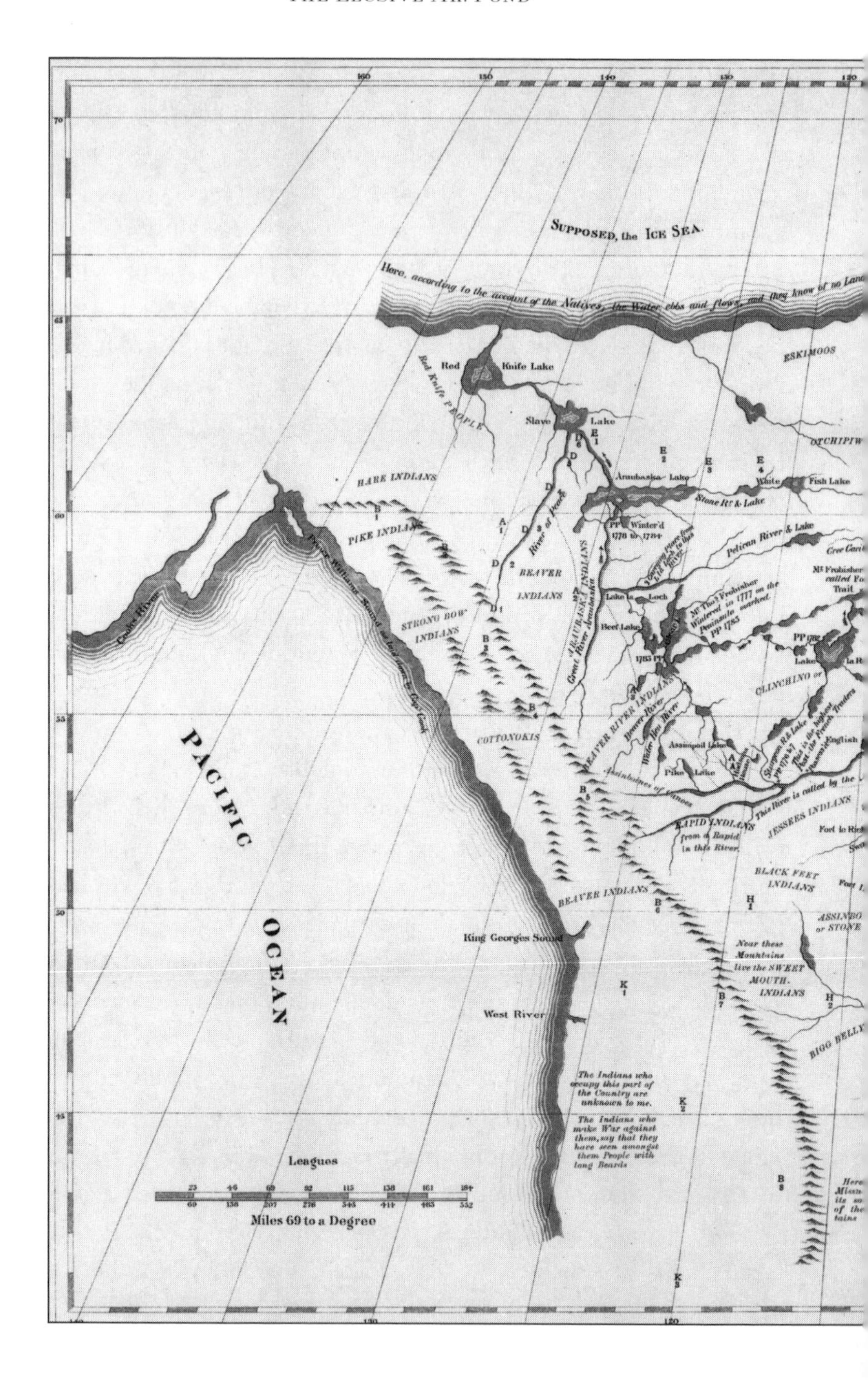
Supposed, the Ice Sea
Here, according to the account of the Natives, the Water ebbs and flows, and they know of no Land
Eskimoos
Red Knife Lake
Red Knife People
Slave Lake
Araubaska Lake
Stone Rr & Lake
White Fish Lake
Hare Indians
Pike Indians
River of Peace
Winter'd 1778 to 1784
Pelican River & Lake
Beaver Indians
Araubaska Indians
Great River Araubaska
Lake la Loch
Strong Bow Indians
Beef Lake
Mr Thos Frobisher Wintered in 1777 on the Peninsula marked PP 1785
Clinchino or
Beaver River Indians
Beaver River
Cottonokis
Assinpoil Lake
Pike Lake
Assiniboines of Canoes
Rapid Indians from a Rapid in this River
Jesses Indians
Black Feet Indians
Beaver Indians
King Georges Sound
Near these Mountains live the Sweet Mouth Indians
West River
Pacific Ocean
The Indians who occupy this part of the Country are unknown to me.
The Indians who make War against them, say that they have seen amongst them People with long Beards
Leagues
Miles 69 to a Degree

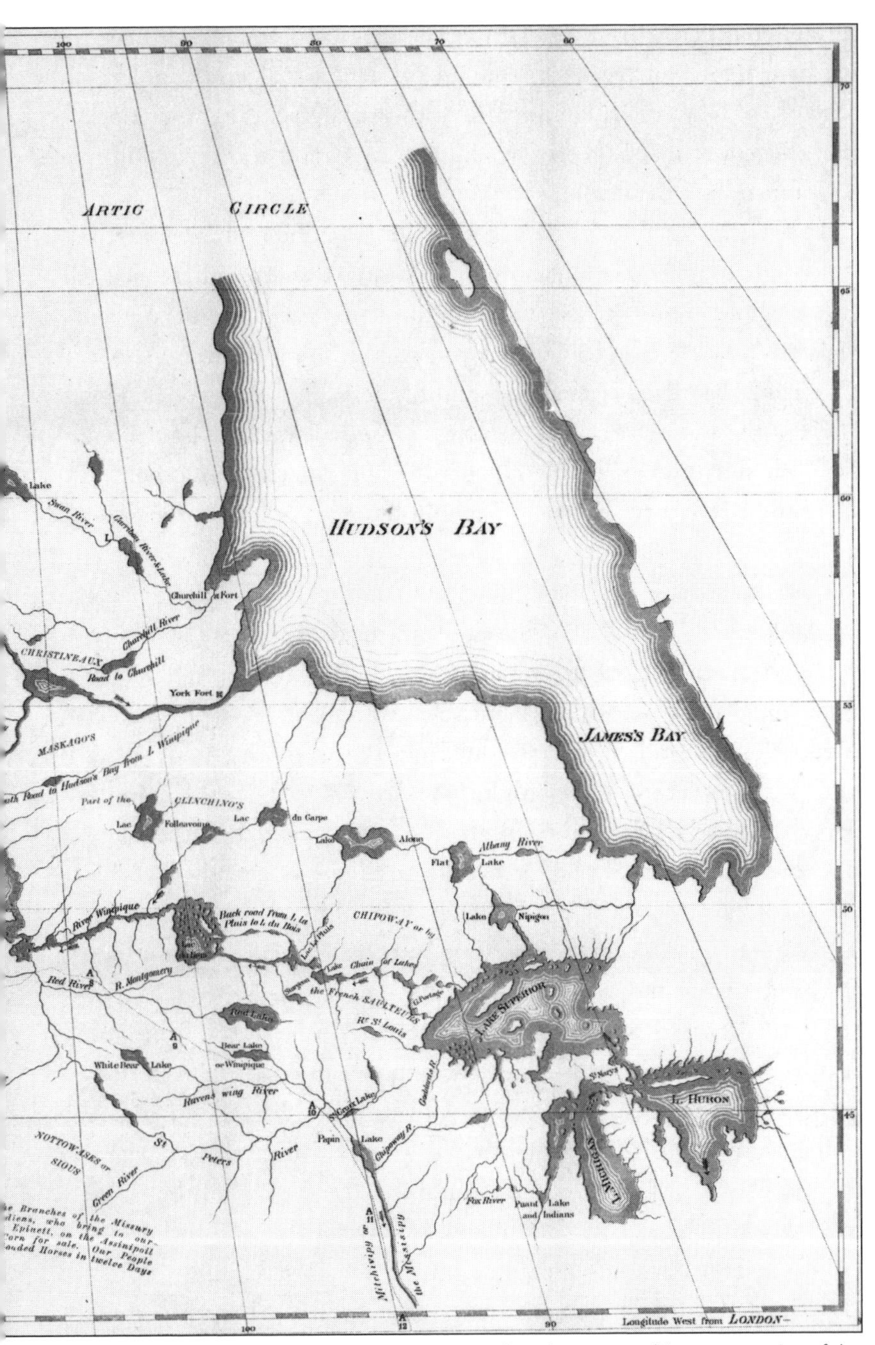

Likely the best map from the North West Company's early partners, this representation of the Nor'Westers' forts and trading realms in the *pays d'en haut* was created in 1785 and presented to the Honourable Henry Hamilton in Quebec. Peter Pond's signature is on the accompanying memorandum, indicative of his prominence among the ambitious traders seeking government protection and support against rivals real and imagined. LIBRARY AND ARCHIVES CANADA facilitate commerce, find a northwest passage, and encourage British trade to China.[10] Such views, from an influential voice, did not ease acceptance of news about Pond's fresh discoveries. With the dab of a pen, Dalrymple could shape the course of discoveries and back any Hudson's Bay Company scheme for these.

We leave Dalrymple for the moment, although he resurfaces later in this account. In parallel to Dalrymple's investigations, another force in the making of empire, Sir Joseph Banks, came to hear about Pond again (as related earlier, Alexander Henry wrote to him about Pond in October 1781). Banks had been elected president of the Royal Society of London in 1778—the same year Captain Cook visited Vancouver Island and Alaska. He nurtured explorers. His network of contacts was as wide as his worldly laboratory. He had a London house in Soho Square and a country place, Revesby Abbey, Lincolnshire.

It was to the latter place that a Captain Bentinck, fresh from Canada, came calling in 1788 to tell him that—and this is in Banks's handwriting—"A Mr. Pond set out from Quebeck in the Spring [of] 1785 Alone with the intention of Crossing America Westward & returning by Siberia, he had before traveld till he met the Tide in a river which ran to the west & supposes he then was within three days Journey of the Sea in the Neighourhood of Jesuits harbor."[11] This document, though fragmentary, is elusive as it provides few details that can be confirmed by other sources. Pond never wrote about this travel adventure himself, but it might be imagined that his concepts for pressing west from Lake Athabasca and Great Slave Lake could take him to Jesuits Harbor, Alaska; Kamchatka, Siberia; and across Russian dominions to Britain before returning to North America. This would be just the opposite of what the American Marco Polo, John Ledyard, set forth to do in 1787–88.[12] Ledyard described himself as "the very football of chance," and to some degree Pond was also at the mercy of those who directed the affairs of the North West Company.

But Captain Bentinck was not alone in advising Banks on Pond's discoveries and intentions. A savant in Quebec City, J. Mervin Nooth, had made a habit of sending Banks the most recent news of natural history discoveries in Canada—all about botanical, zoological, geological matters, and the like. In early November, in order to beat freeze-up in the St. Lawrence River, which would stop all communication with

London until the next April, he sent Banks a flurry of letters that were really reports about new findings—wild rice, geological specimens, and, of particular interest, the lay of the western interior, notably its lakes and rivers.

"A very singular Person of the name of Pond is arriv'd at Quebec," Nooth announced to Banks on 4 November from the capital of Canada.[13] He gave no further details about his encounter with the wilderness explorer. In what way, we might ask, was Pond seen as a "very singular Person"? We can imagine that the grizzled and bronzed Pond, dressed in rough frontier attire and with tall, leather gaiters typical of traders of that day, cut an odd, angular picture among those of the upper echelon of nicely dressed civil servants, learned persons, and literary figures who lived in the colonial capital and did the Province of Quebec's business. This place differed from Montreal, with its banking and shipping, and Pond was there on political and imperial business, to put a face, as it were, on his recent memorandum. It was his first, and perhaps only, visit to Quebec, seat of Lord Dorchester, the governor.

Nooth told Banks where Pond had ventured and what he had found in his travels: "This man has been some Years in the western parts of America on a trading Expedition with the Indians & positively asserts that he has discover'd an immense Lake [Great Slave Lake] nearly equal to Great Britain that communicates in all probability with Cook's River or Sandwich Sound [Alaska]." He continued his account of Pond's travels:

> In the River which was form'd by the Water that was discharg'd from this Lake he met with Indians that had undoubtedly seen Cooks Ships & who had with them a variety of European Articles evidently of English manufacture. The country which Pond pass'd thro' after leaving the neighbourhood of Montreal was altogether level no mountains or even Hills any where appearing till he came near the Lake above mention'd & to which the Traders have given the Name of the Great Slave Lake. The Land every where abounded with Timber & from the Banks of the Rivers they collected an infinite Variety of extraneous Fossils. The most common Animals which they saw were Buffaloes, & the number of these was everywhere incredible. Mr. Pond pretends that he has discover'd a new species of Buffaloe [Wood Bison, *Bison bison*

> *athabascae*] that wants a Tail although at first View it appears to be well furnish'd in that respect. This deception is owing to an exuberant Growth of strong coarse Hair that covers the internal parts of the Buttocks from the Rump to the Hocks. As none of the extraneous fossils are yet brought to Quebec I cannot say any thing respecting them but I dare say there are many nondescripts in the immense tract of Country which Pond & his Party pass'd through.

Pond, Nooth reported, had presented his map of his western journey to Lord Dorchester. Whether or not he spoke to the great man, the architect of the Quebec Act and the most powerful figure in British statecraft directing the affairs of Canada at that time, is not known. As to the map itself, the latitudes were well laid down, thought Nooth generously, "as Pond himself was very capable of ascertaining that circumstance." This is a hint that Pond applied the lines of longitude and latitude himself, but the possibility remains that he had someone else help him in this.

It was always easier in that age to figure out the latitude and, by strange contrast, devilishly hard to determine the longitude: you could not always observe with a glass the satellites of Jupiter, and cloudy days made it impossible; even a chronometer, whose accuracy is so loudly proclaimed these days, could be faulty or in need of correct rating and adjustment. "The Longitude seems to be guess-work and not in any respect accurate enough to be depended on," said Nooth.

> Altho the Country to the southward of the Great Lake was every where cover'd with Trees, the Land to the northward of that immense tract of fresh Water had neither Tree nor shrub, nothing but a very luxuriant Grass cover'd the whole face of the Country. I don't find that in this immense Space of Land which Mr Pond & his Associates travell'd over, they found any trace of mineral Substances, excepting Iron, & this was chiefly Bog Ore such as abounds in the neighbourhood of Three Rivers [Trois-Rivières, Quebec] & which is at present wrought with considerable Advantage at that place.

Nooth had commented on Pond's northernmost travels, beyond the northern or boreal forest to what explorer Sir John Franklin called "the Barrens." And fascinating is the fact, which we learn by deduction, that Pond had not seen the Rocky Mountains; or if he had, Nooth knew nothing about this finding. Did Pond seek to keep secret the forbidding ramparts of the Rockies, the barrier to western discoveries and a route to the Pacific, where Cook's ships had been?

On 7 November 1789, three days after Nooth's remarkable disclosure to Banks of Pond's visit to Quebec, another equally insightful letter, from a different writer to a different recipient, told about Pond, his travels, his map, and his discoveries. The writer, like Nooth, had met Pond in Quebec. His name was Isaac Ogden.

A judge of the Admiralty court in Quebec, the well-placed Ogden, then acting clerk of the Crown and possibly working in or close to the governor's office, took note of Peter Pond. He was precisely the same age as the trader, and he, too, had been born in colonial America of Puritan stock. He wrote a telling letter to his father, David Ogden, also a judge, with deep attachments to New Jersey. The Ogdens had settled in New Jersey after the restoration of Charles II, who had granted the colony to Sir George Carteret, a prominent player in the founding of the Hudson's Bay Company. David Ogden had become a King's Counsel in New Jersey and sat among those directing the affairs of that jurisdiction. But when the storm of the American Revolution broke he found himself first a partisan for the revolutionary cause and then an opponent of a break with King George III. As a Loyalist, he reluctantly sought refuge in London. The Ogdens were well connected to Elizabethtown, New Jersey, also home of Alexander Henry, Peter Pond's trading contemporary in the Northwest. Isaac Ogden likely knew Alexander Henry, and this may have been the connection that brought about his meeting with Pond. In Montreal, Isaac Ogden, had been a guest at the prestigious Beaver Club. He was acquainted with all the great Nor'Westers, including Mackenzie, and was now even more entranced by the prospects for western discoveries advanced by Pond. (That he, in turn, fired the interest of his son, Peter Skene Ogden, in discoveries when the latter was a youth seems undeniable, and the latter went on to an outstanding career as a fur trader and explorer of the North West Company and, subsequently, the Hudson's Bay Company.[14])

In previous correspondence, Isaac Ogden had complained to his father how difficult it was to "a Philosophic Mind"—that is to say a scientific and logical one—to obtain a correct idea of the size of Canada, east to west. The dimensions of the future dominion seemed limitless, without bounds. But since his previous letter he had had an opportunity of seeing a map or chart of that country made by "a Gentleman of observation and Science [Peter Pond], who has actually traversed it and made his Map in it, and with whom I have this week had several Conversations with the Map before me." He continued, "I am [now] able to give you all the Satisfaction that you wish for, exclusive of the Map itself, which I could not get a Copy of, but I hope to send it [to] you next Summer." Isaac had made copious notes, and he described the position of the Mississippi River, the Falls of St. Anthony, the Grand Portage of Lake Superior, and the course of lakes and waters leading to the Saskatchewan, or north to York River on Hudson Bay:

> The Hudson's Bay Company have Posts several hundred Miles west from them, but none to the Northward. Our Traders pass them at one of their Posts about the Lat. 57 & Long. 110. A Chain of Lakes &c continue from thence to the Lat. 58. & Long. 124. when with a small Portage [Methye] they enter into other Lakes and Rivers, which all finally communicate with and empty into a Great Lake called the Slave Lake...and this Lake is the last Water before you come to the Great Northern Ocean in Lat. 68 ½ & in the Long. 132. & There the Water ebbs and flows, of which the Gentleman gave me indubitable Proofs.[15]

In other words, Pond knew, or at least speculated, that the river that drained Slave Lake flowed to the Arctic. This was *De Cho*, the River Big as the Dene called it—the Mackenzie River.

In recounting his meeting with Pond and his examination of Pond's map, Ogden wrote that in 1787 the explorer met with "two Indians who came (as they said) up a River from the Northern Pacific Ocean all the way to the Slave Lake—they brought him a blanket in 1787 which they received from Vessels which were at the Mouth of the River—they said that the River he was in is large to the Place of Discharge and Navigable; so that if we take the Lat. & Long. of the two Rivers, the Courses, and all the other Circumstances into Consideration, little doubt remains that they are the Same."[16] Ogden knew that Cook had sailed north into high latitudes, and Pond's evidence, based on Native testimony, seemed to indicate that a watercourse existed from Great Slave Lake to the North Pacific.

While all these wild imaginings and rich postulations about far-western geography were being advanced by closet philosophers, nosy fixers, interested observers, and responsible statesmen, Pond was completing his last years in the *pays d'en haut*. Twenty years had passed since he entered the trade at Detroit. Now age forty-five, he was at once the most prominent of the partners of the North West Company in terms of being a field general and a master of logistics and, at the same time, probably the least amenable to the powerful company interests that dominated corporate affairs in Montreal. Time and space had distanced him from the up-and-coming powerbrokers of the concern, persons such as Simon McTavish and the younger William McGillivray, who would become in time the new lord of the Northwest. Alexander Mackenzie was not yet a force to be reckoned with, but it is a fact of fascination that he, like Pond, fell afoul of the dominant Montrealers. It was yet again a tug of war between the frontier and the metropolis, and both Pond and Mackenzie were of the frontier before their respective exits from it.

We were last with Pond in 1784–85, on his election to the Beaver Club, and it is to this point in time we return. He seems to have left Montreal in early May 1785, en route to Athabasca via Grand Portage, and at that time we have a rare glimpse of Pond as a humanitarian. It was not uncommon for fur traders to be couriers of medicines, notably vaccines. Mackenzie is known to have carried smallpox vaccine on a medical mission to the interior tribes. How Pond got involved in a parallel mission is an intriguing story, of which few details are known. A disease known locally in Charlevoix, Quebec, as Baie-Saint-Paul malady was of pernicious influence that year. A French surgeon working in the British militia, Dr. Philippe-Louis-François Badelard, investigated it and correctly identified it as venereal disease. The colonial administration, worried that this potentially fatal disease would be conveyed west of Lachine by fur traders and voyageurs, called on the North West Company to guard against such a possibility, and the governor ordered that medicines be carried to the interior for the relief of any persons who might have symptoms of the disorder. To check its spread, the Nor'Westers assured the governor that anyone having the disease would not be permitted to travel west of Lachine. In addition to this measure, Pond agreed to take the medicines to the interior with him that summer.[17] We hear no more of this matter, and it may be surmised that the efforts of the Nor'Westers and Pond were successful. Individual cases of venereal disease were identified among Native and Métis persons from time to time—Louis Riel had it—but widespread effects were not felt. It was smallpox that was the main killer, especially among the Assiniboine.

Pond was not alone, and rivals now were making their appearance, using Methye Portage to transit to the upper Mackenzie River basin. The mastery of the Nor'Westers in Athabasca, built up on Pond's shoulders, was now threatened by a group of upstart Montreal-based traders. In 1785 a syndicate led by John Gregory, Alexander Mackenzie, Normand MacLeod, and Peter Pangman precipitated what Mackenzie described as "the severest struggle ever known in that part of the world." Pond was at the heart of this struggle, his tactic to defend his already flourishing interests.

Our story now follows the brief life of John Ross (about whom, sadly, so little is known). He is, historically, a shadowy figure. His name appears as one of the small traders in the fur trade licences in 1779; we also know that he was one of the traders in the first North West Company, formed in that year.[18] In 1780 he was in partnership with Peter Pangman but was dropped in the Company's 1783 reorganization. Ross then joined Gregory, MacLeod and Company (with whom Mackenzie was connected) in 1785, and when he came into Athabasca that same year he was in opposition to Pond. His job was to draw off his rival's traffic. Accordingly, and brazenly, he set up a post right under Pond's nose, near Pond's House. It was too close for comfort for the wary Pond. We can imagine that Pond watched his rival narrowly, with all due suspicion and not a little anguish as he saw his Native alliances subverted and his own fur collections dribbling away. Pond, we know, always guarded his interests fiercely, and the pre-emptive impulse probably drove him to take action, by indirect means.

In the winter of 1786–87, competition became severe and then predatory between Pond and Ross. At some place and at some date, Ross was "shot in a scuffle with Mr. Pond's men," according to one report. Here was another violent episode of the fur trade, and those who heard of it must have been reminded of Pond's already deteriorating reputation, sullied by implication in the 1782 murder of Jean-Étienne Waden. Word of Ross's murder reached Grand Portage in the summer of 1787 and was brought eastward by Roderick Mackenzie, cousin of Alexander Mackenzie, and William McGillivray, Mackenzie's friend and the nephew of Simon McTavish, called "the Premier" and the most powerful of the Montreal-based Nor'Westers.

The tale of murder was delivered right to the heart of those Montreal interests. So significant was the news of Ross's death to those who directed the trade strategy of the firm (and were conscious of its public reputation) that it was decided, on the spot, to unite the interests of the North West Company and Gregory, MacLeod and Company. The Nor'Westers had been obliged to give way. Mackenzie, in 1801, wrote, "After the murder of one of our partners, the laming of another, and the narrow escape of one of our clerks, who received a bullet through his powder horn...they were compelled to allow us a share of the trade." Philip Turnor, Hudson's Bay Company surveyor, specifically states that a partnership of the two interests was necessary to prevent "great inquiry into the affair." Ross's party continued to trade as it pleased, wrote Turnor, "having no opposers." Traders did not want a trading war, one injurious to their personnel and to their profits, and they especially did not want law and order breathing down their necks.

It was not just news of the murder that came eastward out of the *pays d'en haut*. Two of Pond's men—names unknown to the outside world for some time—were strong-armed by agents of the North West Company and brought the great distance to Quebec for trial. "But," writes W.S. Wallace, in a suitable appraisal, "either the evidence against them was insufficient, or else the court decided that it had no jurisdiction, and they were acquitted."[19]

It took some years to identify the real culprit in the murder of Ross. Turnor chanced on three Canadians building a post on the east branch of the Slave River on 22 July 1791, about four years after the incident. Wallace takes up the story:

> The master of the post was a French Canadian named Péché; and Turnor says of him "he is charged with having killed Mr. Ross up the Athapescow River near to Peter Pond's House." His account

> of the murder is fairly explicit. He says that Péché "was in the interest of and servant to Peter Pond," and Mr. Ross was in charge of goods, indeed a Partner of Peter Pangman, Alexr. Mackenzie and others, the dispute was about some Chepawyans as they were coming to the House to trade. P. Pond and his men being more numerous than Mr. Ross's, they were taking the Indians by force, which Mr. Ross opposed, and in the dispute was shot." This is corroborated by Peter Fidler, who accompanied Turnor, and says in his journal that Péché was "the same man that shot Mr. Ross at Peter Pond's fort a few years back, he then absconded with the Chepewyans and remained with them 3 winters and 3 summers, before he could venture back—frightened of the Gallows, he is the only man in the Canadian employ that understands the Chepewyan language."[20]

Péché (or Peshe, though most correctly Piché[21]) seems to have led a purposely reclusive life in the north country among the Chipewyan for three years, and traded from Slave River. But the evidence of HBC surveyor Fidler, in his journal of 1791, that "Mr. Ross was shot by one Peshe, a Canadian, by order of Pond," seems conclusive.[22] David Thompson, who heard of the event secondhand, corroborates Fidler's statement that Ross was shot by Péché. On the other hand, Thompson's account comes from a remote source, Dr. John Bigsby, so it has to be treated with caution. And this twist was added: "He [Peter Pond] persuaded his men to rob Mr. Ross of a load of furs in open day. In the course of the altercation Mr. Ross was shot, really by accident, from a gun in the hand of a voyageur named Péché."[23]

Whether by accident or not, Pond was involved and implicated. There is no mention of Pond in the report of a special 1788 privy council of the Province of Quebec that considered the province's jurisdiction to try cases of murder in the Native country. Thus, as Innis concluded, evidence against Pond is slight, although the privy council investigation is not conclusive evidence of Pond's innocence.[24] Wallace, with wisdom, writes, "It is perhaps one of the ironies of fate that he should have escaped punishment for the murder of Étienne Waden, in which he was almost certainly implicated, and should have been compelled to retire from the fur trade because of the murder of John Ross, for which he was perhaps not legally responsible."[25] Yet again we have one of the incongruities of history. But whether he was guilty or not, Pond had become an undesirable in a commercial concern that was seeking respectability in its imperial rivalry with the Hudson's Bay Company, which was under the ever-watchful eye of the British authorities in Canada and London.

Pond and other traders lived in a violent world, where intertribal war was endemic and murder was more common than has been imagined. War parties of Cree and Assiniboine from the Swan River department of the North West Company continued to attack the Bloods and Rapids (Gros Ventres) as late as 1803, as Daniel Harmon testifies. Then he turned to the violence between the Nor'Westers and the New North West Company (also known as the XY Company), which was established in the late 1790s and later joined by Alexander Mackenzie. On this latter rivalry Harmon writes: "The North West Co. look upon their opponents...as encroachers of their territories...This jarring of interests keep up continual misunderstandings and occasions frequent broils between the two contending parties, and some times the enmity that exists between them rises to such an unbecoming height as to cause bloodshed, and in several instances even lives have been sacrificed!" He concludes with some moral comments:

> But I am of the opinion that those who have committed Murder in this Savage Country, would if a favorable occasion had offered been guilty of the like horrid crime in the Civilized part of the World—yet there are many in this Country who appear to be of a different opinion. Here it is true they have one advantage if indeed it may be thought one, that they have not below, is: here a Murderer escapes the Gallows, as there are no human laws that can reach or have effect on the People of this Country. However they are, in England about passing laws [the *Canada Jurisdiction Act*] which will equally affect the People of this Country as those in the Canada or any other part of the British Dominions—and it is high time it should be so, or the most of us soon should have cut one anothers throats.[26]

In 1803, almost a decade after Ross's murder, the *Canada Jurisdiction Act* (43, Geo. III, c.138[27]) was passed for the specific extension of British law in the Indian Territory. Its intention was to regulate the lawless conflict between the Canadian trading factions. Under its provisions, justices of the peace could be appointed in the "Indian Territories," and crimes committed there could be dealt with by the courts in Upper and Lower Canada.[28]

In the spring of 1788, Pond left the northwest. From the time of the murder of Waden in 1782, he had been a marked man, and his time in the west was limited. This situation was re-emphasized with Ross's murder five years later, despite Pond's apparent distance from this particular episode. The second death led to his withdrawal or forced retirement from the fur trade. In 1788, Roderick Mackenzie was at Fort Chipewyan, a remote observer of Pond's movements. He later recalled that at that time Pond, "being accused at different times of having been instrumental towards the death of two gentlemen who were in opposition to his interest...was now on his way out of the country on his defence."[29]

But there is another factor to consider regarding Pond's departure from the Canadian fur trade. He was fifty years old when he retired, and in his day that was a more advanced age than it is now. He could never be anything more than a partner with a single share in the North West Company. He no longer had a strong voice in its decision-making councils. He could not lead by example. Age consigned his achievements to an earlier, less proscribed era. Younger and more powerful interests—Mackenzie, Simon McTavish, and William McGillivray—were coming on to dominate the Nor'Westers. The old pioneers—Pond, Alexander Henry, and the Frobishers among others, and all of them at one time independents—were giving way to the new breed. Pond, independent to the core, found all partnerships uneasy except those he could control. He bridled at arrangements external to his interests that cut across his profits and his autonomy. If this was not so at the beginning, in his earliest trade partnership with Felix Graham and, later, with Alexander Henry and others, by the mid-1780s Pond was fuming with dissent and angry at how others were upstaging him, gathering more to themselves than he thought they deserved.

Evidence for this point of historical perspective comes from a scrap of correspondence in the annals of the North West Company. In late 1787, Pond had a correspondence with trader Patrick Small at Île à la Crosse. Small was father to Charlotte Small and thus David Thompson's father-in-law, a noteworthy association as it turns out. Two matters were of special concern in the letters: geographical aspects of the Athabasca country, and the business affairs of what Small calls "two concerns of men and goods put into general stock." Pond, writing to Small on 3 December 1787, says that Mackenzie left Athabasca suddenly that year. Pond was suspicious of Mackenzie's actions, and he obviously sensed that Mackenzie intended to gain some sort of advantage by early action. Pond was mistrustful, perhaps rightly so. Writing to Simon McTavish about this matter, Small noted: "I am quite surprised at the wild ideas Mr. Pond has of matters which Mr. Mackenzie told me were incomprehensively extravagant."[30] His comment that "he [Pond] is preparing a fine map to lay before the Empress of Russia,"[31] suggests he is referring to Pond's dreams of northern and westerly discoveries that would put the Canadian traders in touch with the Russians near Cook Inlet. There can be no other explanation, and it is surely odd that Mackenzie was to profit by a geographical insight he sought to disparage.

In reply to Pond, Patrick Small answered as satisfactorily as he could: he tells Pond that he is unjustified in believing "that anything was ever thought of contrary to the mutual interest of all concerned."[32] We read between the lines that the distrustful Pond suspected Mackenzie of acting in his own interest, in a style quite in conflict with the interests of the company. Pond could have made a representation to the rendezvous of partners at Grand Portage, but the distance there and back may have precluded such a visit, and Small reminded him that if he did go, he would have to be expeditious.

The noted explorer and mapmaker David Thompson based his assessment of Pond on information he received from Small, who was his father-in-law. Thompson never met Pond. Nonetheless, he was never short of opinions and judgments, and he had this to say about the famed trader:

> He was a person of industrious habits, a good common education, but of a violent temper and unprincipled character; his place [and here Thompson was wrong] was at Fort Chipewyan on the north side of the Athabasca Lake, where he wintered three years. At Lake Superior he procured a Compass, took the courses of the compass through the whole route to his wintering place; and for the distances adopted those of the

> Canadian canoe men in Leagues, and parts of the same, and etching off the Lake shores the best he could. In the winters, taking the depot of Lake Superior [Grand Portage] as his point of departure, the Latitude and Longitude was known as determined by the French Engineers. He constructed a Map of the route followed by the Canoes. Its features were tolerably correct; but by taking a league of the canoe men for three geographical miles (I found they averaged only two miles) he increased his longitude so much as to place the Athabasca Lake, at its west end near the Pacific Ocean. A copy of this map was given to the agents of the North West Company.[33]

Pond was not included in the 1790 reorganization of the North West Company, and he probably turned in his share in the Company for sale to some younger man, to be nominated by the partners in accordance with the conditions regulating disposal of stock. William McGillivray, twenty-six years Pond's junior, was the clerk nominated to purchase his former share.[34] The price paid was £800. The sale of his share may not have extinguished his right to receive from the Company the equivalent to the annual net produce of this share. John Finlay's North West Company documents from 1805 specify that even though he (Finlay) had relinquished his shares to the corporation, he was still entitled to receive his due.[35] But because Pond sold his share directly to McGillivray, the parallel may not obtain. Even so, until the document of sale surfaces—and it may, regrettably, never do so—we are left wondering if Pond's exit was as final and complete as it has been assumed.

Pond's departure had important consequences for Alexander Mackenzie. He profited mightily from Pond's pioneering enterprises and geographical ideas, building a career and reputation on business activities suggested by Pond's theories and actions. Mackenzie was self-conscious about his abilities, and his sunny disposition did not bear the dark side that is everywhere part of Pond's character. "I was led, at an early period of life, by commercial views, to the country North-West of Lake Superior, in North America," writes Mackenzie, "and being endowed by Nature with an inquisitive mind and enterprising spirit; possessing also a constitution and frame of body equal to the most arduous undertakings, and being familiar with toilsome exertions in the prosecution of mercantile spirits, I not only contemplated the practicability of penetrating across the continent of America, but was confident in the qualifications, as I was animated by the desire to undertake the enterprise."[36]

Pond undoubtedly lighted the path for Mackenzie. The older man knew more about the geography of Athabasca than any other, but he was an amateur at the business of exploration and he did not have the explorer's zeal that Mackenzie possessed—the desire to find out more by specifically organized expeditions. Pond imagined what lay beyond; of that there can be no doubt, and his imaginings often exceeded the reality. He was not the first nor would he be the last explorer to be hoist on his own petard—and he got into a terrible muddle about Cook's River, which turned out to be an inlet. But Pond seems to have unlocked the secrets of the upper reaches of the Mackenzie River system. The great river of the Athabasca district bears three different names, one for each of its important segments: first, the Peace River, which flows from the Rocky Mountains and does not actually pass through Lake Athabasca but, rather, ends just downriver from it; second, the Slave River, running from Lake Athabasca to Great Slave Lake; and third, the Mackenzie River proper, which flows from Great Slave Lake to the Arctic Ocean. Pond relied on his own conjectures and such other information as he could cobble together. He contended at one time that Great Slave Lake drained to Pacific tidewater. His acquaintances in Quebec City had various interpretations of what Pond told them—and what he showed them on his map. One has it that Great Slave Lake flowed to the Arctic Ocean; another, to the Pacific at Cook's River, having flowed around the north end of the Rockies to the Pacific.

Pond continued to produce maps of the northwest. One, dated 6 December 1787, he presented to Lord Dorchester (Sir Guy Carleton) at Quebec. Dorchester sent it to London in November 1790. By this time, however, a simplified version of Pond's map of December 1787 had already been published in the *Gentleman's Magazine* of March 1790. This map is of unique importance in the Pond story, for it disclosed the general geography of northwestern America. It advertised Pond's achievements. It gave him a place in the history of discoveries. It bears lines of longitude, obviously superimposed on what Pond had sketched out in generality. This handsome map shows one river flowing north from "Slave Lake"—actually Great Slave Lake—to the Arctic Ocean. It shows another

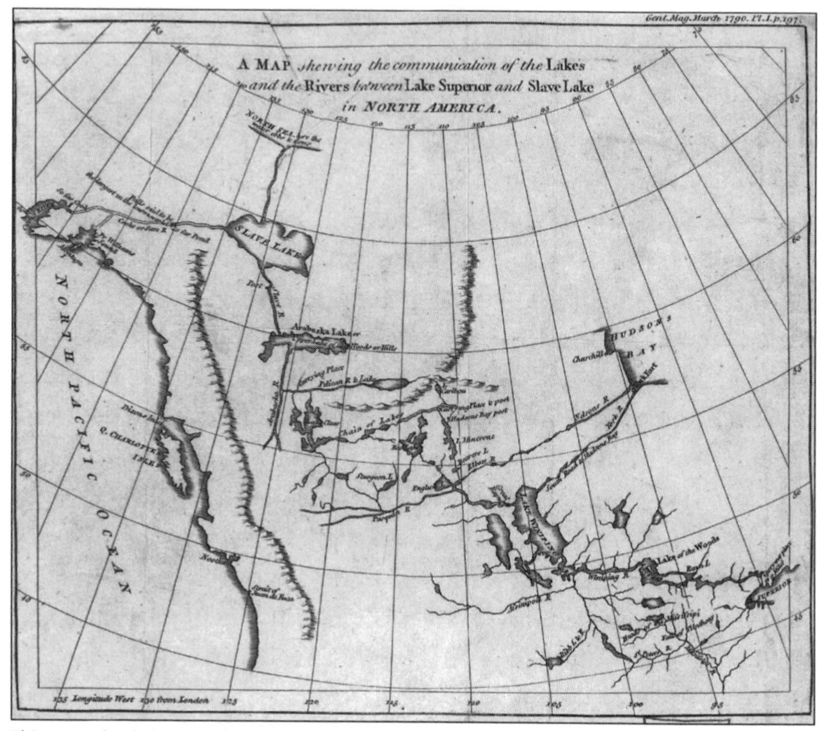

This exceedingly important map appeared in the March 1790 issue of *Gentleman's Magazine*, a London publication of learned information. It is the only map detailing Pond's knowledge of this part of North America to be published in engraved form. Lines of latitude and longitude give it scientific ballast, though who supplied them is anyone's guess. LIBRARY OF CONGRESS, GEOGRAPHY AND MAP DIVISION

running from the western end of the same lake to the Pacific shore at Cook Inlet, and a third branch flowing to Prince William Sound. There is a note on this elusive river, "so far Pond," and at its saltwater extremity, "so far Cook." Between these "so far" points was no easy passage, for on the map is marked "Falls said to be the largest in the known world." Pond did not add that detail; it appeared in John Meares's voyage account, also published in 1790, and Dalrymple may have added it to the map. Information about the fabulous falls was entirely speculative, but the existence of such an obstacle—a Niagara Falls plus—implied that no commercial route for navigation could exist in such high latitudes. The other part of the puzzle concerning this westward flowing, cascading stream was whether it linked with Cook's River, which Captain Cook contended drained out of the cordilleran mountains. Those looking at Pond's map in *Gentleman's Magazine* were misled into believing that a communication to the Pacific Coast from the rivers and lakes of Canada might not be so difficult after all. But Pond showed Great Slave Lake some six or seven hundred miles west of its actual location. His longitudes were wildly in error.

Pond drew yet another version of his map, intended for the Empress of Russia, Catherine II, as Patrick Small mentioned in his letter to Simon McTavish. This he prepared for the first explorer who could reach the Pacific Coast from Athabasca, meet up with Russian traders, and pass it to them as proof of Canadian commercial advances. Or, if possible, that first explorer could trek all the way across Russia to present the map in person. He hoped fortune would attend such a venture. This is what Mackenzie later spoke of on the eve of his departure from Fort Fork on the Peace River, 8 May 1793, bound for the Pacific, when he told his cousin Roderick, "I send you a couple of Guineas. The rest I take with me to traffick with the Russians...May all happiness attend you. Adieu, Dear Roderic."[37] Today, that version of Pond's manuscript map lies in the National Archive in Kew, England, "a melancholy relic of thwarted hopes."[38]

These maps show that Pond had become aware of Cook's discoveries. What is now called Cook Inlet, Alaska, was thought by the captain to be a river flowing from the east, and Pond's 1787 maps strongly suggest that it drained from a gigantic Great Slave Lake. In 1789, Alexander Mackenzie explored the river leading out of that lake and found it flowed to the Arctic, as Pond's first maps had indicated. Pond's willingness to change on the basis of Cook's unsubstantiated discovery dramatically hurt his credibility as a mapmaker and cast further doubts upon his character.

Word of Mackenzie's 1789 travels soon reached London by way of the commercial network and the imperial infrastructure; toward the end of 1790, the first disconcerting rumours suggested that Mackenzie had shown a flaw in Pond's theory that waters from Great Slave Lake flowed to the Pacific. The news passed quickly among those in Whitehall, the City, and the scientific circles who cared about such things. It was shared among the likes of Evan Nepean, the undersecretary of state; Dalrymple, the hydrographer; Samuel Enderby, the whaling magnate; and Daines Barrington, influential doyen of British discoveries in the Pacific.[39] In Montreal, Isaac Ogden learned of Mackenzie's intentions and reported to his father in London: "Another man by the name of McKenzie was left by Pond at Slave Lake with orders to go down the River, and thence to Unalaska, and so to Kamshatsha, and thence to England through Russia, etc. If he meets with no accident, you may have him with you next year."[40] Philip Turnor, the Hudson's Bay Company surveyor, recorded in his journal, "Mr McKenzie says he has been at the Sea but thinks it the Hyperborean [Arctic] Sea, but he does not seem acquainted with Observations which makes me think he is not well convinced where he has been." Turnor may have thought Mackenzie did not know where he had been, but in fact this is not the case. Mackenzie was well aware that he had reached the Arctic Ocean, and the only feature of this text is that Turnor, a trained surveyor, was trying a bit of one-upmanship at Mackenzie's expense. In fact, Mackenzie recognized the inadequacies of his scientific capabilities, and he went to London and spent the next winter, that of 1790–91, learning astronomical surveying, the reading of the moons of Jupiter, and the calculations of the *Nautical Almanac*. When he returned to the *pays d'en haut*, he was as skilled as Turnor and far more free and able to undertake vigorous discoveries.[41] From this time forward, Pond's star was in the descendant in London, Mackenzie's in the ascendant.

And how did Mackenzie give Pond the *coup de grace*? Hidden deep among the incoming correspondence of Lord Dorchester was a letter from Mackenzie that was not known to the general public until long afterward. On 17 November 1794, in Montreal, Mackenzie wrote to the famous Canadian governor about his two expeditions of discovery. Of the first and failed attempt to get to Pacific tidewater he says, "I followed the course of the Waters which had been reported by Mr. Pond to fall into Cooks River, they led me to the Northern Ocean." And "Tho' this Expedition did not answer the intended purposes, it proved that Mr Ponds assertion was nothing but conjecture, and that a North West Passage is impracticable."[42] There is nothing malicious or ill-intended in Mackenzie's recounting. Pond was merely being supplanted by another explorer who had come in his wake, found new realities, and opened new prospects—the age-old story of discovery.

Pond was similar to Mackenzie in many respects: he had been a leader in a new fur domain and had made a fortune not only for himself but also for the North West Company. Athabasca had been its certain success story, perhaps the most important up to the time of Mackenzie's rise from near obscurity to prominence as a trader and explorer. Is it possible that Pond felt aggrieved? That he had not received his due? Others had profited from his primacy, and now he was too old to pursue other fur trading schemes that were bottled up by the North West Company or by the Hudson's Bay Company. John Jacob Astor had not made his appearance, promoting the American fur trade south and west of Michilimackinac, and later to the mouth of the Columbia River. The British and Americans had yet to solve the knotty problem of the occupation of the British posts south of the Canadian–American border. Pond was out of luck and out of opportunity. The corporation he had helped to make had outflanked him. He was barred from any further activity; that would have been demanded of him when he sold his shares to McGillivray, the powerful and rising lord of the Northwest, Mackenzie's dear friend, and a close friend, besides, of Pond.[43]

Pond had reason to be disgruntled. Dorchester, who had a keen eye for problems that went on in the Province of Quebec, had knowledge that Pond left the province owing to his dissatisfaction with the North West Company. His intention, Dorchester said, was to seek employment in his native United States. He gives no further details. In large measure, Pond found himself a victim of the dissolution of the old British Empire in America. Like the Royal Marine John Ledyard, who was at Nootka Sound with Captain Cook in 1778, or like Benedict Arnold, who sought advancement in what he considered would be a better professional service, Pond was an opportunist, and a good one. We cannot claim that his being a New Englander or Yankee stood in his way, for then we should have to include in our evaluation the likes of Peter Pangman, both Alexander Henrys, Simon Fraser, and Daniel Harmon—all born in British American colonies and all, in time, prominent in the fur trade. He had, rather, run out of close allies in Montreal fur trade circles. His independence of action, which had been his strength for ever so long, had no future in the tight world of the McTavishes and McGillivrays. Even Mackenzie felt the pinch. And so Pond, who had been at Montreal when it fell to British arms, now left the city for the last time.

8

The Outlier Returns

In early March 1790, with his fiftieth birthday just behind him, Pond returned to the town of his boyhood. To get there we imagine that he went south by familiar tracks and ferries from Montreal by way of Burlington, Vermont; then down to Albany, and south again toward New York, taking a convenient cut over the mountains to his Connecticut home and kin. Thirty-four years had passed since he first left Milford, to his parents' alarm, to serve in the Connecticut regiment and fight for King George and the British Empire. Now he returned to a prominent state of the Union. Peter Pond may have found that much had changed. Or perhaps not much had changed at all: having moved through so many different political, economic, and social circumstances, this continental traveller may well have thought that only his individual self and needs counted for much in the larger equations of life, independence, and nationhood.

Any glittering commercial prospects that still fired his imaginings were fading fast on the northern frontier: his ties with the Nor'Westers were cut without any possibility of retying. But he still held some secrets of the geography and possibilities of the great northern land, though these were time sensitive and subject to correction or refutation. Should Mackenzie, his pupil in the exploring line, come out of the north with a scientific map, one based on accurate longitudes, Pond's current knowledge as well as his justifiable bragging rights would soon be as dust. Thus, Pond was keen to advertise his geographical findings about the continental interior and far northwest. All he had to support his uniqueness in history as an explorer was his remarkable map, on which he had placed, according to his knowledge of the same, the rivers and lakes of the greater northwest and his own notations recounting his own crossings of this immense tract of wilderness. Who might be interested in this visual representation of the greater northwest? He knew what step to take next.

Map in hand, he immediately called upon that great figure, the eminent divine Dr. Ezra Stiles, president of Yale College in nearby New Haven, Connecticut, and among the most learned men of his day. The date was 8 March 1790, a Monday. Stiles, a Congregational clergyman, lawyer, librarian, and teacher, was, like Pond, Connecticut born. They were near contemporaries, one a master of the fur trade; the other, the more senior, a master of collegiate affairs. Among his many passions,

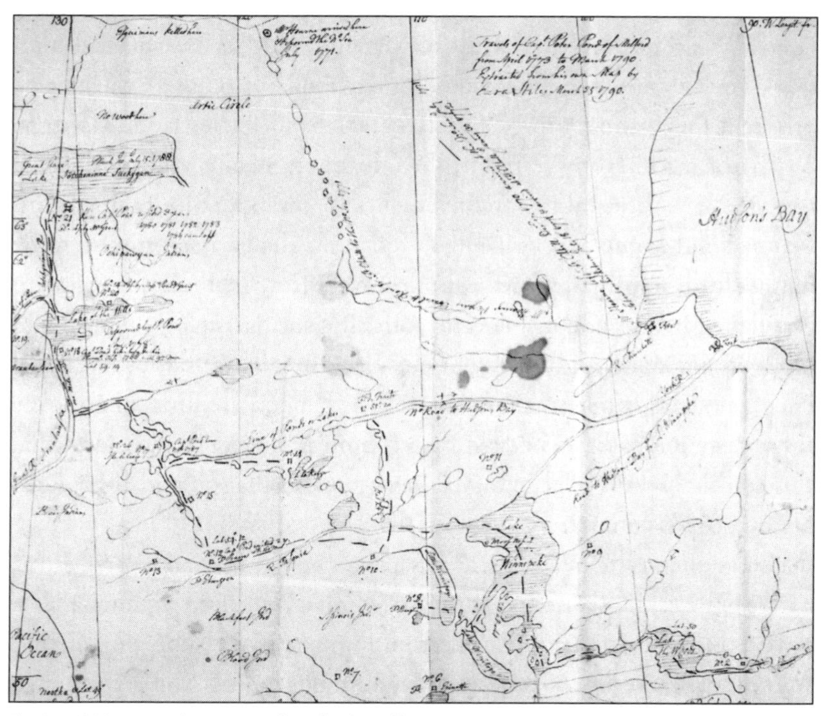

The inquisitive President Ezra Stiles of Yale College interviewed Pond about his fabulous travels, profitable trade in the interior and groundbreaking explorations into distant lands. Immensely interested in Pond's achievement, Stiles created this representation of his voyages, indicating his various posts, the rivers then known, the forts, and the tribes. GENERAL COLLECTION, BEINECKE RARE BOOK AND MANUSCRIPT LIBRARY, YALE UNIVERSITY

Stiles held high the torch of American independence; in fact, he had been a dedicated supporter of the American revolutionary cause, whose passions still flared.

We can imagine the conversation that took place in comfortable academic surroundings between the eminent Stiles and the hard-headed Pond, the former asking searching questions about wilderness geography, economic prospects, and aboriginal ways and languages—passions of that age of inquiry; the latter giving concrete details on all these matters and others besides. In answer to a certain question, Pond could point to a detail on his map, which was spread before them. That map was a visual representation of his own travels and an indication of what he knew about the wilderness. It was the first step to a greater understanding of the secrets Pond had unlocked. Stiles got to work directly and copied the map.

On 25 March, Stiles, always the careful scholar, noted by signature the fact that the map he drew, or copied—entitled "Travels of Capt. Peter Pond of Milford from April 1773 to March 1790"—was a faithful representation of, or extract from, Pond's own map, the one lent to the Yale president for copying.[1]

Stiles made further study of Pond's map as late as 7 April. The summer passed, and we know that on 15 September Stiles paid a return visit to Pond at Milford, presumably to return the original map, to show him the version he had made, and to converse further about northwestern geography. In addition to the geographical particulars that Pond had laid down on paper or told him of in person, Stiles would have been interested in tracing where the new international boundary, negotiated only seven years previously, separated British from American jurisdiction, what Canadian fur posts existed on United States sovereign lands, and what Native peoples inhabited these wilds.

Library and Archives Canada has a true copy of this map, dated 1909, and it has been reprinted in G.C. Davidson's *The North West Company*. Stiles took notes as Pond recounted to him his travels, pointing out the various locations on his map, and the notes give a chronology of Pond's "Residences," listed here by way of review:

1773	Wintered at St. Peters R. in the sources of Mississippi, 3 leagues below

1774	The falls of St. Antoine
1775	Two years at Fort Dauphin on S.W. side of L. Winnipeg
1776	At Fr Prairie
1777	Ditto
1778	At Arabauska and came to Montreal 1779
1779	Montreal (but see below, 1781)
1780	Montreal
1781	Montreal with time at Fort la Ronge in 1782, 1783 at Mischamakinak and Montreal
1785	at Arabauska 3 years to
1786	No 21 in summer, Excursions
1787	ditto, and Came out of the Indian country 1788
1788 & 1789	at Montreal and Quebec and returned to Milford March 1790[2]

The above may be taken as a reasonable recounting of Pond's adventures. Also noteworthy is Pond's identification of Samuel Hearne's arrival at the Northern Sea in July 1771. Hearne linked these discoveries to the fort at the mouth of the Churchill River. Also of importance, and to the south, is the line of ponds or lakes that formed the northern road to Hudson Bay and the post at the mouth of York River. South of that again lies the Saskatchewan River system, the Pasquia River—Pond shows it leading to Fort Sturgeon—and the passage north via Methye Portage to the "Great River Arubaska." Thence north, downriver, to Lake of the Hills, which drains to the forks where the Peace River joins and flows north to Great Slave Lake, where Pond was for much of January to July 1788. Here he was near the Arctic Circle and on the barrens, as Sir John Franklin later called them; "no wood here" is shown on Pond's map. Far to the left is Nootka Sound on the Pacific Ocean, in latitude 49° North and about 125° West.

What are we to make of this version of the map? Here we closely follow Innis, who himself had canoed most of these streams or passed by them on a river barge. Innis said that the rivers held sway over the human activities and preoccupations of Canada. "The map copied by Stiles," he remarks, "...provides an excellent basis for a study of the posts and the trade routes but has serious limitations as to latitude and longitude." Innis points out that Pond did not include a map of the prospective outlet of Great Slave Lake through a river to the Pacific Ocean:

> After learning of Mackenzie's failure he probably destroyed the large map which he had shown to Ogden and submitted a rough revised map to Stiles. His reversal of opinion after the map of 1785 that was the occasion for numerous projects to prove the existence of a direct line of communication from Athabasca River to Cook's inlet and which Alexander Mackenzie disproved had a sad ending. He left Canada with all his later conclusions disproved. Had his conjecture proved correct he would have been accorded a place among the great discoverers of Canadian history. But it was proved wrong and his former friends and supporters probably regarded him as a traitor.

There can be no quarreling with Innis on this. Nor can we disagree with his statement that Mackenzie found that he was also mistaken. "But youth was on his side and he lived to make the journey to the Pacific by the Peace River. The latter achievement offset the disappointment incidental to the voyage down the Mackenzie river."[3]

Meanwhile, just as the inquisitive Stiles was poring over Pond's latest version of his map, and working out the discoveries indicated on its sheet, a number of unforeseen circumstances occurred that made Pond's findings more poignant, more significant to the learned world and to international politics. In March 1790, *Gentleman's Magazine* published the report, already alluded to, about Pond's discoveries and printed what amounted to an update of new findings under the heading "A Map shewing the communication of the Lakes and the Rivers between Lake Superior and Slave Lake in North America." The latter was set out in Mercator's projection and disclosed that whole water world of links and portages from Grand Portage to "Arabaska Lake," then the Slave River to the North Sea ("here the water ebbs and flows"), and west from Slave Lake to Prince William's Sound, possibly, or Cook's River (in fact, Cook Inlet), showing Cook's discoveries. The whole Northwest Coast appears as a surprisingly simple lineal affair, with only the Queen Charlotte Islands, that favourite haunt of the maritime fur traders seeking the sea otter, shown in an insular form, and that inaccurately. Even Vancouver Island is not shown as an island; only "Nootka" appears, and the Strait of Juan de Fuca, but without details.[4]

This, then, was the state of English knowledge of the Northwest Coast when news, alarming and fragmentary, arrived in London's corridors of powers and on the fractious benches of the House of Commons early that same year, announcing that British ships, cargoes, captains, and men had been seized by the high-handed Spanish at far-distant Nootka Sound and sent into captivity in the Mexican port of San Blas. The merchant mariner John Meares, head of an association of merchants trading from China to the Northwest Coast in the sea otter business, arrived hotfoot in London with the news. Quizzed under oath by the Board of Trade, he gave testimony sufficiently convincing and authoritative that it formed the basis for the government of William Pitt the Younger to demand compensation and apology for this outrage from the Spanish government. Meares also, on request of the Ministry, presented a memorial to Lord Grenville detailing these proceedings.

In the June edition of *Gentleman's Magazine*, all these particulars were disclosed to the public, and in the July issue fresh details from Nootka Sound reported that American vessels were trading to China and that the Spanish were taking care not to molest their trade: in fact, the *Lady Washington*, a Boston vessel under Captain Kendrick, had made two voyages without let or hindrance. The Spanish, it appeared, had erected a fort at Nootka, stationed a frigate there to protect their own trade, and prevented other Europeans from trading there, just as they pleased. Other English ships captured there that previous year had all been sent to Mexico in the same manner as the first that was taken, with the crews placed in irons. And not least in the litany of disclosures was the fact that Kendrick, in command of the *Lady Washington*, "discovered a very extensive sea up the straits of Juan de Fuca, stretching to the East."

Here was news indeed, shocking to those who had concluded, against empirical evidence, that no such sea existed. Juan de Fuca, a shadowy pilot in the employ of Spain, had vouchsafed that he had made such a passage (though stopped by cold and other obstacles) in 1592, and now, all of a sudden, curiosity was revived in the prospects of a northwest passage in these latitudes. Pond was on the margins of all this, but the report of his discoveries, and the map showing his route and his prospects for further geographical disclosures, tying in as it did with Captain Cook's findings, added piquancy and mystery to the question of what lay on that long, western flank of what Elizabethan strategists liked to call "the backside of America."

In the months before news of the Spanish seizure of ships at Nootka Sound reached London, Alexander Dalrymple, the hydrographer to the East India Company (whom we met in Chapter 7), had been pressing on government the necessity of finding a northwest passage. Recent evidence from British mariners involved in the sea otter trade off the Northwest Coast of America pointed to the possibility of some sort of western entrance to such a passage in latitudes ranging from 48° to 60° North—that is, somewhere near where Juan de Fuca, Admiral de Fonte, or Lorenzo Ferrer Maldonado had suggested that it existed.[5] James Cook in 1778 had dismissed the idea a little casually. In his voyage of discovery he had not bothered to look in on the coast around 47° North latitude, where such a strait was rumoured to exist according to Fuca. Dalrymple, with new geographical details at his disposal, was understandably dubious of Cook's doubts that such a passage ran eastward from Cook's River. He wanted proof. He had studied what John Meares had to say on the topic, and mariner Nathaniel Portlock's contribution. Both had recently published large books on the North Pacific trade. "The opinion therefore of a N.W. Passage is strongly confirmed by the concurrence of the ancient Reports, the Indian Maps, and the opinion of those who have recently visited the N.W. Coast," Dalrymple confidently wrote. He also knew of Samuel Hearne's travels westward from Churchill, and he knew of the Canadian traders' reports of the distances from Quebec to Lake Superior and then on to far-off Great Slave Lake, a total (by estimate) of 5,250 miles.

Dalrymple then made reference to someone who can only be Peter Pond, "the Canadian Trader" who had given a position for the Island in Arathapescow (Great Slave) Lake. (We do not know exactly what documents Dalrymple had from or about Pond, though the Ogden letter, published in the March 1790 edition of the eminent *Gentleman's Magazine*, is the probable source of Dalrymple's understanding of these matters.) At first Dalrymple commented in sneering tones about Pond's lack of scientific location finding. He got particularly nasty about Pond's inability to reveal the difference between real and approximate claims to the longitude of Great Slave Lake:

> By Hudson's Bay the Discoverers would profit by the information of Mr. [Philip] Turnor whom the Hudson's Bay Company have sent into those parts and from whose Astronomical abilities we may reasonably expect competent Information, whereas Peter Pond's allegation (as reported by Mr. Halland [John Frederick Holland, a land surveyor]) "that the *Observations* of the Latitude of his *last Journey* agreed to a second with the positions in his *former* map" laid down by Estimation, betrays his *ignorance* or impudence and invalidates any Reports coming from him.
>
> Supposing some person of knowledge and veracity to be sent with him it is probable Pond would *hide* that Person as is at present alleged of a person whose merits raised his Jealousy.
>
> It is also to be considered that Pond is a native of the United States, and cannot therefore be deemed to be attached to this Country. He also pretends to the Sovereignty of the Lands adjacent to the Arathapeskow Lake, so that by encouraging him we may be fostering a Viper in our bosom.[6]

Dalrymple distrusted Pond and dismissed his geographical findings. He seems also to have concluded that if a passage existed, it was likely not a strait or clear waterway. Rather, it would be a series of lakes and even portages that linked Hudson Bay to the Pacific.

However, Dalrymple soon warmed to the Canadian traders and to Pond's contributions to discoveries as a result of advice he received from Captain George Dixon. Dixon had been on the Northwest Coast with Nathaniel Portlock's expedition on behalf of the King George's Sound Company, an independent London-based firm that had winkled permission from the East India Company to trade with the West Coast Indians for sea otter skins. Dixon thought the Canadian traders coming out of the interior would be a good counterweight to Russian pretensions in western North America. For this reason, he proposed a sea expedition from Hudson Bay. This would be linked with an overland expedition from Canada, something Governor Carleton had imagined so many years before, as mentioned in Chapter 3. In short, the project was by sea and by land, Dalrymple was at the centre of the grand scheme, and Pond's discoveries had given it legitimacy. Here was the origin of transcontinental

Canadian dominion, and the Dalrymple files on this show how Pond's star was rising in the firmament, if only to be eclipsed rather quickly by events and geographical disclosure.[7]

Let us look at the prospective land expedition first. The British government, having considered plans for such an expedition, made arrangements for Captain John Frederick Holland to cross the continent to Great Slave Lake. He was then to follow the river to the Pacific (they seemed assured that it would flow in that direction). Holland was the son of Samuel Holland, surveyor general of British Dominions in North America, and as early as 1767 the senior Holland, who knew James Cook, pressed on government the necessity of sending an official exploratory expedition to find a northwest passage overland. His proposal, like Carleton's, was shelved. His son, fired with the same idea as his father, arrived in Quebec in the fall of 1790 to lead an expedition, but he was too late. The plans were cancelled when news reached Quebec and London that Mackenzie had explored the Mackenzie River in 1789 and found its course very different from that suggested by Pond.[8]

As for the sea expedition, Dalrymple's urgings led to the Hudson's Bay Company sending an expedition under the command of Charles Duncan, a former lieutenant in the Royal Navy. How did Duncan enter the picture? His story is one of the many threads that make up the historical fabric. He is a minor figure but, like Pond, makes his appearance at the critical hour. He was a brilliant sailor, having previously rounded perilous Cape Horn in the small *Princess Royal* en route to Nootka Sound. He traded there and returned to England after the crisis with the Spanish, in which he lost his vessel to the Spanish Dons. Duncan had entered Juan de Fuca Strait in 1788 in search of sea otters. He drew a chart of the entrance to the strait, indicating the Vancouver Island and mainland sides, the latter at Cape Flattery. He even noted Fuca's Pillar, a unique geographical formation at the entrance, which Juan de Fuca had described to an inquisitive Englishman, Michael Lok, in 1596. This was a new find, with credit to Duncan,[9] but it was not until Meares wrote about it in his 1790 book, and arrived in London early that year to complain about the Spanish at Nootka Sound, that disclosure of the strait became a subject of public discussion.[10]

Dalrymple must have met Duncan upon his return to London in August 1789. He had Duncan's chart engraved; it carries the date January

1790.[11] He also thought Duncan the perfect candidate to find a northwest passage by water, tracing Juan de Fuca's route in reverse, as it were, from Hudson Bay west to the Pacific. Duncan was ready to venture on another cruise and, thinking the prospect suggested by Dalrymple attractive, undertook the voyage. But all he voyaged to was rock and ice. He sailed to Hudson Bay without geographical profit. He returned to London an ill and disappointed man.

In Dalrymple's time—and Pond's too—it had become abundantly clear that no waterway existed between latitudes 47° and 60° North. To put the matter entirely to rest, Captain George Vancouver, RN, was sent on his voyage of discovery to the Northwest Coast the following year. He proved the nonexistence of a waterway in 1792 and 1793. He was also sent as British commissioner to meet with his Spanish counterpart, Bodega y Quadra, and clear up points regarding British property seized at Nootka Sound. That story has been told elsewhere, but the point here is that Vancouver's voyage was a natural scientific extension of the discoveries, naval and mercantile, of those who had sailed in advance of him or made overland expeditions in search of just such a passage. Gradually the ring of science was tightening on this geographical puzzle, and if Mackenzie tightened it by land, Vancouver did so by sea.

Similarly, the events that led to the so-called Spanish Armament—that is, the equipping and manning of a large British fleet to convince the Spanish that they could not get away with such arbitrary measures in a place where the British did not recognize a Spanish *mare clausum*—has been the subject of much historical description and need not concern us here except to say that the British soon had made their point, obliged the Spanish to back down, and forced a mutual abandonment of Nootka, leaving it largely to the local Mowachaht and Muchalaht people. The American merchant mariners came to dominate the sea otter business, bringing in arms and ammunition, iron and copper, cloth and rum with great success in their fast brigs and schooners, and opening up the China trade to the Stars and Stripes. Meanwhile, those who followed in Pond's wake in Athabasca, including Mackenzie, continued to profit from the remarkable beaver trade of those northern lands. As Mackenzie was to propose, in terms that Pond had earlier hinted at, bases of operation could be established on the Northwest Coast, trade in fishing and whaling could be developed, and closer and enhanced business by sea with the Orient could be undertaken. In all it was a grand scheme of northern empire, connecting the North American continent to Asia, using the North Pacific Ocean as the great link between the Occident and the Orient. The crush of history left Pond in the dust, as it were, and the attention shifted to Meares and to Mackenzie; to the Hudson's Bay Company and its possible link with the East India Company, promoted by Dalrymple; and to a greater global enterprise than Pond could have imagined. His influence had been a flash in the pan and was now extinguished.

In 1791 there was a faint possibility that Pond might re-enter the fur trade and resume his efforts as an explorer. At least one cluster of Montreal-based traders was after his talents. On 13 November of that year, John Howard wrote a letter to Pond from Montreal. In it he simply intimated that a partnership had been formed and "offered to him to join without pointing out to him any Share that he would hold, if he chooses to join us." The business was to be called "Company for the N [orth] W [est]." This, obviously, was to be in opposition to the North West Company.[12] The syndicate seems to have been London-based and consisted of John Howard, Jacob Jordan, and Samuel Birnie. Jordan's backers, Brickwood Pattle and Company, had their roots in London. The syndicate also had connections with American business interests, notably Dr. Bache, an agent who was under instructions to purchase twenty thousand wampum as well as two hundred pipes and other items. This Dr. Bache is likely William Bache, of Philadelphia, grandson of Benjamin Franklin and a prominent figure in his own right. A meeting in New York between Pond and Bache was hoped for, and Bache was given full scope to arrange the terms at which Pond would be engaged. Obviously he was a hot talent. However, Pond's response to this call is not known. We do not know whether the meeting with Bache occurred. Nor do we know if Pond went into the interior.

Sometime in late 1792 or early the next year, the Secretary of War in President George Washington's administration, the corpulent Major General Henry Knox, met with Pond and a Captain William Steedman in Philadelphia, then the federal capital. The subject of their meeting was the security of American interests and, by definition, the pacification of Native peoples in the Northwest Territory, particularly in what is now Indiana and Ohio. Knox wanted to use Pond as a special agent and had plans to make Pond, apparently known to him as a soldier and an Indian agent, a captain in the United States Army.[13]

Fully ten years after the Treaty of Paris had secured American independence in 1783, the Union Jack still floated over some northern posts on United States soil. Britain had solemnly promised to give them up but showed no intention of abandoning the rich fur trade (and, truth to tell, on their part the Americans had not honoured the payment to Loyalists for lost lands and property). The key to holding the posts, which were a means of protecting the Canadian fur trade for Britain, was the influence of the Native tribes. To unite these tribes or form a grand alliance of them was British policy, its purpose being to form a buffer against American frontier advancement. To achieve this end, the British continued to promise aboriginal nations a return to their own authority. Thus it was that the British traders poured firewater, fabrics, tobacco, war paint, scalping knives, and beads into the area and liberally distributed arms and ammunition. One American authority, reflecting on this state of affairs, remarked, "The hand that sells the whiskey rules the tomahawk."[14]

President George Washington concluded that British Indian agents were the source of all the hostilities, all the murders, and his intelligence sources had more than a shadow of right on their side. Many atrocities were carried out against frontiersmen in Ohio. American citizens and settlers demanded protection. American interior policy seemed to be in a shambles. A treaty at Fort Harmar (near present-day Marietta, Ohio) only intensified the anger of some tribes and strengthened their resolve. Thus it was that late in 1791 a tragedy unfolded in the valley of the Wabash River. Major General Arthur St. Clair, the senior United States military officer and governor of the Northwest Territory (created by the Northwest Ordnance of 1787), carried with him the high hopes of Washington and Knox. The gout-stricken St. Clair was no inexperienced fighter; indeed, he had served under Amherst at Louisbourg and Wolfe at Quebec. St. Clair was at the head of two regular regiments and some militia, a largely untrained and bickering army. He led a punitive expedition into the Wabash River valley and was routed at the Battle of the Wabash, 3 November 1791, with terrible losses (637 soldiers killed to 50 of their enemy). Miami war chief Little Turtle (Michikinakoua) and Shawnee war chief Blue Jacket (Weyapiersenwah) were known to be the Native leaders.[15] President Washington, when told of the disaster, relieved

St. Clair of command (he had warned him against surprise), though he allowed him to carry on as governor. But the administration wanted answers. How had this happened? And where had the Army's cannon gone to? These were the particular and painful circumstances that led Knox to summon Pond and Steedman.

On 9 January 1793 Knox drew up lengthy instructions for "Captains Peter Pond and William Steedman." "Having verbally acquainted you with the general causes of the existing hostilities between the United States and certain Western tribes of Indians," he wrote, "it will not be necessary to recapitulate, particularly, the same to you in writing. This war is irksome to the President and General Government, as well as to the people, generally, of the United States. It has, however, been brought on by events which the government could not control." Knox went on to state that the government wished to be at peace with these Western tribes, "to be their friends and protectors—to perpetuate them on the land." However, "the desire, therefore, that we have for peace, must not be inconsistent with the national reputation. We cannot ask the Indians to make peace with us, considering them as the aggressors: but they must ask a peace of us. To persuade them to this effect is the object of your mission."[16]

Pond and Steedman's instructions as secret agents called for them to travel by way of Genesee, where Reverend Kirkland, who had a mission among the Six Nation Iroquois, might be able to supply them with runners and guides, to Niagara and Detroit. At Detroit, Pond and Steedman were to assume the characters of traders, "a business Mr. Pond is well acquainted with," noted Knox. They were told to mix with the Miami and Wabash, and to learn from them the disposition of more distant tribes. Knox wanted peace, and to get this he was proposing a grand council. His plan was that the most influential chiefs would be persuaded to repair to the United States posts on the Ohio, and from there they might gather at Detroit or even Niagara. United States troops were promised to provide protection for the chiefs if they came forward to parley; the fear here was of reprisal from the whites who were anxious to get back at them for crimes against persons and property. Knox also wanted to know the number of warriors and the tribes that had attacked General St. Clair and, more importantly, what their future intentions were. That tragedy had stamped itself on the United States government.

Pond and Steedman were now agents of American western destiny, and of intended peace and pacification. They each received an advance of $800 plus assurance that, on their return, reasonable expenses would be paid by government. A liberal compensation was also promised on their return, a lovely bait to strengthen their loyalty as well as their purpose. "It is unnecessary, at this time, to say what the sum shall be: but you may be assured, in any event, it shall be in proportion to the hazard and fatigue of the business; and, if successful, also in proportion to the services you may render."[17]

At the same time, the British had the effrontery to build a new post, Maumee, south of Detroit. As mentioned above, British governors continued to hold out to their Native allies the promise of a homeland under their protection, but this hope was fading fast, and not just because of the U.S. Army's pacification, supported as it was by American agents (of whom Pond and Steedman can be counted, if in fact they proceeded on their mission). The United States government also sent John Jay to London to obtain from the British a promise that they would finally withdraw from their posts on American soil. Jay has been pilloried for much of his diplomatic work on other matters of controversy. In this case, although he got a promise of British withdrawal, and a signed treaty to this effect dated 19 November 1794, the British continued to occupy the posts and to cultivate the Native alliance.

At the same time, however, the U.S. government adopted an even more aggressive policy to deal with the "Indian menace," and General Anthony Wayne, the Revolutionary hero, succeeded General St. Clair at the head of the army. General Wayne's force defeated the tribes at the Battle of Fallen Timbers, south of present-day Toledo, Ohio, on 20 August 1794, and compelled them to sue for peace. The resulting Treaty of Greenville, 1795, brought peace to the Ohio Territory. It closed a difficult chapter in the history of United States administration in the Old Northwest, and it also signified the end of Indian military capabilities east of the Mississippi.

We do not know the roles Pond and Steedman played in these matters. But the old order that Pond had seen at Michigan, Prairie du Chien, and Minnesota was disappearing quickly. The Washington administration, coercive in its treatment of tribes hostile to the government, gave way to that of Thomas Jefferson, with no respite to the indigenous cause, and by 1829 every tribe on American soil from Lake Michigan as far west as the Mississippi had taken treaty—that is, succumbed to U.S. Native administration and, with it, the loss of their domain. "So the treaties were executed at last," wrote a U.S. agent, "and a passage had been acquired across the country from Lake Michigan to the Mississippi." To this he added: "South of the Wisconsin [River] the Indians now own only reservations, which as soon as the white people settle on all the ceded lands, will be sold to us, and the Indians will retire above the Wisconsin, or cross the Mississippi, where the bear, beaver, the deer, and the bison invite them."[18]

The last of these treaties, dated Prairie du Chien, 1829, was concluded with the Chippewa, Ottawa, Potawatomi, and Winnebago, some of the same nations Pond had encountered four decades before. This was an epoch in North American history unrivalled in the pacification of the tribes, at least to that time, and the early years of it as well as the closing ones saw Pond on the scene—with a big yawning gap in the middle, those years of his trade in northern latitudes.

Pond lived out his final days in Milford. It was a time of rest and reflection, and a time, too, to craft his own record of events and to place himself, as it were, in history. He began to write his memoirs, perhaps in response to pleadings from Dr. Stiles or, equally plausibly, because he was inspired to do so by reading various travel accounts that had become early classics of North American history.[19] The illustrations and maps of these must have been enchanting to him, a visual feast. In such literary study Pond might have seen his own life and travels pass before his eyes, for described in these narratives were familiar haunts and routes he knew personally from fur trade sorties into the wilderness. Perhaps he read of La Salle's sailing voyages on the upper Great Lakes and travels south to Texas, and of the restless Louis Hennepin and his explorations in the continental interior.

Two books of particular interest to him were the colourful travels and, its sequel, the memoirs of the soldier Louis-Armand de Lom d'Arce de Lahontan, Baron de Lahontan (1666–1715). A nobleman whose fortunes had declined through no fault of his own, Lahontan was one of the famed two hundred soldiers sent by the King of France in 1688 to subdue what was regarded as "the Iroquois menace" in the vicinity of the Great Lakes and to protect and defend French trade in the interior. His first voyage "to the land of the Iroquois" was to Niagara, and the falls, with a strong force of the king's soldiers sent to show the flag and demonstrate French power. This military unit was a fist in the wilderness, and in strict keeping with French colonial policy. Under Count Frontenac, governor of New France, with whom he was on intimate terms, Lahontan had then been sent to Detroit (then Fort Saint-Joseph) as commandant. He developed a strategic plan for the defence of French trade in the interior, including the building up of key, garrisoned posts.

Pond would have seen in Lahontan's pages the places of his own early travels, and the gap in time between Lahontan's and his own was not all that great—less than a century. From Detroit, Lahontan made another great journey, this one in 1688, using the Great Lakes and especially the Green Bay portage and Fox River to get to the upper waters of the Mississippi. With soldiers and a brigade of six canoes he passed through country later well known to Pond. Lahontan had crossed from Michilimackinac, his place of departure, to Lake Michigan and Green Bay, used the Fox River and portages, then passed down the Wisconsin River to the Mississippi and thence into territory possibly unexplored. Along the way, the Native peoples had expressed wonder at his surveying techniques, which they found incomprehensible. He reported that they considered his graph meter to be "Divine, being unable to guess how we could know the distance of places without measuring them [on the ground] by Cords and Rods without there were some Supernatural Assistance."[20] Here were European and Native geographies in conflict.

Details of his second expedition of discovery are lost to time; it may be that he was looking for the Western Sea or perhaps trying to reach Hudson Bay. But he kept a journal, penned out on birchbark. His widely read *Nouveaux voyages dans l'Amérique septentrionale* and the subsequent *Mémoires de l'Amérique septentrionale*—which includes supplementary dialogues with an Indian chief that contributed to the image of the "noble savage"—were first published, in French, in 1703, and in English translation the very same year. These travel narratives were in extraordinary vogue in Europe and North America, rivalled only by those of the French traveller Louis Hennepin, a Recollet.

Pond might have read that first English edition of Lahontan or, more likely, a more recent one. But after reading Lahontan and perhaps Hennepin, Pond would have realized that these writers often lifted whole pages from one another, multiplied errors, and gave erroneous descriptions of tribes and geographical particulars. Falsification was a characteristic of these works, and plagiarism a noted general feature of eighteenth-century travel literature in America.

The second travel account of interest to Pond was that of Jonathan Carver, already mentioned, who, like Lahontan, had canoed these same rivers and made his own discoveries in the headwaters of the Mississippi. What Pond thought of the gullible Carver, who was often fooled by Native intelligence, is not known. Carver had described a vast area of rock, streams, and lakes that was familiar to Pond, though he failed to credit Major Robert Rogers with the idea of a northwest passage. Pond, who had fought so strenuously to work out the then unclear geography of a water passage to the western ocean, would have been puzzled by Carver's mischievous oversight—mischievous, because it appears that he did not want to draw any attention to his feeble attempt to fulfill the ambition that spurred almost all travellers and that enlivened all discussions in learned circles about a possible, if delusive, shortcut to Japan and China.

As to writing his own history, we have Innis to thank for the following, which deserves reprinting here:

> One cannot forget the old man noting down his story, becoming confused as to the sequence of events, with so much to write and such difficulty in writing it, remembering the campaigns of the Conquest, the ginger bread and "small bear", the cold tents, the fighting at Ticonderoga under Abercrombie, his old comrades in arms, his trips to the West Indies, the duel, the trade, on the Mississippi and in the Northwest, chuckling to himself as he remembered the stories of the trade, the Indians, and the voyageurs, remembering with the detail which always comes with physical effort, the good and fat ducks, the warm ground, his garden at Athabaska, the pull upstream of the canoes, the portages, the gentle gliding stream "as we desended it we saw maney rattel snakes swimming across it and kild them.[21]

In late 1806, Captains Meriwether Lewis and William Clark returned to St. Louis, having completed their overland expedition to the Pacific. What impact news of this transit of the continent via the Missouri River, the Rocky Mountain passes, and thence to the Columbia River and back had on Pond cannot be known. But one can speculate, as John C. Jackson has done with insight, that Pond followed with keen interest the stories of how the Americans had wintered among the Mandan on the Missouri, how they had seen the sources of that river in the chain of Stoney Mountains, and how they had seen the river beyond, flowing to the Pacific, that Native informants had called the *Naberkistagon*.[22] Scholar John Logan Allen writes,

> The implications for a potential commercial water route were clear, and they were made even more clear when Peter Pond... produced a map based on his own sojourns in the Canadian West. On Pond's map, the Rockies were shown as a single ridge of mountains positioned around the 113th meridian of longitude. Near the headwaters of the Missouri appeared the source of a river Pond called the "Naberkistagon": the origins of the name are uncertain but what was meant by it is not. It was the Oregon or River of the West, and the commercial route to the Pacific must have seemed obvious to those who viewed Pond's map.[23]

As with the maps of Hearne, Fidler, Thompson, and others, the representations of the interior provided by British cartographers supplied important source materials for the shaping of American images of the west.

Jefferson had got his idea for Lewis and Clark's Corps of Discovery Expedition from Mackenzie's achievements, certified in print by his famous book of travels, *Voyages from Montreal*.[24] At the same time, the Spanish were making claims to great western discoveries by sea. In the last fleeting fragment of documentary evidence we have of Pond during his lifetime, we find Thomas Jefferson asking a fellow member of the American Philosophical Society, his friend Dr. Caspar Wistar, about these wild claims of western discovery by a Spanish officer. Wistar replied, "I shall write this day to Mr. Peter Pond (who is mentioned by Mr. Mackenzie) on the subject [proximity of the Saskatchewan to the upper Missouri], he lives in Connecticut & I believe will give any information in his power, without any particular explanation respecting the reason for asking it."[25] If Pond gave an answer to Wistar's inquiry there is no surviving evidence. But the fact that a leading man of learning would consult Pond speaks to his renown and authority on this subject. His knowledge of continental geography, and more particularly its river systems, was perhaps unmatched at this time.

Pond died in Milford on 6 March 1807. He was in his sixty-seventh year, which must have been near to the average life expectancy of males in that time, if not beyond it. He was buried in the town cemetery, the grave unmarked, that being quite a common thing in that day and age.

We know that Peter and Susanna Pond had at least two children, as the 1906 Ponds of Milford genealogy attests. One of them, a son, Peter Pond the third, born in 1763, seems to have accompanied his uncle Charles in naval operations during the American Revolution. This Peter Pond died childless; he perished at sea off Barbados in 1803. A daughter, Elizabeth, or Betsey as she was known in the family, was probably born before her father left Milford in 1763.[26] She married into the Durand family in 1779 and had eleven children. Peter Pond thus had eleven grandchildren, some of whom did well in marriage and various professions in New York, Paris, and even Moscow.[27]

It is said that Peter Pond died impoverished. Our authority for that is the historian of the fur trade, and Pond's contemporary, Roderick Mackenzie. But Mackenzie gives no authority for his statement, and there is no other confirmation: it may have been wild hearsay. Was it an attempted slur on Pond's good name? Possibly. (I have even read in an unauthoritative source that he led a dissolute life toward the end. I can find no justification for this either.) There is no reason to believe that he did not husband his declining assets carefully, and even if he were poor in latter days, perhaps he was given aid and assistance by his immediate family and other kin. In fact, we have evidence contrary to Mackenzie's statement. Sophia Mooney, undertaking research on Peter Pond genealogy, learned from one of Pond's granddaughters, Mrs. S.E. Siegel of New York City, that "it does not appear that Sir Peter as he was always called was in want of money." Sophia Mooney takes up the story:

> I asked my aunt about her G[rand] Father—she said I never saw him but once—when I was about 6 years old—I saw a splendid looking man coming up the St[reet] dressed in a velvet coat,

> knee britches, silk stockings, low shoes with buckles, ruffles at his hands, and carrying a cane. I called to my Mother to look at the Prince coming up the St[reet]. He turned in at the gate. I let him in and ran to my Mother telling her a prince had come—she came in, and lo it was her Father. After a long talk with my Mother, he gave me a Gold piece and I never saw him again. His name was Peter Pond—his wife's name was Susan Newell.[28]

In this connection I like what Ivan Doig, noted writer, said regarding his research about James Gilchrist Swan in the book *Winter Brothers*: "You have met him yourself in some other form—the remembered neighbor or family member, full of years while you just had begun to grow into them, who had been in a war or to a far place and could confide to you how such vanished matters were. The tale-bringer sent to each of us by the past."[29]

He was unheralded and underappreciated in his own time. He did not cut a dramatic or flamboyant figure and, in any event, was part of a society that did not exalt such things. Perhaps, had he been a civic giant or a noted clergyman, some sort of obituary notice would have survived. Or perhaps, if he had been one of the rich or the eccentric or even the devious, some death column would have noticed his passing. But no, that was not his lot either. Thus he slipped from this world without a whimper and without a bang. His life's end left so little for a historian to plunder, and even his grave is unmarked and unknown. But the town of Milford has latterly proclaimed him as one of its great pioneers and famed citizens.

As to Pond's liaisons with Native women, we have confirming evidence. Sophia Mooney learned about Pond's "country wife," whose name is lost to history. She recounted the details to R. McLachlan of the Numismatic and Antiquarian Society of Montreal, the honorary curator at the then notable Chateau de Ramezay Museum. Her letter to him does not survive, but his reply, dated 18 December 1905, does. It provides graphic details and is worth quoting at length: "I have no doubt...about the story that his wife was a squaw [sic] or more likely a halfbreed. Nearly all the old NorWesters took to themselves Indian wives and in this way there grew up a large community whom our French Canadians call Métis or bois brule...A number of our prominent families are connected with these halfbreeds. Sir Donald Smith now Lord Strathcona married a half-breed. As a rule these families have not turned out well. Many of them partake of the Indian craving for stimulants and consequently they give way to that failing."[30]

Pond's name survives in numerous schools and heritage sites in Canada. One of them, Peter Pond National Historic Site, lies at the junction of the Sturgeon-weir River and the North Saskatchewan. It is three miles west of Prince Albert and includes the remains of Fort Sturgeon. Pond apparently spent two winters there. Another place name is Peter Pond Lake, in Saskatchewan, named after him. Pond Inlet near Iqaluit is not named for Peter Pond, though is often mistakenly believed to be. A few bars and at least one shopping centre have been named for Pond in Fort McMurray, where he, like the industrial activities of this oil patch, is larger than life. But of all historical sites connected with him, that of Methye Portage is most important. As Judge Frederic Howay, a member of the Historic Sites and Monuments Board of Canada, said at the unveiling of the plaque in a schoolyard in Fort McMurray in September 1938, it was "a spot far more important in the story of Canada than those whose names are emblazoned in large letters."[31]

Before closing, it may be useful to review how some of Pond's contemporaries or near contemporaries viewed him (all of these have been quoted above). They generally regarded him with a mixture of admiration and suspicion: admiration for his energetic activities; suspicion for his association with murders and for his American background. East India Company hydrographer Alexander Dalrymple dismissed him on grounds of his unscientific nature and apparently duplicitous ways and doubted his loyalty to the Crown.[32] We have seen how Alexander Henry, who used Pond's discoveries for his own benefit and without acknowledgement, called him a "trader of some celebrity."[33] Dr. John Mervin Nooth, who met him in Quebec, thought him "a very singular person."[34] Judge Isaac Ogden favoured him as "a Gentleman of Observation and Science."[35] Trader Roderick Mackenzie said Pond "thought himself a philosopher, and was odd in his manners."[36] St. John de Crevecoeur, the French authority on North American history, who was living in New York and who copied Pond's map for his historical associate, His Grace of La Rochefoucauld, in March 1785, said this of Pond: "This extraordinary Man has resided 17 years in these Countries...from these discoveries as well as from the reports of Indians, he assures himself of having at last discovered a Passage to the

N[ord] O[uest] Sea. He has gone again to ascertain some important observations."[37]

Alexander Mackenzie obviously was jealous of Pond's pre-eminence and of his discoveries, actual and suggested: thus, apart from recounting some details of Pond's travels and trade prospect, he gave no other opinion on the man who might be called his mentor in the discovery line. Explorer and surveyor Thompson, who never met Pond, was critical of his abilities as a mapmaker, pointing out Pond's unscientific methods and instruments. At the same time, he credited Pond's map with being the spur that drove the British government to consider more seriously than it had hitherto done the necessity of exploring overland to the Pacific—a necessity that vanished once Mackenzie had made his remarkable voyages of discovery. But Thompson's famed word portrait of Pond, probably obtained from Patrick Small, which describes him as "a person of industrious habits, a good common education, but of a violent temper and unprincipled character," has stuck.[38] This frank and unfavourable attitude forms a common thread in the works of later writers, including Charles Lindsey, historian of Ontario boundaries; Marjorie Wilkins Campbell, biographer of William McGillivray; and Edwin E. Rich, historian of the Hudson's Bay Company.[39]

Pond's first biographer, Innis, the noted student of the Canadian fur trade, called Pond's achievements "in many ways remarkable but...not of a sensational character."[40] Innis preferred to see Pond as one of many Nor'Westers who contributed to the commercial lifeblood of the fur business based on Montreal. In fact, Innis wrote his biography so as to explain the nature and difficulties of the North West Company, of which Pond was a formative force and a later source of difficulty to the partners. This suited Innis's needs but failed to put flesh on the bones of a unique and individual life.

Pond was an unusual man, more energetic, more combative, more aggressive, and more capable of organizing than most traders. I like what Wisconsin historian Louise Phelps Kellogg, expert on French and British regimes in the Old Northwest, said about him—that he had all the virtues and defects of his calling: "He was bold, enterprising, courageous, and persevering, but ruthless in competition, sacrificing all for success."[41] Lured by profits from rich northern furs, he pushed farther north and west than any other trader in the 1770s and 1780s. Overcoming competition from rivals and problems of supply over lengthy distances, he and his men pushed their wares into little-known river valleys and lakes of the northwest. They made them tributary to the commerce of Montreal. In so doing he induced rivals into his lucrative trade but dealt with them often with a heavy hand.

Others benefited from his geographical findings. He was the first European to cross Methye Portage to the Athabasca River and Lake Athabasca. That discovery linked the Mackenzie watershed with the rivers flowing to Hudson Bay. In this achievement, Pond succeeded where others, especially Thomas Frobisher, had failed. He was a master of fur trade logistics, honing his skills in this important line of business using techniques learned in military operations during the Seven Years' War. Pond's use of supplies, including pemmican, and his good organization were keys to his success: they enabled him to travel farther and to trade better than his predecessors. They also set the pattern for the concern's exploitation of the Athabasca country.

His business activities led to the first organization named the North West Company. They also opened what Alexander Mackenzie called the "new Eldorado," around which the company's prospects for the 1790s and afterward revolved. Pond's reputation for violence, however, invited the suspicion of other traders both inside and outside the concern and eventually forced his withdrawal from the company. He never faced trial, and he may have been falsely accused. No documents survive to show that Pond resisted the charges brought against him, and his retreat from the fur trade and from Montreal suggests that he knew there was no use in fighting against perception and even malice. Retirement came to him out of necessity, and post-retirement years found him back at the place of his birth and youth. The wilderness had not consumed him; rather, it had afforded him much in the way of opportunity. And with the unique personal gifts that were his, it may safely be said that he had exploited that opportunity to its limits.

Say about him what they will, his achievement placed him among the greats of early North American history. Pond's maps and suggested course of the waters of Athabasca are enduring testaments to him as a pioneer in the last great fur-bearing area of North America. Pond disclosed to the outside world the general features of the Mackenzie River system. His greatest gift, however, was to the ungrateful and selfish Alexander

Mackenzie. His findings fired the young Scot with the possibilities of discovery in the north and the lure of glory that led him to follow the course of the great river to its mouth in 1789 and overland to the Pacific in 1793. Peter Pond, as will be seen in our concluding chapter, sprang open the secrets of the far northwest, inspiring by his actions in the tough business of fur trading in new zones a necessary quest to find the rivers of commerce that would bring the Empire of the St. Lawrence to Pacific tidewater and thence to the gates of Cathay.

EPILOGUE

In Pond's Tracks, a New Athabasca

For some eight years after its founding, Pond's House stood as the fountainhead of Montreal-based commerce in high, northwestern latitudes. The stream of Canadian business steadily flowed from it and to it. In the long scheme of human settlement and activity, its life was admittedly short, existing only from 1778 to 1788 and then reverting to wilderness. Even so, these were formative years for the North West Company, as it expanded to the north and northwest, and were, in fact, years critical to the firm's survival.

By the time Pond left the post for the last time—on 15 May 1788 after the late breakup of the ice that year—a network of posts had been established downstream in the upper Mackenzie River system. Under Pond's direction, outlier posts had been set up, intelligence gathered about Native movements, and geographical features spied out. In all things the needs of the consumers and the suppliers had to be taken into consideration, for the Nor'Westers and their rivals were totally dependent on the sure and steady flow of furs to their posts. In time, Pond's House was supplanted by other more useful and prodigious posts farther downstream, throughout the watershed, north toward the Arctic Ocean, and westward to the ramparts of the Rocky Mountains. As with so many fur posts, its history is incandescent.

Alexander Mackenzie, having worked under Pond's tutelage, assumed command at Pond's House in the fall of 1788, only to find trade falling off. Yes, the previous summer's hunt had been good, but over the next few years the returns diminished, and he came to the conclusion that the Cree, with whom the principal trade was conducted, were unsatisfactory trading partners. (This is an interesting comment from one who had taken a Cree woman, The Catt, in the custom of the country, but it also tells us a good deal about the hard-driving, highly critical Mackenzie.) Let Mackenzie's own words speak on this: "The Crees here were very troublesome in the Summer, but Mr. MacLeod kept them in check. The greater part of them have not appeared Since my arrival. Some of them are gone to war. These Crees cannot be depended upon nor is there much trade to be expected from this fort, and that was one of the reasons that made me think of changing it."[1]

Thus it was that Mackenzie decided to move the post to a point near the estuary of the Athabasca River where it meets Lake Athabasca. He called it Fort Chipewyan, in honour of the Chipewyans who he anticipated would be more energetic and eager traders than the Cree had been at Pond's House. Mackenzie entrusted the building of this post to his cousin Roderick. It was a great establishment, built on the south shore of Lake Athabasca. Streams running to the north and west became arteries of fur trade expansion. However, in 1804 a new Fort Chipewyan was constructed on the north shore and the original fort of that name fell into decay. The new Fort Chipewyan was located at the hub of a drainage basin and was not only the "grand magazine of the north" but also the base of operations for land explorers—Mackenzie, John Franklin, John Richardson, George Back, and others.[2]

These were the dark years of Athabasca's history, for not only had Native numbers been reduced very substantially by smallpox epidemics—it has been estimated that the epidemic of 1781–84 reduced Chipewyan numbers by 90 percent, an unimaginable holocaust—but listlessness and reduced initiative were everywhere present among the Native peoples. The Cree and Chipewyan clustered around Pond's House when it was reestablished in 1784, but the record also shows that the Nor'Westers used measures of coercion to get them to hunt. They increased liquor

There were two incarnations of Fort Chipewyan on Lake Athabasca. The first, on the south shore, allowed the fur traders to be nearer to Native traders and suppliers. The second was constructed on the north shore in 1804 while the original fell into decay. The daily diet for the fur traders here was fish, although wildfowl provided some necessary culinary variety. LIBRARY AND ARCHIVES CANADA, ACC. NO. 1986-45-1

and tobacco inducements. They forcibly obtained furs and provisions from compliant Chipewyans by taking women and children as hostages. William Sloan says, "When hostage-taking was risky and the Indians aggressive and proud, as in the case of the Beaver, the traders used liquor to get what they wanted."[3]

In those years and for some time after, the Chipewyan continued to be drawn to the Bay traders' posts—a trek that consumed as much as seven months, Mackenzie calculated. To his regret, even the building of a post on Lake Athabasca was not enough to assure him of the regular trade connection with these people. His letters on the subject express continued doubt about this first wave of commercial expansion and reorganization in the upper Mackenzie River area. It was natural in the circumstances to have second thoughts and added worries. Pond's House had outlived its usefulness, and a new scheme had to be sought out, but logistics continued to imperil the scheme. The farther north you went, the farther incoming goods and outgoing furs had to be carried. The rub was that ice came earlier on the river, in October, and broke up later, in mid- to late May, than it did farther south. Thus the season of navigation and supply was truncated. From Grand Portage the goods would be sent inland to the Saskatchewan, then to Île à la Crosse, and thence again to Lake Athabasca, taking usually from early July to mid-October. Accidents to men and canoes did occur, delaying progress. Of his passage to Athabasca from the rendezvous at Grand Portage in 1788, Mackenzie wrote to the agents of the North West Company, "I had a very favourable voyage into the country until within a short distance of the Isle a la Crosse when one of the Canoes got injured and Sunk. By this unfortunate accident I lost two men and eleven pieces of goods. After repairing these damages as well as we could we continued our voyage and arrived at this Department on the 29 September, which was our fifty second day from Lac la Pluie, and the shortest voyage I believe that has been performed to this quarter with loaded Canoes."[4] The main line of Canadian commerce, from Montreal to Lake Athabasca, was kept up by brawn and fortitude.

After the harrowing days of the 1790s, Fort Chipewyan took on a new aura. It became the Nor'Westers' stronghold in Athabasca. The place acquired the reputation as a great emporium of the north, and it also provided a glimmer of European civilization in these latitudes, sometimes grandiloquently called the Athens of the North, boasting as it did a fine library and the latest London newspapers, months old. Travellers passing by found it a place of pleasant relief, the nearest thing to a London club of social and literary companionship. But it was more than this: it was a depot and node of commerce just as important as Grand Portage and Michilimackinac had been to the same fur traders, though of an earlier era. Fort Chipewyan excelled because of its location, and tribes came to it over the barrens or from the Rocky Mountain ramparts or the upper tributaries of the Mackenzie River system. It grew rich on the fur trade, and even after 1833, when the beaver felt hat fell out of fashion among persons who wore such things and demand for beaver fell, the fort kept up a trade in peltry outward bound, and the customary inflow of goods continued—cloth, iron items, guns and ammunition, liquor and tobacco, trinkets and ornaments, and much else besides.

Most posts the Nor'Westers had built north, or downriver, of Pond's House had long lives, and many grew into towns. Pond had sent out many of his traders to set up tributary posts: Cuthbert Grant had a temporary one on the north shore of Lake Athabasca for a time during the winter of 1785–86; he occupied a more permanent one on Great Slave Lake's south shore in the fall of 1786; and in 1786–87, Pond sent

Charles Boyer to Peace River and Alexis Derry to Great Slave Lake to establish trading forts. Space does not allow a full recounting, but some basic points will illuminate the general statement of northern expansion and the course of empire in high latitudes.

Always with an eye to the possibilities of trade with the Pacific Coast, and the rivalries of the Russians and Americans there, the Nor'Westers continued the age-old project of finding a serviceable commercial route. Geographical features seemed always against them in this, but even so the riddles posed by mountains, mountain trenches, and rivers flowing to the Pacific had to be solved. Carver had talked about the River Oregon, and the Spanish mariner Bruno de Hezeta had spied the mouth of that same stream, the Columbia River, in 1775. John Meares made much of this a subject of public notoriety in his 1790 book. The Nootka Sound crisis boosted interest even further. Pond had pointed to a waterway leading to Cook's River, and Native evidence that he gathered doubled his belief in the possibility of this. He cannot be faulted for this: he did not do the empirical work on the ground. That fell to Alexander Mackenzie. This Scot, we know, had been sent by the North West Company to take over from Pond, and from him had learned the latest intelligence about the lay of the rivers of Athabasca and the upper basin of what we now call the Mackenzie River. When Alexander Mackenzie set out from Fort Chipewyan in the late spring of 1789, with dangerous and impeding ice sheets still here and there on the waters of Lake Athabasca, he had every intention of getting to the Russians at Unalaska or some other post on the Gulf of Alaska. But his incredible summer voyage led him north to the Arctic Ocean and not across to the elusive Pacific. He confided to his cousin about this "River Disappointment." But Mackenzie was not to be denied. He took his time; re-educated himself in astronomical observation so that he could read the moons of the planet Jupiter and then determine, using nautical almanacs and tables, his exact longitude; and then set out again on his western mission.

In the fall of 1792 he sent a party to erect an advance base, Fort Fork, on Peace River. After wintering there, and as soon as the ice broke up, he went upriver against some of the most harrowing waters in all of explorations history, facing disasters of one sort or another, to say nothing of intended desertions of the men that he so gallantly led, and eventually found himself where east- and north-flowing waters were in surprisingly close proximity to those that flowed, obviously, in another direction—to the west. Making this grand portage of watersheds, he followed a tributary of what he thought was the Columbia River (it was actually the Fraser). Proceeding southward until local tribes generously told him not to proceed farther downstream—for it would surely lead to his party's destruction in what is now known as Hells Gate—he then struck off to the west, through what he described as "a sea of mountains," and finally came to the farthest west, down Dean River to Dean Channel, where he made his famed inscription "Alexander Mackenzie from Canada by Land 22nd July 1793." He had completed Pond's dream and got through to the

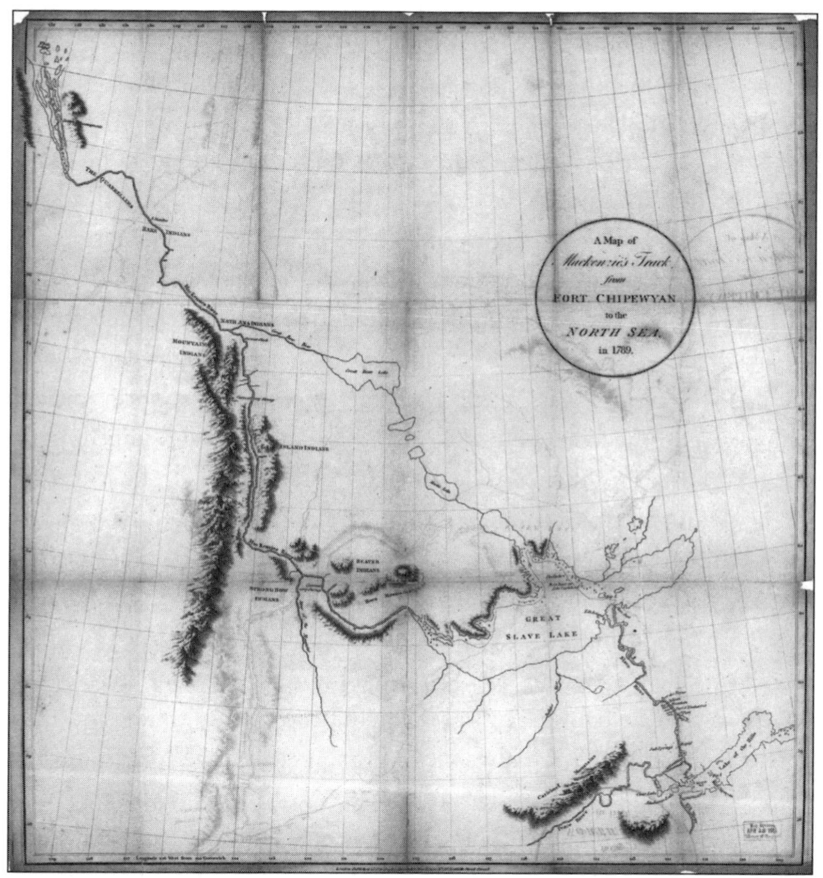

To Alexander Mackenzie went the laurels that success brings. This etching is based on Mackenzie's own drawing of his extraordinarily demanding (and quick) 1793 journey to Pacific tidewater from his advance post on the Peace River. It fails to indicate the rises in elevation that were equal to the obstacles of dangerous river travel. Mackenzie achieved what Pond had hoped to do, but he was a much younger man than the veteran colonial soldier turned fur trader. LIBRARY OF CONGRESS, GEOGRAPHY AND MAP DIVISION

Western Ocean, as he called it, though in more southerly latitudes. Still, he was at 52° 23' North latitude, and there was no northwest passage here either.[5] But what he had found was equally significant in uncovering the mysteries of this quarter: he thought he had located, as he told Lord Dorchester in a letter of 17 November 1794, a part or the whole of "the River of the West."[6] By using this name, Mackenzie indicates that he knew of the tortuous history of all those men, going back to the earliest sailor-explorers of eastern North America, and all the ill-made maps that had laid down just such a great stream somewhere in the west. Discovering "the River of the West" was his heroic triumph.

Mackenzie, as Pond before him, lit the trail for others. Trade followed exploration. Exploration induced dreams of empire. North West Company partners sent Simon Fraser and John Stuart to build forts in the cordilleran plateau, the first in what is now British Columbia. Fraser traced Mackenzie's new-found stream only as far as it was navigable, then scrambled around rocks and stages built by aboriginal people at Hells Gate until he came at last to navigable waters, where he surged on the mighty Fraser River to the sea near Musqueam, south Vancouver. David Thompson, the mapmaker, found a river—the Columbia—running to the Pacific in more easterly and then southerly latitudes, and thereby opened a communication with the Great Ocean. The Nor'Westers had uncovered the secrets of the rivers of the west. At the same time, they forged the new northern economy, precursor of transcontinental business linking London, Montreal, the cordilleran plateau, and, by shipping, China.

Meanwhile, the Nor'Westers were expanding their posts in Athabasca—and doing so against competition from other Montreal-based firms and against the great rivals from Hudson Bay. Mackenzie had become the champion for brokering a deal between the North West Company and the Hudson's Bay Company to allow an access of trade via Hudson Bay. His hope was to reduce transportation costs for incoming items and outgoing furs. But for a number of reasons, including Hudson's Bay Company resistance and British ministerial indifference, he could never bring this grand design to fruition, so other measures were undertaken, including partnerships with American merchant traders who would carry furs to Canton or to Europe. The main route was still via British commerce based on Montreal, and this was a healthy trade.

But Mackenzie, who, like Pond, was ahead of his time, was concerned with logistics and attendant costs and the need to curtail the latter. He, like Pond, became disaffected with the masterminds of the North West Company. For that reason he set up, with the connivance of others, the New North West Company in 1799. The two firms waged war against one another in Athabasca, where rival posts were often set up within a stone's throw of one another, and elsewhere. It was not until the death of Mackenzie's opponent Simon McTavish, in 1804, that the two companies buried their differences and formed a new, larger association. Posts were consolidated and trading relationships rearranged under the new circumstances. Athabasca became the largest department of the North West Company, with more employees and more fur exports than other districts. Commercial triumph seemed at hand.

But the North West Company was forced to continue knocking on the doors of the British government in Whitehall, peppering statesmen and undersecretaries of state with urgent appeals for protection in the face of many rivals. Mackenzie had been the most eloquent spokesman but was by no means the only one. He had warned of American commercial expansion on the southern bounds of North West Company trade. He and others had appealed for a charter as a guarantee of the government's good will. At one time a strong claim was made for a trading corridor from the *pays d'en haut* to Hudson Bay. Those appeals fell on deaf ears. Not until the War of 1812 did the government supply Royal Navy support for a trading vessel destined for the mouth of the Columbia River. By the time the vessel arrived, the Nor'Westers had obliged their rivals, the Pacific Fur Company owned by John Jacob Astor, to sell out its interests.

Meanwhile, the North West Company sent militia units to Michilimackinac and Prairie du Chien to back its trade by armed force. These militia units, which employed men of the company, Metis, and Natives, were officered by partners and clerks in the North West Company and accompanied by a unit of the Royal Artillery. They held Prairie du Chien against an amphibious United States Army force that had come upriver from St. Louis. This was the last desperate phase of the British military alliance with the tribes of the Old Northwest, and when peace was established by the Peace of Ghent, British statesmen shamefully abandoned the nations south of the line to their fate. The consequences are well known.[7]

At the same time, an old rivalry reasserted itself, bursting onto the scene with great force. The last stages of the struggle between the North West Company and the Hudson's Bay Company were fought out in Athabasca, where the formidable HBC decided to make its last stand. The rival posts were scenes of many conflicts. The internecine rivalry between Canadian traders had strengthened the Nor'Westers' purpose and resolve, which initially helped them face the new challenges from the Bay traders. The Nor'Westers maintained, against the charge of the Hudson's Bay Company, that they on every occasion exerted influence to preserve the lives and property of the Bay traders from the violence of the Native tribes.[8] However, the Bay sent some of its strongest traders to Athabasca to compete with the Nor'Westers. In part, this was because the region was, at that time, the place of the greatest fur trading yields and the greatest Native consumption of imports. North West Company fortunes waned quickly, and when the company lost its great business in Athabasca to its rivals, its plea for union in 1820 was inevitable.[9]

There were many legal considerations underpinning the rivalry, for Methye Portage marked a boundary between watersheds. George Simpson (later Sir George Simpson, the field director of the Hudson's Bay Company) crossed it in September 1820 and wrote in his journal, "Portage La Loche [Methye Portage] is the height of land that divides the waters which discharge themselves into Hudson's Bay from those that run into the Frozen Ocean, and is considered the N.W. boundary of the Honble. Hudsons Bay Coy. Territories."[10] Simpson came out in the spring of 1821, just as the details of the union of the two great trading rivals were being announced, to report that the North West Company was already in revolt against its agents—that is, the partners and traders in the interior were strenuously objecting to the Montreal and metropolitan powers that were negotiating the history of the firm, and the union with the Hudson's Bay Company. In fact, some of the North West Company traders in Athabasca, realizing the game was up, were already drifting away to the Hudson's Bay Company. All of this signified the end of an era.

Following the union of the companies in 1821 a state of quietude fell over

Athabasca. The Hudson's Bay Company inherited the North West Company's powerful imperium west of the Continental Divide and began to consolidate its holdings throughout this vast quarter. Governor Simpson put in place sustained yield policies of fur resources, and this allowed for a rationalization of posts, and the closure of some. But always there existed a need for new fur habitats to exploit. Thus expeditions of exploration were mounted: Samuel Black's examination of the Finlay River, one of the two major tributaries of the Peace River, was one;[11] and to the southwest was Peter Skene Ogden's companion work on the Snake River. Exploration sped commercial expansion, adding new markets and making new Native allies and partners. In all this, threats of foreign rivalry lay behind Company machinations. Black's quest was designed to answer Russian encroachments from the coast of southeast Alaska; Ogden's expedition to counter American mountain men and other free traders. All of these considerations had been hinted at by Pond in his 1785 memorandum. Mackenzie, too, had proclaimed similar concerns to government in his memoranda and visits to office holders in Whitehall.

At the mouth of the Columbia River, the British were well positioned to exert their imperial influence, with preference for trade over dominion. Until 1846, the commerce of the Pacific cordillera lay open to the Hudson's Bay Company. However, the arrival of American settlers overland was a wave that the British could not stay, and thus old Oregon was divided. The northern realm, developed by Mackenzie, Fraser, and Thompson, became a formal part of the British Empire. The rest was lost. The negligence and spinelessness of successive British administrations were the culprits.

During all these years the commerce of the north, when not carried on overland in long treks, was conducted by canoe, the swiftest means of transportation in summer. Simpson wanted to use carts and horses over an improved track of the Methye Portage; that way, loaded boats could replace canoes and cargoes having to be portaged by human labour. Improved access over these portages was always a consideration to the businessman. But by the 1860s, steam navigation was making its appearance, first on the Saskatchewan and later on the Slave and Mackenzie Rivers. Barge traffic followed naturally from this, and the Hudson's Bay Company posts on these rivers were serviced in this fashion during the navigational season.

Athabasca continued to offer a powerful pull to commercial interests long after the fur trade ceased prominence. Missionary activities by the Oblates in the latter nineteenth century brought Christianity and schooling. Further explorations were undertaken, principally by Abbé Émile Petitot. Dominion land surveyors and others working for the Geological Survey of Canada recorded the details of the land and resources. Agents of the Dominion of Canada entered into treaty (Treaty Number 8) with the Cree, Chipewyan, and Beaver tribes in 1899. The floatplane transformed northern communications, as did radio and, later, television. Eventually, in 1905, territorial status was acquired by the Northwest Territories, headquartered at Yellowknife on Great Slave Lake. Oil was discovered in the riverbed of the Mackenzie at Norman Wells, uranium and pitchblende were uncovered and, much later, diamonds, too. Steam navigation came to the Mackenzie. World War II spurred northern development, partly to defend the Alaskan frontier. The Cold War brought further defense preparations. The Mackenzie Valley pipeline proposals indicated the way ahead for commercial expansion, bringing northern resources to southern markets. Other commodities had replaced fur. But, as in the time of Pond, the realities were the same: how to get supplies in in bulk, how to win Native support and cooperation, and how to work efficiently in a harsh northern climate.

Pond left a significant legacy, for he was at the cutting edge of a system of modernization that brought with it its own hazards and difficulties. He thought nothing of these things at the time. To him, profits based on the fur trade counted for all. But he also had an explorer's mindset, for he was fascinated by geographical realities and prospects—and what lay on the other side of the hill. In all these ways he stood apart from other work-a-day traders. But as with so many other powerful figures of history, the times favoured him. The circumstances allowed him to maximize his advantages in the face of many difficulties. He seized these opportunities once offered. It might, in other circumstances, have fallen to others to be so favoured. But this was Pond's achievement, and it is important to note that other traders saw in Pond the possibilities of such great success in northern trading; they entrusted him with special assignments. He did not disappoint. As with all great figures of history, no matter how quizzical and even unpleasant or unlikable the individual, success brought its own reward. In his latter years he had disappeared from the scene, haunting the margins of history, all but forgotten. But time and distance give us a clearer view of the man. As a subject for biography he may remain an elusive quarry, but we come away from this examination with an appreciation of how character and circumstance intertwine in the oddest of ways, and how new frontiers are examined and developed by agents who may have had destiny on their side and certainly unique personalities to carry on their obligations and challenges. It is for this reason that commercial opportunists and exploring geniuses will continue to work the margins of the known world, making slow, even incremental, additions to what might have been thought, even yesterday, to be an impossibility.

Acknowledgements

Every book has its own story, this one beginning with an invitation from *Dictionary of Canadian Biography* editors Francess G. Halpenny and Jean Hamelin to write the entry on Pond. As seductive inducement they provided a rough file on Pond—bits and pieces collected by Pond's only biographer Harold Adams Innis, assisted by W. Stewart Wallace, the University of Toronto librarian. All they fervently asked was for me to take a fresh look at Pond from all the sources newly made available, none of them I recollect from the Hudson's Bay Company Archives, then recently transferred to the Archives of Manitoba from Beaver House, in the old City of London (where, if I might digress, I had happily researched in the late 1960s, the musky smells of furs drifting up to me from the warehouse which lay below the archives room—as good an inspiration to any Canadian historian as could be imagined. And, oh yes, there was the not-to-be-forgotten treat: tea with a biscuit was served free of charge from a trolley, its tinkling arrival proudly announced by the strike of an old ship's bell. Those days are sadly passed). The key repository for Pond documents, then as now, is the Library and Archives Canada in Ottawa. Many of these documents, and related items I collected for the entry on Pond for the *Dictionary of Canadian Biography*, published in English and French in Volume 5 (1983), I later deposited in the Archives of Alberta, Edmonton. Since then new documents and historical materials have been added to the historical base. Particular mention might be made of a surviving North West Company journal kept during a latter year of Pond in Athabasca, published as The *English River Book*, edited by Harry Duckworth. From these documents and others listed in the bibliography, this work derives. If somehow I have inadvertently missed any key sources I should be glad of notice of the same, for inclusion is any further edition.

I owe debts to researchers who have been on the trail of Peter Pond, notably Reuben G. Thwaites, Charles Gates, W. Stewart Wallace, Harold Innis, and John Chalmers. The late John Foster of the University of Edmonton invited me to prepare a paper on Pond and the Athabasca country; this he published in the journal *Alberta* in 1983 (see bibliography). Colleagues at Wilfrid Laurier University, notably the geographer, Jody F. Decker, and the communications specialist, Paul Heyer, urged me to think that Pond deserved a book. More recently, William Buxton of Concordia University stoked the fires of interest about Innis and the North West Company. I then took my research to Connecticut, Pond's own jurisdiction. I was fortunate in discovering two local authorities: Richard Platt, historian of Milford, Connecticut, generously answered my questions about Pond's hometown and Pond family genealogy. William N. McDonald, a resident of Milford and devotee of Pond's life and contributions to history, provided copies of correspondence that sheds light on Pond's later years. Mr. McDonald maintains a well-known website for the Peter Pond Society, whereat much information and the text of my *Dictionary of Canadian Biography* entry may be found. The website led me to John C. Jackson's text, "Peter Pond's Map" typescript of 2007. This site also contains much information about Pond, especially about the lands and waters where he was, for a time, a Caesar of the wilderness. Professor George Colpitts of the Department of History, University of Calgary, extended collegial benefits to me during a stay in that illustrious Department of History. That visit helped define the final text, notably Pond's role in the North West Company and his activities in opening Athabasca to the commerce of the wider world.

In addition, I thank the staffs of the following institutions for easing my research: in the United States: Yale University Library Manuscripts and Documents Division, also the Beinecke Rare Book and Manuscript Library of Yale University; Sutro Branch, California State Library, San Francisco; in the United Kingdom: British Museum Library, Maps

Collection; Scott Polar Research Institute, Cambridge; University of Cambridge Library, The National Archives, Kew, Surrey; and in Canada: Rare Book and Special Collections, University of British Columbia; Glenbow Museum in Calgary; Library and Archives of Canada; McCord Museum of McGill University; and University of Victoria Libraries. Parks Canada's historians and staffs have helped over many years, and I recall with pleasure the assistance given by the late Robert S. Allen and also by Susan Buggey. David Armour, historian of the Mackinac Island State Park Commission, and Brian Dunnigan, maps curator of the Clements Library, University of Michigan, helped in regard to Michilimackinac and Fort Niagara. Those on-the-spot scholars of Alberta's history, Daniel Kyba and Jane Ross, provided information about the site of Pond's Fort. Thanks are due to Bob Beal, Edward Dahl, Richard C. Davis, James S. Dean, Bruce Greenfield, J. Liane Kennedy, and the late Hugh MacMillan. Thanks also to Robert Caldwell and Fred Gaskins, both canoe enthusiasts of note and great voyageurs of our own age. I thank persons who read this work in draft, including George Colpitts, Harry W. Duckworth, Paul Heyer, John Jenkins, William McDonald, and Richard Platt. To these persons and to others I express thanks. I, alone, remain responsible for any errors of fact or interpretation.

Notes

Author's Preface

1. Barry Gough, *First Across the Continent: Sir Alexander Mackenzie* (Norman: University of Oklahoma Press; Toronto: McClelland and Stewart, 1997).

2. See, for example, Jon Whyte, "Peter Pond, His True Confession," in *Stories from Western Canada*, ed. Rudy Wiebe (Toronto: Macmillan of Canada, 1972).

Chapter 1: Peter Pond and the Riddles of History

1. John S. Galbraith, *The Hudson's Bay Company as an Imperial Factor, 1821–1869* (Berkeley and Los Angeles: University of California Press, 1957), 3.

2. William H. Goetzmann, *New Lands, New Men: America and the Second Great Age of Discovery* (New York: Viking Penguin, 1986), 128.

3. Lawrence J. Burpee, ed., *The Search for the Western Sea: The Story of the Exploration of North-western America* (Toronto: Macmillan of Canada, 1935), 2:327–28.

4. This seemingly attractive theme owes much to Thompson as instigator. For one of several texts by Thompson in which he deals with Pond and his legacies, see Victor G. Hopwood, ed., *David Thompson: Travels*

in *Western North America, 1784–1812* (Toronto: Macmillan of Canada, 1971), 152–53.

5. Jack M. Sosin, *Whitehall and the Wilderness: The Middle West in British Colonial Policy, 1760–1775* (Lincoln: University of Nebraska Press, 1961), 99.

6. Kenneth Roberts, *Northwest Passage* (Chicago: J.G. Ferguson, 1936), 71.

Chapter 2: Crucible of War

1. Mortality list of the Rev. Bezaleel Pinneo (minister of First Church, Milford), Susan Woodruff Abbott, *Families of Early Milford, Conn.* (Baltimore: Genealogical Publishing, 1979). Heretofore it was generally believed that Peter Pond was the oldest of eight children of his family (although Harold A. Innis placed the number at nine, as shown in note 3 below).

2. Charles Gates, ed., *Five Fur Traders of the Northwest* (St. Paul: Minnesota Historical Society, 1965), 18.

3. My narrative here is reconstituted from Harold A. Innis, *Peter Pond, Fur Trader and Adventurer* (Toronto: Irwin and Gordon, 1930),1–2, but for the reader's fuller information the following is printed: "The date of arrival of the first Pond in New England has not been definitely established, but it is probable that he was one of two sons of William Pond, a neighbor of John Winthrop, of Groton, Suffolk who arrived with the latter at Salem, Massachusetts in the 'great fleet' of 1630. Winthrop refers in one of his letters to John Pond and it is probable that the other son was Samuel and that he migrated from Salem with various Dorchester settlers to Windsor, Connecticut. In any case a Samuel Pond married Sarah Ware at Windsor on November 18, 1642, and a son, named Samuel Pond, was born on March 4, 1648. Six years later on March 14, 1654 the father died leaving his widow a small estate of 130 pounds. She apparently moved to Branford, Connecticut, and on July 6, 1655 married John Linsley at that place. The son became one of the charterers of Branford and in 1672 became a freeman at Hartford. He was deputy to the General Court for Branford in 1678, 1682–3 (seargeant of 'ye trainband' in the latter year), and 1687, and was made lieutenant in 1695. On February 3, 1669 he was married to Miriam Blatchley of Hartford and on July 1, 1679, a son, Samuel Pond, the third, was born. On June 8, 1704 this son was married to Abigail Goodrich, of Branford, a daughter of Bartholomew Goodrich, who had been made lieutenant in 1695. A son, Peter Pond, was born

at Branford on January 22, 1718. The latter married Mary Hubbard, a daughter of Zachariah Hubbard of Boston, probably in 1739, and Peter Pond, the second, was born in Milford on Jan. 18, 1740 the eldest of nine children." Further genealogical research might unearth other details but I have been content to rely on Innis.

4. See Innis, *Peter Pond*, 148–49. Although it has been suggested that this Mr. Prudden was the Reverend Mr. Peter Prudden, the historian of Milford, Richard Platt, advises me that there was none such. There was, however, an earlier Peter Prudden (1601–1656), a reverend, who was the leader of the band that settled Milford and was also the town's first minister. There were a few Peter Pruddens later. A descendant, the Rev. Job Prudden (1715–1774), was the first minister of Second Church.

5. Gates, ed., *Five Fur Traders*, 21–23. On this campaign, see Innis, *Peter Pond*, 6–13, and Lawrence H. Gipson, *The Great War for the Empire: The Victorious Years, 1758–1760*, vol. 7 of *The British Empire Before the American Revolution* (New York: Alfred A. Knopf, 1949), 229–33.

6. Gates, ed., *Five Fur Traders*, 25.

7. William N. Fenton, *The Great Law and the Longhouse: A Political History of the Iroquois Confederacy* (Norman: University of Oklahoma Press, 1998).

8. The following narrative is based on Sir William Johnson's instructions and outward letters, mainly to Amherst, in James Sullivan, ed., *The Papers of Sir William Johnson*, vol. 3 (Albany: University of the State of New York, 1921), 33–120. See also the next note.

9. Daniel Baugh, *The Global Seven Years War, 1754–1763* (Harlow, UK: Pearson, 2011), 386–87, provides a confident review of these numbers.

10. Here and elsewhere for the Fort Niagara campaign I have relied on the visual evidence supplied in Seymour I. Schwartz, *The French and Indian War, 1754–1763: The Imperial Struggle for North America* (Edison, NJ: Castle Books, 1994), 112–14, where plans of the fort, French and English, are printed.

11. Innis, *Peter Pond*, 13. See also Gates, *Five Fur Traders*, 25 and notes.

12. Pond incorrectly says, in his journal, "a fort Cald fort Ereyo." See Gates, ed., *Five Fur Traders*, 26n4.

13. For these manpower figures I have used Francis Parkman, *France and England in North America*, vol. 2, *Count Frontenac and New France Under Louis XIV, A Half-Century of Conflict, Montcalm and Wolfe* (New

York: Library of America, 1983), 1448. Parkman cites the various sources he used in coming to this numerical rendering.

14. Ibid., 1450.

15. Details cited here come from Arthur Britton Smith, *Legend of the Lake: The 22-Gun Brig-Sloop* Ontario, *1780* (Kingston: Quarry, 1977), 20.

16. Quoted in Douglas Edward Leach, *Arms for Empire: A Military History of the British Colonies in North America, 1607–1763* (New York: Macmillan, 1973), 477.

17. Information Ezra Stiles learned from Reverend Prudden about the Pond brothers, Innis, *Peter Pond*, 148–49.

Chapter 3: Wilderness Tangles: Robert Rogers, Jonathan Carver, and the Northwest Passage

1. Richard White, *The Middle Ground: Indians, Empires, and Republics in the Great Lakes Region, 1650–1815* (Cambridge: Cambridge University Press, 1991), 256–60.

2. Fenton, *Great Law and the Longhouse*, 224–39. Also, George Hamell, "Wampum," in *Encyclopedia of North American Indians*, ed. Frederick E. Hoxie (Boston: Houghton Mifflin, 1996), 662–64.

3. Alice E. Smith, *The History of Wisconsin*, vol. 1, *From Exploration to Statehood* (Madison: State Historical Society of Wisconsin, 1973), 62.

4. George L. Beer, *British Colonial Policy, 1754–1765* (New York, 1907), 214.

5. The system of licences continued until 1777, when it was suspended.

6. On the evolution and implementation of this policy, see, among other studies, Sosin, *Whitehall and the Wilderness.*

7. Sir Guy Carleton to Lord Shelburne, 2 March 1768, in Burpee, *Search for the Western Sea*, 1:303.

8. The following rests on Harold McGill Jackson, *Rogers' Rangers: A History* (n.p., 1953), 150–68. Pond does not mention Rogers.

9. Glyndwr Williams, *The British Search for the Northwest Passage in the Eighteenth Century* (London: Longmans, 1962), 172, 182.

10. James P. Barry, *Old Forts of the Great Lakes: Sentinels in the Wilderness* (Lansing, MI: Thunder Bay Press, 1994), 30.

11. Alan V. Briceland, "British Exploration of the United States Interior," in *North American Exploration*, vol. 2, *A Continent Defined*, ed. John Logan Allen (Lincoln: University of Nebraska Press, 1997), 318.

12. David A. Armour and Keith R. Widder, *At the Crossroads: Michilimackinac During the American Revolution* (Mackinac Island, MI: Mackinac Island State Park Commission, 1978), 16–17.

13. Analysis of Carver's work lies elsewhere. See Percy G. Adams, *Travel and Travel Liars, 1660–1800* (Berkeley and Los Angeles: University of California Press, 1962), 83–84. Also, for discussion, the introduction to John Parker, ed., *The Journals of Jonathan Carver and Related Documents, 1766–1770* (St. Paul: Minnesota Historical Society Press, 1976), which provides a publications history; and Paul Alkon, "Did Minnesota Have an Eighteenth Century and If So, When?" in *Studies in Eighteenth-Century Culture*, ed. Patricia B. Craddock and Carla H. Hay (n.p.: Colleagues Press, 1991), 267–88.

14. These five concepts rank above all others in the European fictions of the late eighteenth century about the waters of western North America, including the western entrance to the Northwest Passage. For discussion, see Barry M. Gough, *Fortune's a River: The Collision of Empires in Northwest America* (Madeira Park, BC: Harbour Publishing, 2007), 342–49, and references to sources there given.

15. Here I have relied closely on Jackson, *Rogers' Rangers*, 155–56.

Chapter 4: Trader and Emissary to the Sioux

1. Innis, *Peter Pond*, 19.

2. Barry, *Old Forts*, 27–28.

3. Here I follow Innis closely. Innis, *Peter Pond*, 19.

4. Innis, *Peter Pond*, 20.

5. Now Ste. Anne de Bellevue.

6. Grace Lee Nute, *The Voyageur* (1935; St. Paul: Minnesota Historical Society, 1955), 39.

7. W. Kaye Lamb, ed., *The Journals and Letters of Sir Alexander Mackenzie* (London/Toronto: Hakluyt Society/Macmillan of Canada, 1960), 85.

8. From Henday's journal, 30 May 1755, written on the Cumberland River at Fort Pasquia or Paskoyac; quoted in Harold A. Innis, *The Fur Trade in Canada: An Introduction to Canadian Economic History* (1930; New Haven, CT: Yale University Press, 1956), 97.

9. The word, as verb, is found in Old French as *régaler* and in Latin as *regalus,* or royal. Three meanings of *régal* are (1) the great feast or sumptuous repast, (2) a choice of food or drink, a delicacy, and (3) refreshment.

10. Quoted in Hugh MacLennan, *Rivers of Canada* (Toronto: Macmillan of Canada, 1974), 183.

11. W. Kaye Lamb, ed. *Sixteen Years in the Indian Country: The Journal of Daniel William Harmon, 1800–1816* (Toronto: Macmillan of Canada, 1957), 55.

12. Alexander Henry, *Travels and Adventures in Canada and the Indian Territories Between the Years 1760 and 1776*, ed. James Bain (1901; New York: Burt Franklin, 1969), 41.

13. John Long, *Voyages and Travels of an Indian Interpreter and Trader…* (London: printed for the author, 1791), 16.

14. Innis, *Peter Pond*, 25–26.

15. Ibid., 27.

16. Nute, *Voyageur*, 60.

17. Ibid., 60–61.

18. Smith, *History of Wisconsin*, 63–64. See also Wayne E. Stevens, *The Northwest Fur Trade, 1763–1800* (Urbana: Illinois Studies in the Social Sciences, University of Illinois Press, 1928), 144–61.

19. St. Ignace, now a city, derives from the arrival of the Jesuit Jacques Marquette and a group of Wendat who had been driven out of Huronia by the Iroquois. The mission St. Ignatius Loyola was the result. Marquette, before leaving with Jolliet for the Mississippi, also established St. Francis Borgia, a mission for similarly displaced Odawa, or Ottawa, an Anishinaabe group related to the Ojibwa, or Chippewa. A fur post and garrison were subsequently built there, but the whole was eclipsed by subsequent developments at Fort Michilimackinac. The Wendat relocated to Detroit.

20. Innis, *Peter Pond*, 30–31.

21. Ibid., 32.

22. Bruce Greenfield, "Creating the Distance of Print: The Memoir of Peter Pond, Fur Trader," *Early American Literature* 37, 3 (September 2002): 428–29.

23. Long, *Voyages and Travels*, 151.

24. Parker, ed., *Journals of Jonathan Carver*, 16–17.

25. Innis, *Peter Pond*, 43.

26. Ibid., 43–44.

27. Paul C. Phillips with J.W. Smurr, *The Fur Trade* (Norman: University of Oklahoma Press, 1961), 1:579.

28. Ibid., 1:598–99.

29. Nowadays the Sioux prefer the terms Dakota, Nakota, and

Lakota, meaning "allies," when referring to themselves. From the seven bands or "council fires" (or "seven fireplaces"), three divisions developed as some of these groups moved south and west, and dialectical and cultural differences occurred: the eastern division, the Santee Sioux (a name derived from "Dwellers at the Knife," referring to a lake of the Mille Lacs where flint for making knives was found), otherwise known as the Dakotas; the middle division, the Yankton and Yanktonais, or Nakota; and the western division, the Teton Sioux, or Lakota, who are divided into seven sub-tribes: Oglala, Brûlé, Miniconjou, Hunkpapa, Without Bows, Blackfoot, and Two Kettles. See Edwin Thompson Denig, *Five Indian Tribes of the Upper Missouri: Sioux, Arickaras, Assiniboines, Crees, Crows*, ed. John C. Ewers (Norman: University of Oklahoma Press, 1961), 14–40, and especially notes by Ewers. Also see Karen D. Lone Hill, "Sioux," in Hoxie, *Encyclopedia of North American Indians*, 590–93.

30. Innis, *Peter Pond*, 44.

31. Gates, *Five Fur Traders*, 46; Reuben G. Thwaites, *Wisconsin Historical Collections*, 18 (1903): 341.

32. Innis, *Peter Pond*, 150–51, provides other details based on account books.

33. Gates, *Five Fur Traders*, 46–47; Innis, *Peter Pond*, 46, 151.

34. Innis, *Peter Pond*, 47.

35. Ibid., 48.

36. Evolution of British policy based on Michilimackinac in these years is discussed in White, *Middle Ground*, 400–410.

37. We have an example of this from about the year 1800. At Rivière aux Morts, the young men and women of the Cree (then dominant in those parts) went on their customary expedition to York Factory, on Hudson Bay, to trade and obtain necessaries. They left old people and young children behind to pass the summer. "It happen'd once during the absence of the party a large war party of the Scioux fell upon this helpless camp and destroyd a great number of old men women and children. The others arrived but too late to revenge themselves upon the enemy." Barry Gough, ed., *The Journal of Alexander Henry the Younger, 1799–1814* (Toronto: Champlain Society, 1988–92), 1:18–19.

38. See, further, Gates, *Five Fur Traders of the Northwest*, 57n38. He notes that, of the two northern tribes mentioned, the Assiniboine broke away from the Yankton and went north to Lake Winnipeg and the Assiniboine and Saskatchewan Rivers; the Dog Rib, who were Athapaskan, moved to the vicinity of Great Slave and Great Bear Lakes.

39. Innis, *Peter Pond*, 57–58.

40. Ibid., 58.

41. Ibid.

42. Ibid., 61–62.

43. Ibid., 63.

44. Ibid., 64–65. The next paragraphs, describing the grand council at Michilimackinac, follow Innis, *Peter Pond*, 65–66.

45. Ibid., 47–66; Armour and Widder, *At the Crossroads*, 27, 44.

46. In the history of Native missions in North America, a parallel exists and is worth pursuing by the serious student of history: when the Jesuit DesMet moved across the Northwest, he was frequently bidden by Natives who approached him with requests that he come first to their tribe and their village.

Chapter 5: Among the Canadians on the Saskatchewan, and the Rivals from Hudson Bay

1. Thompson comments abundantly on pemmican and the importance of Cumberland House. See Joyce and Peter McCart, *On the Road with David Thompson* (Calgary: Fifth House, 2000), 73–74.

2. The source of this is the letter written by two directors of the North West Company, Benjamin and Joseph Frobisher, to General Haldimand, Governor of Canada, 4 October 1784 (Q/24-2, p. 409ff., Library and Archives Canada). This letter is printed in *Report on Canadian Archives 1890* (Ottawa: 1891), 50–52.

3. Lamb, ed., *Journal and Letters of Sir Alexander Mackenzie*, 69.

4. For the history of this depot, see Carolyn Gilman, *The Grand Portage Story* (St. Paul: Minnesota Historical Society Press, 1992). In Algonquin parlance it was called *Kitchi Onaigaming*. The French gave it the name Grand Portage. Also useful is Solon J. Buck, "The Story of Grand Portage," *Minnesota History Magazine*, 5 (February 1923): 14–27.

5. Lamb, ed., *Journal and Letters of Sir Alexander Mackenzie*, 70.

6. Alexander Mackenzie, *Voyages from Montreal* (London: 1801), viii. Mackenzie's history of the trade, usually credited to his cousin Roderick, does not always accord with that given by the Frobishers (see note 2 for this chapter). As an example, the Frobishers do not mention Curry by name. It is unlikely that Mackenzie knew Curry, who was much older than he, but it is clear from what Mackenzie says about him that he admired his courage and logistical sense. These were qualities that Mackenzie and Pond possessed, qualities that set them ahead of many of

their fellow fur traders. That Curry was content with only one profitable trading expedition is a compelling detail. His one trading season fulfilled his expectations and needs. Or perhaps he was too frightened to return.

7. Besides Mackenzie's account, the above history of the adventurers and the founding of the North West Company derives from the Frobisher memorandum to General Haldimand, 4 October 1784, mentioned in note 2 above.

8. Quoted in Glyndwr Williams, ed., *Andrew Graham's Observations on Hudson's Bay 1767–91*(London: Hudson's Bay Record Society, 1969), 264.

9. The development of HBC interest in this area, in competition with Montreal traders, can be traced in a number of works, most recently Theodore Binnema, *Common and Contested Ground: A Human and Environmental History of the Northwestern Plains* (Norman: University of Oklahoma Press, 2001), 110–14.

10. Including Andrew Graham, chief at York Fort, who insisted on a higher quality of reporting. What follows here on Matthew Cocking derives from Irene M. Spry's biography of him in *Dictionary of Canadian Biography* (Toronto/Laval: University of Toronto/Université Laval, 1979), 4:156–58.

11. Binnema, *Common and Contested Ground,* 110–14 (Tomison quote at p. 110).

12. Paul C. Thistle, *Indian-European Trade Relations in the Lower Saskatchewan River Region to 1840* (Winnipeg: University of Manitoba Press, 1986), 42.

13. Edward Umfreville, *Present State of Hudson's Bay*, ed. W.S. Wallace (1790; Toronto: Ryerson Press, 1954), 91.

14. Thistle, *Indian-European Trade Relations,* 3.

15. Marjorie Wilkins Campbell, *The North West Company* (New York: St. Martin's Press, 1957), 7, 19; also, Jennifer Brown, *Strangers in Blood: Fur Trade Families in Indian Country* (Vancouver: UBC Press, 1980), 39.

16. Henry, *Travels and Adventures*, 251.

17. Smith, *History of Wisconsin*, 62. The Cadottes worked in concert with the North West Company and, later, the American Fur Company as well as with Henry.

18. Arthur S. Morton, ed., *The Journals of Duncan M'Gillivray* (Toronto: Macmillan of Canada, 1929), xxvi–xxviii.

19. Binnema, *Common and Contested Ground*, 111.

20. Ibid., 113.

21. Ibid., 111.

22. Information on Cocking and Hearne is derived from Douglas MacKay, *The Honourable Company: A History of the Hudson's Bay Company*, rev. ed. (Toronto: McClelland and Stewart, 1966), 109.

23. Henry, *Travels and Adventures*, 260.

24. Ibid.

25. Fort des Prairies and the Forts des Prairies are often used interchangeably, the reason being simply that the fort was so important to the trade of the forks of the Saskatchewan that it was the nucleus of others set up in the area. The North West Company's district, Fort des Prairies, or "Shuskachivan," was a vast and important entity for the concern in the late 1770s, but Pond's development of Athabasca quickly supplanted it. See Gough, ed., *Journal of Alexander Henry the Younger*, 1:xxix–xxx; also George C. Davidson, *The North West Company* (1919; New York: Russell and Russell, 1967), 280.

26. Henry, *Travels and Adventures*, 266n21.

27. Ibid., 263n.

28. Bain, in editing Henry's *Travels and Adventures* (275n4), said the "fort Pond 1775" was actually a few miles south of the lake, on Ochre River. See also Davidson, *North West Company*, 37n26.

29. Arthur S. Morton, *A History of the Canadian West to 1870–71*, 2nd ed. (Toronto: University of Toronto Press, 1973), 311.

30. Material in the preceding paragraphs is drawn from Barry Gough, "Peter Pond," *Dictionary of Canadian Biography*, 5 (1983): 681–86.

31. See Davidson, *North West Company*, 40, where the map references are given.

32. Harry W. Duckworth, ed., *The English River Book: A North West Company Journal and Account Book of 1786*, Rupert's Land Record Society Series (Montreal: McGill-Queen's University Press, 1990), xv.

33. Lamb, ed., *Journals and Letters of Sir Alexander Mackenzie*, 73.

Chapter 6: Athabasca Odyssey

1. Mackenzie, *Voyages from Montreal*, lxii–lxiii. Material throughout this chapter is drawn from Gough, "Peter Pond."

2. Edwin E. Rich and A.M. Johnson, eds., *Cumberland House Journals and Inland Journal, 1775–82* (London: Hudson's Bay Record Society, 1951–52), 1:235–36; Duckworth, ed., *English River Book*, xv.

3. Eric W. Morse, *Fur Trade Canoe Routes of Canada/Then and Now*, 2nd ed. (Toronto: University of Toronto Press, 1979), 42–44.

4. *Natural Resources Canada, June 1929* (periodical). Copy in Howay papers, file 24-11, Rare Books and Special Collections Library, University of British Columbia.

5. Here I have relied verbatim on Davidson, *North West Company*, 40.

6. William Sloan, "The Native Response to the Extension of the European Traders into the Athabasca and Mackenzie Basin, 1770–1814," *Canadian Historical Review*, 60, 3 (1979): 284.

7. Morse, *Fur Trade Canoe Routes of Canada*, 97.

8. Lamb, ed., *Sixteen Years in the Indian Country*, 114.

9. Lamb, ed., *Journals and Letters of Sir Alexander Mackenzie*, 127–28.

10. Lamb, ed., *Sixteen Years in the Indian Country*, 114–15. The comment on editorial matters is by Lamb.

11. Louis Primeau may have used it before Pond, but there is no concrete evidence to this effect. There were often unknown precursors of discovery who pose tantalizing prospects for the historian, but in the absence of authentic data we have to fall back on the known details, not the wild possibilities. That other traders may have preceded Mackenzie to the Pacific shore by a year or two has been suggested but, again, there is no hard evidence.

12. Mackenzie, *Voyages from Montreal*, lxxxvii. Also Lamb, ed., *Journals and Letters of Sir Alexander Mackenzie*, 128–29.The modern reading is 58° 40' North.

13. Lamb, ed., *Sixteen Years in the Indian Country*, 114–15.

14. Lamb, ed., *Journals and Letters of Sir Alexander Mackenzie*, 129.

15. Quoted in Karlis Karklins, *Trade Ornament Usage Among the Native Peoples of Canada: A Source Book* (Ottawa: National Historic Sites, Parks Service, Environment Canada, 1992), 137.

16. Alan Rayburn, *Dictionary of Canadian Place Names* (Toronto: Oxford University Press, 1997), 16–17.

17. James G. MacGregor, *The Land of Twelve-Foot Davis: A History of the Peace River Country* (Edmonton: Institute of Applied Art, 1952), 386, which gives the surveyor's location as T. 108-10-W5. This may not be an accurate enough designation to pinpoint the actual spot—assuming it has not been swept away by flood, collapse, or other ravages. I am told that archaeologists have searched for it in vain.

18. J.N. Wallace, *The Wintering Partners on Red River from the Earliest Records to the Union in 1821* (Ottawa: Thorburn and Abbott, 1929), 11.

19. We have no firm data on what Pond grew at Pond's House, where, admittedly, he might have been able to grow potatoes and similar.

I am extrapolating from what is said to have grown at York Fort at about the same time. Note that farther south, at Moose and Albany forts, "potatoes, turnips and almost every species of kitchen garden stuff, are reared with facility." Umfreville, *Present State of Hudson's Bay*, 13–14.

20. Sloan, "Native Response to European Traders," 284.

21. Fidler Journal, B.104/a/1; cited in Edwin E. Rich, ed., *Colin Robertson's Correspondence Book, September 1817 to September 1822* (Toronto: Champlain Society, 1939), xviii.

22. Lamb, ed., *Journals and Letters of Sir Alexander Mackenzie*, 77.

23. Mackenzie, *Voyages from Montreal*, xii.

24. Barry M. Gough, ed., *The Journal of Alexander Henry the Younger*, 1: xxx. Also, W. Stewart Wallace, ed., *Documents Relating to the Northwest Company* (Toronto: Champlain Society, 1934), 26–64, 194–95.

25. Duckworth, ed., *English River Book*, xxii–xxiii, 42, and passim.

26. Gough, *First Across the Continent*, 54–55; see also William Sloan, "Aw-gee-nah, the English Chief," *Dictionary of Canadian Biography*, 6:20.

27. See on this the careful reconstruction by Wallace, *Wintering Partners on Peace River*, 13.

28. Rich and Johnson, eds., *Cumberland House*, 5–6.

29. Ibid.

30. Ibid., 6.

31. Quoted in Innis, *The Fur Trade in Canada*, 213.

32. Log of the *Welcome*, in Askin Papers, Detroit Public Library, entries cited by Harold Innis, "Peter Pond in 1780," *Canadian Historical Review*, 9, 4 (December 1928): 333. The *Welcome*, rated at 45 tons and with a capacity of 66 persons, was owned by the Irishman John Askin and had been built at Michilimackinac five years previous. In 1777 this sloop was armed with two swivels and two blunderbusses, and was manned by eight including a Master to command, one boatswain and a gunner. She plied a regular beat between that place and Detroit, maintaining a lifeline of food, guns and ammunition, and messages. In this vessel, officers and men of the garrison made regular transits. Armour and Widder, *At the Crossroads*, 66. She was one of eleven vessels and one row-galley listed by the Naval Department at Detroit, Captain Alexander Grant, Commander of the Upper Lakes. When at Michilimackinac the *Welcome*, and the eleven other vessels that came under the king's regulations, fell under the authority of the commandant.

33. Innis, *Peter Pond*, 116. Henry's correspondence is in Richard H.

Dillon, ed., "Peter Pond and the Overland Route to Cook's Inlet," *Pacific Northwest Quarterly*, 42 (1951): 324–29.

34. Gerald S. Graham, *British Policy and Canada, 1774–1791: A Study in 18th Century Trade Policy* (London: Longmans, Green, 1930), 86–90, 99.

35. Lamb, ed., *Journals and Letters of Sir Alexander Mackenzie*, 74.

36. Edgar I. Stewart and Jane R. Stewart, eds., *Ross Cox, The Columbia River* (Norman: University of Oklahoma Press, 1957), 169–70.

37. Lamb, ed., *Journals and Letters of Sir Alexander Mackenzie*, 74.

38. Jody F. Decker, "Tracing Historical Diffusion Patterns: The Case of the 1780–82 Smallpox Epidemic Among the Indians of Western Canada," *Native Studies Review*, 4, 1 and 2 (1988): 1–24; Elizabeth A. Fenn, *Pox Americana: The Great Smallpox Epidemic of 1775–82* (New York: Hill and Wang, 2001).

39. Lamb, ed., *Journals and Letters of Alexander Mackenzie*, 74–75. Also, on revival of trade, Davidson, *North West Company*, 11–12.

40. Biographical details are drawn from J.I. Cooper's biography of Waddens (his spelling) in *Dictionary of Canadian Biography*, 4 (1979): 757.

41. Lamb, ed., *Journals and Letters of Sir Alexander Mackenzie*, 75–76.

42. Her petition for the apprehension of Pond and Lesieur by military officers at the back posts, dated 29 May 1783, British Library Add. Mss. 21879, pp. 122–25. See also Davidson, *North West Company*, 41n42.

43. Affidavit of J. Fagniant, British Library Add. Mss. 21879, referenced in Series B (Haldimand Papers), vol. 219, p. 113, Library and Archives Canada. Translation of this in Innis, "Some Further Material on Peter Pond," *Canadian Historical Review*, 16, 1 (1935): 63.

44. W. Stewart Wallace, "Was Peter Pond a Murderer?" in *The Pedlars from Quebec and Other Papers on the Nor'Westers*, ed. W. Stewart Wallace (Toronto: Ryerson Press, 1954), 19–24.

45. Morton, *History of the Canadian West*, 335.

46. See the biographical details and fur trading assignments of Lesieur in Duckworth, ed., *English River Book*, 156–58. Also Lamb, ed., *Journals and Letters of Sir Alexander Mackenzie*, 423.

47. Lamb, ed., *Journals and Letters of Sir Alexander Mackenzie*, 77–78, recounts the details of Pond contending he deserved more than others were prepared to allot to him. I stand with Pond on this. The corporate majority held against him. In the circumstances, and given that he could

not "go it alone" against such an association, he was obliged to accept, if reluctantly.

48. Duckworth, ed., *English River Book*, 10–11. Compare, however, Sloan, "Native Response to European Traders," 291, who confuses the two incidents.

Chapter 7: Maps, Dreams, and Empire

1. Innis, "Some Further Material on Peter Pond," 61–64.

2. Lamb, ed., *Journals and Letters of Sir Alexander Mackenzie*, 9.

3. Joseph B. Tyrrell, ed., *David Thompson's Narrative of his Explorations in Western America* (Toronto: Champlain Society, 1916), 27–29, 172–73.

4. Henry R. Wagner, *Peter Pond, Fur Trader and Explorer*, Western Historical Series No. 2 (New Haven, CT: Yale University Library, 1955), 32.

5. Tyrrell, ed., *David Thompson's Narrative*, 28, 173.

6. Memorial enclosed in Hamilton to Sydney (Secretary of State for the Home Department), 9 April 1785, CO 42/47, p. 329r. Also, Memorial of Peter Pond, 18 April 1785, C.O. 42/47, pp. 649–52 (also Q., 24-2, Library and Archives Canada). A segment of Pond's memorial is printed in Morton, *History of the Canadian West*, 346.

7. Reprinted in Davidson, *North West Company*, 32.

8. Williams, *British Search*, 231.

9. Edwin E. Rich, *The History of the Hudson's Bay Company* (London: Hudson's Bay Record Society, 1958–59), 1:584.

10. I have drawn on an excerpt of this as published in Vincent Harlow and Frederick Madden, eds., *British Colonial Developments 1774–1834* (Oxford: Clarendon, 1953), 35–36.

11. Printed in Dillon, ed., "Peter Pond and the Overland Route to Cook's Inlet," 328. Original in Banks papers, Sutro Library, San Francisco.

12. Among many studies of Ledyard, see, in this context, Stephen D. Watrous, ed., *John Ledyard's Journey Through Russia and Siberia, 1787–1788* (Madison: University of Wisconsin Press, 1966); James Zug, ed., *The Last Voyage of Captain Cook: The Collected Writings of John Ledyard* (Washington, DC: National Geographic Society, 1995), 155–233; Gough, *Fortune's a River*, 17–40; and Edward G. Gray, *The Making of John Ledyard: Empire and Ambition in the Life of an Early American Traveler* (New Haven, CT: Yale University Press, 2007), 136–69.

13. Quoted in Gough, "Peter Pond." Nooth's correspondence is in Dillon, "Peter Pond and the Overland Route to Cook's Inlet."

14. Gloria Griffen Cline, *Peter Skene Ogden and the Hudson's Bay Company* (Norman: University of Oklahoma Press, 1974), 5–10.

15. Isaac Ogden to David Ogden, 7 November 1789, forwarded to Evan Nepean, 23 January 1790, C.O. 42/72, 495–98, National Archives, Kew, England. A lengthy extract was printed in *Gentleman's Magazine*, 60 (March 1790), 197–99, together with a sketch map, simplified from Pond's map of December 1787. Another extract of Ogden's letter is printed in Dillon, "Peter Pond and the Overland Route to Cook's Inlet," 324–28.

16. Isaac Ogden to David Ogden, 7 November 1789.

17. Benjamin Frobisher to the Honourable Henry Hamilton, 2 May 1785, in *Report on Canadian Archives 1890*, 54.

18. Here I rely on Wallace, who searched diligently for firm details of John Ross and found very little. Wallace, *Pedlars from Quebec*, 24.

19. Ibid., 25.

20. Ibid., 25–26.

21. I have retained the common spelling of this name as it appears in the contemporary sources, but recent research identifies the name as Piché. See the valuable biography of this hard-drinking, troublesome interpreter and trader at Great Slave Lake and other North West Company posts in Lloyd Keith, ed., *North of Athabasca: Slave Lake and Mackenzie River Documents of the North West Company, 1800–1821* (Montreal: McGill-Queen's University Press, 2001), 415–17. He died a miserable, painful death at Hay River when, while he was providing two Natives with liquor, a falling ember from his pipe ignited a keg of gunpowder. The Natives were killed immediately; the trader lingered for ten days and then died of his injuries. He may in addition to his drunkenness have suffered mental disabilities. James McKenzie found him "a little crack brained and as variable as the wind." (quoted in Ibid., 416)

22. Ibid. See also Tyrrell, ed., *Journals of Samuel Hearne and Philip Turnor* (Toronto: Champlain Society, 1934), 394n; Innis, "Some Further Material on Peter Pond," 62.

23. John J. Bigsby, *The Shoe and Canoe: or Pictures of Travel in the Canadas; with Facts and Opinions on Emigration, State Policy, and Other Points of Public Interest* (London: Chapman and Hall, 1850), 1:117.

24. Innis, *Peter Pond*, 153, which I repeat here in full:

Regarding the murders of Waden and Ross of which Pond has been accused, the evidence against him is extremely slight. In "A report of the special privy council to consider its powers to try cases of murder in the Indian territory and a number of cases so tried including that of Francois Nadeau and Eustache Le Comte for the murder of John Ross at Arabaska" Q.36-1, 276–310, there is no mention of Pond. The report dated June 9, 1788 includes minutes of proceedings from May 20th, 1788 to May 29th 1788 and represents a first inquiry into the whole question of the right to try cases of murder in the Indian Territory. There is no mention of the murder trial of Waden as establishing a precedent and while this is not conclusive evidence of Pond's innocence it does show that evidence of his guilt was not sufficient to even raise the question of jurisdiction of the judicial machinery of the province of Quebec.

25. Wallace, *Pedlars from Quebec*, 26.

26. Lamb, ed., *Sixteen Years in the Indian Country*, 69–70.

27. Mentioned in the introduction by Chester Martin to Edwin E. Rich, ed., *Journal of Occurrences in the Athabasca Department by George Simpson, 1820 and 1821, and Report* (London/Toronto: Hudson's Bay Record Society/Champlain Society 1938), xvi. See also Hamar Foster, "Long-Distance Justice: The Criminal Jurisdiction of Canadian Courts West of the Canadas, 1763–1859," *American Journal of Legal History*, 34 (1990): 1–48.

28. Here I rely literally on Lamb, ed., *Sixteen Years in the Indian Country*, 70.

29. "Reminiscences of Roderick McKenzie," in *Les bourgeois de la Compagnie du Nord-Ouest: Récits de voyage*, comp. L.F.R. Masson (Quebec: 1889–90), 1:18.

30. In Wagner, *Peter Pond*, 34.

31. Patrick Small to Simon McTavish, 24 February 1788 (repository not given), printed in Wagner, *Peter Pond*, 34–35.

32. Ibid.

33. William E. Moreau, ed., *The Writings of David Thompson*, vol. 1: *The Travels, 1850 Version* (Toronto: Champlain Society, 2009), 171–72; also, with variants, Hopwood, ed., *David Thompson*, 150–51.

34. Marjorie Wilkins Campbell, *McGillivray, Lord of the Northwest* (Toronto: Clark, Irwin, 1962), 51.

35. Declaration of John Finlay, retiring from the North West Company, 1 May 1805, Collection Baby, R 11960-0-2-F (formerly MG 24, L3, vol. 40), Library and Archives Canada.

36. Mackenzie, *Voyages from Montreal*, preface.

37. Lamb, ed., *Journal and Letters of Sir Alexander Mackenzie*, 453.

38. Glyn Williams, *Voyages of Delusion: The Quest for the Northwest Passage* (New Haven, CT: Yale University Press, 2003), 363.

39. Williams, *British Search for the Northwest Passage*, 235.

40. Banks papers, Sutro Library; Dillon, "Peter Pond and the Overland Route to Cook's Inlet," 328.

41. Mackenzie never contended, as Turnor did, that waters flowing out of Great Slave Lake exited in Hudson Bay. Turnor was misinformed and ignorant of the fact. He even misguided the management of the Company in London when he wrote, "A Mr. McKenzie with Six men... think they have discovered a river running out of the Slave Lake into Hudsons Bay upon which discovery the Canadians talk of trying to get a free trade into Hudsons Bay." Quoted in Barbara Belyea, *Dark Storm Moving West* (Calgary: University of Calgary Press, 2007), 27.

42. Alexander Mackenzie to Dorchester, 17 November 1794, C.O. 42/401, National Archives, Kew, England; printed in T.H. McDonald, ed. *Exploring the Northwest Territory: Sir Alexander Mackenzie's Journal of a Voyage by Bark Canoe from Lake Athabasca to the Pacific Ocean in the Summer of 1789* (Norman: University of Oklahoma Press, 1966), 119–21.

43. McGillivray named one of his Métis sons after his friend Peter Pond.

Chapter 8: The Outlier Returns

1. F.B. Dexter, ed., *Literary Diary of Ezra Stiles, D.D., LL.D, President of Yale College* (New York: Scribner's, 1901), 3:383, 385. Wagner, *Peter Pond*, 37–38.

2. These particulars do not conform entirely to data on the map, and the disputed details may be followed by the curious in Davidson, *North West Company*, 37–50.

3. Innis, *Peter Pond*, 140–41.

4. *Gentleman's Magazine*, 60, pt. I (June 1790): 487–90; 60, pt. II (July 1790): 664.

5. Gough, *Fortune's a River*, App. 1. For the influence of these

theories, and reports of Russian discoveries by sea, on British postulations at the time, see Williams, *British Search*, 138–62.

6. Memorandum by Alexander Dalrymple on the Route for Discoveries, 2 February 1790, Canadian Archives, Q, vol. 49, printed in Burpee, *Search for the Western Sea*, 2:596–601.

7. These papers are conveniently printed in a compendium of documents on northwestern exploration in Douglas Brymner, ed., *Report of Canadian Archives 1889* (Ottawa: Queen's Printer, 1890), 29–38.

8. Holland's report, 10 November 1790, C.O. 42/77, pp. 274–5v, National Archives, Kew, England.

9. Further particulars are in Barry Gough, *Juan de Fuca's Strait: Voyages in the Waterway of Forgotten Dreams* (Madeira Park, BC: Harbour Publishing, 2012), 100–104.

10. Captain Charles William Barkley, in the *Imperial Eagle*, sailing southeast from Nootka Sound in 1787, saw the opening and called it the Strait of Juan de Fuca, for it resembled Juan de Fuca's description of it, as given to Michael Lok in 1596 and published in *Purchas His Pilgrims* (1625).

11. The original drawing is not extant.

12. Samuel Birnie letterbook, 7 January 1792, Library and Archives Canada. See also Wagner, *Peter Pond*, 103.

13. I have never found confirmation that Pond was made captain, but Gates says assuredly that he was commissioned a captain in the army sometime in 1790 or 1791, after his return to the United States. Gates, ed., *Five Fur Traders*, 14. I am inclined to believe him. Certainly Henry Knox referred to him as Captain Pond, and so did Ezra Stiles on an earlier occasion.

14. A.P. Whitaker, quoted in Thomas Bailey, *A Diplomatic History of the American People* (New York: F.S. Crofts, 1940), 59.

15. See biographies of these two war chiefs, given under their real names, in *Dictionary of Canadian Biography*, vol. 5 (1983): 593–95 and 852–53.

16. *American State Papers, Class 11, Indian Affairs,* vol. 1, 227; in Wagner, *Peter Pond*, 98–102.

17. James Ripley Jacobs, *The Beginnings of the U.S. Army, 1783–1812* (Princeton: Princeton University Press, 1947), 164.

18. Quoted in Barry M. Gough, *Fighting Sail on Lake Huron and Georgian Bay: The War of 1812 and Its Aftermath* (Annapolis, MD: Naval Institute Press, 2002), 116.

19. Innis, *Peter Pond*, 141.

20. Louis-Armand de Lom d'Arce de Lahontan, *New Voyages to North America* (London: 1703), 2:15. John Logan Allen, ed. *North American Exploration*, vol. 1: *A New World Discovered* (Lincoln: University of Nebraska Press, 1997), 461.

21. Innis, *Peter Pond*, 141–42.

22. John C. Jackson, "Peter Pond's Map" (typescript, 2007), copy from William McDonald.

23. John Logan Allen, "To Unite the Discoveries: The American Response to the Early Exploration of Rupert's Land," in Richard C. Davis, ed., *Rupert's Land: A Cultural Tapestry* (Waterloo, ON: Wilfrid Laurier University Press, 1988), 82.

24. Many historians have discussed this matter. See, particularly, Allen, "To Unite the Discoveries," in Davis, ed., *Rupert's Land*, 79–93. For details of Mackenzie's travels, his book, and his subsequent influence see Gough, *First Across the Continent*, passim.

25. Caspar Winstar to Thomas Jefferson, 13 July 1803, in Donald Jackson, ed., *Letters of the Lewis and Clark Expedition with Related Documents, 1783–1854* (Urbana: University of Illinois Press, 1978), 1:108.

26. Thwaites, *Wisconsin Historical Collections*, 315; Pond genealogy in *Connecticut Magazine*, 10 (1906): 161–76; also, Wagner, *Peter Pond*, 25–26. Information from William McDonald. See also Alvy Ray Smith, *Dr. John Durand of Derby, Connecticut, and His Family* (Boston: Newbury Street Press, 2003), 94, 179, 181.

27. Sophia Mooney (Mrs. N.G. Pond) to R. McLachlan, 15 December 1905, copy supplied by William McDonald.

28. Ibid.

29. Ivan Doig, *Winter Brothers: A Season at the Edge of America* (New York: Harvest/HBJ, 1980), 3.

30. R. McLachlan, 18 December 1905, copy from William McDonald.

31. F.W. Howay, Address for Methye Portage at McMurray, 15 September 1938, F.W. Howay Collection, Box 32, Rare Books and Special Collections, University of British Columbia Library.

32. Memorandum by Alexander Dalrymple on the Route for Discoveries, 2 February 1790, Canadian Archives, Q, vol. 49, printed in Burpee, *Search for the Western Sea*, 2:596–601.

33. Henry, *Travels and Adventures*, 251.

34. Quoted in Gough, "Peter Pond."

35. Isaac Ogden to David Ogden, 7 November 1789, forwarded to Evan Nepean, 23 January 1790, C.O. 42/72, 495–98, National Archives, Kew, England.

36. "Reminiscences of Roderick McKenzie," in *Les bourgeois de la Compagnie du Nord-Ouest*, 1:3.

37. In Raymonde Litalien, Jean-François Palomino, and Denis Vaugeois, *Mapping a Continent: Historical Atlas of North America, 1492–1814*, trans. Kathe Röth (Montreal/Sillery, QC: McGill-Queen's University Press/Septentrion, 2007), 260.

38. Moreau, *The Writings of David Thompson*, vol. 1: *The Travels*, 171; also, with variants, Hopwood, ed., *David Thompson*, 150.

39. Richard H. Dillon began his compilation of correspondence about Pond in the Joseph Banks papers at the Sutro Library, San Francisco, with the claim "The influence of Peter Pond upon his contemporaries was out of all proportion to the recognition offered him by historians of the present" (Dillon, ed., "Peter Pond and the Overland Route to Cook's Inlet," 324).

40. Innis, *Peter Pond*, 113.

41. Louise Phelps Kellogg, "Peter Pond," *Dictionary of American Biography*, 15 (1935): 61.

Epilogue: In Pond's Tracks, a New Athabasca

1. Alexander Mackenzie from "Athabasca" (the "old establishment on the Athabasca River" or Pond's House) to agents of the North West Company, Grand Portage, 15 February 1789, in Lamb, ed., *Journals and Letters of Alexander Mackenzie*, 436.

2. Of the many works published on Fort Chipewyan, particularly valuable is James Parker, *Emporium of the North: Fort Chipewyan and the Fur Trade to 1835* (Regina: Alberta Culture and Multiculturalism and Canadian Plains Research Center, 1987). Among its treasures is Patricia A. Myers' analysis of recent literature on fur trade history in relation to aboriginal peoples, a subject that falls outside the bounds of my inquiries here.

3. Sloan, "Native Response to European Traders," 282–83.

4. Lamb, ed., *Journals and Letters of Sir Alexander Mackenzie*, 436.

5. Mackenzie to Simcoe, 10 September 1794; Lamb, ed., *Journals and Letters of Sir Alexander Mackenzie*, 455–56.

6. Mackenzie to Dorchester, 17 November 1794, C.O. 42/101,

National Archives, Kew, England; McDonald, ed., *Exploring the Northwest Territory*, 120.

7. See Barry Gough, "Michilimackinac and Prairie du Chien: Northern Anchors of British Authority in the War of 1812," *Michigan Historical Review*, 38, 1 (September 2012): 83–105.

8. W. McGillivray to H.I. Mose [Moses?], 17 June 1798, North West Company Letter Book, MG 19, B1 (1), 28, Library and Archives Canada.

9. Sloan, "Native Response to European Traders," 299.

10. Edwin E. Rich, ed., *Journal of Occurrences in the Athabasca Department*, 37.

11. As will be seen from the following, man has rearranged the geography that the early explorers examined. "Rising in the Omineca Mountains in the north central part of the province, this river was once part of the two major tributaries (the Parsnip is the other) of the Peace River, before the construction of the W.A.C. Bennett Dam in 1968–9 and the subsequent creation of Williston Lake. The river was named after John Finlay of the North West Company, who had travelled up it in 1797." Rayburn, *Dictionary of Canadian Place Names*, 127.

Bibliography

1. Pond's Narrative, Original and Printed Editions

First, some comments on Pond's narrative. Pond penned the manuscript some time after he reached the age of sixty. Many years later, in 1868, Sophia M. Mooney, wife of Nathan Gillette Pond, discovered it in the kitchen of former Connecticut governor Charles Hobby Pond; she rescued it from destruction. Pond's account stops in 1775, and Mooney reported that some pages had been torn off at the end. It may be speculated that many sheets had been used to start kitchen fires. Whether much is missing is debatable. Henry Raup Wagner in his *Peter Pond: Fur Trader and Explorer* contended that probably not many pages of the manuscript were lost. Wagner advanced a tempting but unsupported suggestion (odd for a lawyer) that Pond broke off the story because 1775 marked the beginnings of the American Revolution. I subscribe to the argument put forward by Professor Charles M. Gates of the University of Washington in the 1965 edition of his *Five Fur Traders of the Northwest* that "Mr Wagner offers a conjecture but no proof. No one knows how much, if any, of the manuscript now in the possession of Yale University was destroyed."

But speculation is no sin, and, if Pond completed the manuscript to, say, the conclusion of his work in the *pays d'en haut*, then we can say that the lion's share was indeed lost. We wonder, or speculate, what he told Alexander Mackenzie, and what Mackenzie did upon receipt of advice from Pond. Did Pond recount the details of his visits to Montreal, and to William McGillivray, who bought out his share—thus ending his old association with the North West Company? What did Pond say about his encounter with that great worthy and paragon of learning

Ezra Stiles? And, in doing so, did he ever mention the great Connecticut traveller and dreamer John Ledyard? I hope so, and I also hope that he had included expansive discussions about the nature of the fur trade, particularly of its northwestern reach to the Mackenzie River basin and to the Arctic Ocean. It is a sad fact that only a segment of Pond's memoir of travels survives. What we have may well be a handsome quotient of the whole. But we are still left wondering about the missing segment, which is one of the true losses of fur trade history. In larger measure, this is the tragedy of the history of the North West Company: so much material does not survive, giving a beneficial bias for these critical years to the rival Hudson's Bay Company.

Pond's original manuscript is in Yale University Library Manuscripts and Archives Division, New Haven, Connecticut. (It was in private hands for decades but was acquired by donation in 1947.) A number of copies of this have been made. Pond's narrative has been published in a variety of forms. A transcription by the text's first finder, Mrs. Nathan Gillette Pond, was published in *Connecticut Magazine* (New Haven), 10, 2 (1906): 239–59, as "Journal of 'Sir' Peter Pond—Born in Milford, Connecticut, in 1740." A fragment of the narrative was published in the *Journal of American History* (New Haven), 1 (1907): 357–65. The first authenticated edition of Pond's narrative—what we might call its first critical edition, with annotations—was published by Reuben G. Thwaites in *Wisconsin State Historical Collections*, 18 (1908): 314–54. Louise Phelps Kellogg, expert on early travel accounts in Wisconsin, assisted Thwaites in this endeavour. To date, however, the most easily accessible and best-edited text is the new transcription by June D. Holmquist, Anne A. Hage, and Lucile M. Kane, which was published in the second edition of Charles Gates, ed., *Five Fur Traders of the Northwest* (St. Paul: Minnesota Historical Society, 1965), 18–59. This was prepared from a 1965 copy of the Peter Pond narrative held by Yale University. (Note: The first edition of *Five Fur Traders of the Northwest*, 1933, contains a less authentic transcription.) I have used the 1965 edition.

2. Pond's Maps

Several, but not all, copies, or more correctly states, of Pond's cartographic representations survive (see the website of Calgary's Glenbow Museum for digital copies). These are:

1. British Library's Map Library (London), Add MSS 15332: C, D, and E. Note: C and D are not copies of each other and vary in small detail; E, in Manuscripts Division, is the accompanying remarks in French on the map presented to the United States Congress on 1 March 1785.

2. National Archives (Kew, England), C.O. 42/77 (Holland's report); C.O. 700 (America North and South 49).

3. Ministère de la Défense, Service historique de la Marine (Vincennes,

France), Recueil 67, pièce no. 30 (anciennement 208 (4044[b]). Copied by St. John de Crevecoeur for His Grace of La Rochefoucauld, New York, 1785.

4. Library and Archives Canada (Ottawa), MG 55/23, no. 47.

3. Other Maps Attributed to Pond or Based on Information Supplied by Him

Other maps contemporaneous with Pond's time and based on data supplied by Pond are:

1. Map attributed to Pond and published in *Gentleman's Magazine*, 60 (March 1790): 197. The original does not survive.

2. Map by Ezra Stiles entitled "Travels of Peter Pond," dated 25 March 1790, in Yale University, Beinecke Rare Book and Manuscript Library (New Haven, CT), Stiles Misc. Papers Drawer 3. This is not by Pond but by Stiles, compiled from information provided by Pond.

4. Manuscript Sources Arranged Alphabetically by Repository

Archives of Manitoba, Winnipeg: Hudson's Bay Company Archives: North West Company Papers

HBCA A.11/117 (Philip Turnor correspondence to HBC Committee)

HBCA B.104/a/1 (Fidler Journal 1799)

HBCA B.49/a/22 (Cumberland Post Journal)

HBCA B.239/b/50 and 52 (Turnor correspondence with Joseph Colen, 1791)

F.2/1, English River Book, 1786 (published as *The English River Book,* ed. Harry Duckworth—see below)

British Library, London

Add MS 15332 A, B, C, D, E. Pond memorials

Haldimand Papers, Add MS 21879 (Petition and deposition, enclosed in Allan Morrison to Governor Haldimand, 29 May 1783, re: murder of Waden in the upper country by Peter Pond, a trader, and Toussaint le Sieur, Waden's clerk, praying that these two be taken into custody. See also below, Library and Archives Canada, for similar)

Stowe 793 ("Mackenzie's Journal to the North and Northwest Coast of America," 1789)

Buffalo and Erie County Historical Society, Buffalo, NY

C64-4 (Porteous papers), John Askin accounts, 1775. List of supplies and trade goods headed "Adventure to the N.W. per Messrs. Pond & Greeves, Grand Portage, 22 July 1775"

Detroit Public Library, Burton Historical Collection

John R. Williams papers, Felix Graham and Peter Pond fur trade accounts, 1773–75, showing quantities and values of goods Pond received from Graham and others, also peltries delivered

Library and Archives Canada, Ottawa

MG 11, (CO 42) Q, 24-2 (Pond's memorial of 18 April 1785)

MG 36-1: 280–310; and 49 (Dalrymple memorandum and Holland letter on exploring the interior parts of the northern and western quarter of North America, February 1790)

MG 19, B1 (1), North West Company Letter Book

MG 19, C1, 32A, various papers related to the fur trade

MG 23, GIII, 8, 7 January 1792, various papers related to the fur trade

RG 4, B28, 115, 1780: 1; 1783: 1. R 11960-0-2-F (formerly MG 24, L3, vol. 40): Collection Baby, various papers related to the fur trade

Series B (Haldimand Papers), vol. 129, p. 113 (Fagniant affidavit); in regard to the latter, see item in British Library, London, above

Montreal Public Library

Jonathan Carver, Journal, copy of that in the British Library; typescript provided to author by the late B.C. Payette

National Archives, Kew, England

C.O. 42/47, pp. 649–52 (Pond to Hamilton, 18 April 1785)

C.O. 42/72, pp. 495–98 (Isaac Ogden's letter, 7 November 1789, forwarded to E. Nepean 23 January 1790)

C.O. 42/77, pp. 274–75v (Holland's report, 1790)

C.O. 42/101 (Mackenzie to Dorchester, 17 November 1794)

C.O. 700/America North and South 49 (Copy made by, and signed by, Peter Pond, dated Araubaska 6 December 1787): "[Map] of North America and Eastern part of Asia, showing Captain Cook's track in the *Resolution* and *Discovery*"

United States Archives, College Park, MD

Papers of the War Department, 1784–1800. Major General Henry Knox, instructions to Pond and William Steedman, 9 January 1792

University of British Columbia Library, Rare Books and Special Collections, Vancouver

F.W. Howay Collection, some items notably on Methye Portage and Alexander Mackenzie re historical commemoration and historic sites

University of Toronto Library, Thomas Fisher Rare Book Library

Mss. coll. 30

Wallace (J.N.) Collection, Mss. James Nevin Wallace, Encyclopedia of the Fur Trade, Biographical and Geographical, 3 vols., unpublished

Yale University, Beinecke Library, New Haven, CT

Ezra Stiles papers, itinerary, 6: 406–7

5. Printed Documents and Editions

Bigsby, John J. *The Shoe and Canoe: or Pictures of Travel in the Canadas; with Facts and Opinions on Emigration, State Policy, and Other Points of Public Interest.* 2 vols. London: Chapman and Hall, 1850.

Dexter, F.B., ed. *The Literary Diary of Ezra Stiles, D.D., LL.D, President of Yale College.* 3 vols. New York: Scribner's, 1901.

Dillon, Richard H., ed. "Peter Pond and the Overland Route to Cook's Inlet." *Pacific Northwest Quarterly*, 42 (1951): 324–29.

Duckworth, Harry W., ed. *The English River Book: A North West Company Journal and Account Book of 1786.* Rupert's Land Record Society Series. Montreal: McGill-Queen's University Press, 1990.

Gough, Barry, ed. *The Journal of Alexander Henry the Younger, 1799–1814.* 2 vols. Toronto: Champlain Society, 1988–92.

Henry, Alexander. *Travels and Adventures in Canada and the Indian Territories Between the Years 1760 and 1776.* Edited by James Bain. 1901. New ed. New York: Burt Franklin, 1969.

Hopwood, Victor G., ed. *David Thompson: Travels in Western North America, 1784–1812.* Toronto: Macmillan of Canada, 1971.

Jackson, Donald, ed. *Letters of the Lewis and Clark Expedition with Related Documents, 1783–1854.* 2 vols. Urbana: University of Illinois Press, 1978.

Keith, Lloyd, ed. *North of Athabasca: Slave Lake and Mackenzie River Documents of the North West Company, 1800–1821.* Montreal: McGill-Queen's University Press, 2001.

Lamb, W. Kaye, ed. *The Journals and Letters of Sir Alexander Mackenzie.* London/Toronto: Hakluyt Society/Macmillan of Canada, 1960.

———, ed. *Sixteen Years in the Indian Country: The Journal of Daniel William Harmon, 1800–1816.* Toronto: Macmillan of Canada, 1957.

Lom d'Arce de Lahontan, Louis-Armand de. *New Voyages to North America.* 2 vols. London: 1703.

Long, John. *Voyages and Travels of an Indian Interpreter and Trader...* London: printed for the author, 1791.

Mackenzie, Alexander. *Voyages from Montreal on the River St. Laurence Through the Continent of North America to the Frozen and Pacific Oceans in the Years 1789 and 1793, with a Preliminary Account of the Rise, Progress, and Present State of the Fur Trade of That Country . . .* London: 1801. Reprinted with an introduction by Roy Daniells. Edmonton: Hurtig, 1971.

McDonald, T.H., ed. *Exploring the Northwest Territory: Sir Alexander Mackenzie's Journal of a Voyage by Bark Canoe from Lake Athabasca to the Pacific Ocean in the Summer of 1789.* Norman: University of Oklahoma Press, 1966.

McKenzie, Roderick. "Reminiscences." In *Les bourgeois de la Compagnie du Nord-Ouest: Récits de voyage*, compiled by L.F.R. Masson. 2 vols. Quebec, 1889–90.

Moreau, William E., ed. *The Writings of David Thompson*. Vol. 1, *The Travels, 1850 Version*. Toronto: Champlain Society, 2009.

Morton, Arthur S., ed. *The Journals of Duncan M'Gillivray.* Toronto: Macmillan of Canada, 1929.

"North-western Explorations." *Public Archives of Canada Report, 1889*: 29–38; *1890*: 48–66.

Parker, John, ed. *The Journals of Jonathan Carver and Related Documents, 1766–1770*. St. Paul: Minnesota Historical Society, 1976.

Rich, Edwin E., ed. *Colin Robertson's Correspondence Book, September 1817 to September 1822.* Toronto: Champlain Society, 1939.

———, ed. *Journal of Occurrences in the Athabasca Department by George Simpson, 1820 and 1821, and Report.* London/Toronto: Hudson's Bay Record Society/Champlain Society, 1938.

Rich, Edwin E., and A.M. Johnson, eds. *Cumberland House Journals and Inland Journal, 1775–82.* 2 vols. London: Hudson's Bay Record Society, 1951–52.

Stewart, Edgar I., and Jane R. Stewart, eds. *Ross Cox, The Columbia River*. Norman: University of Oklahoma Press, 1957.

Sullivan, James, ed. *The Papers of Sir William Johnson*. Vol. 3. Albany: University of the State of New York, 1921.

Tyrrell, Joseph B., ed. *David Thompson's Narrative of His Explorations in Western America*. Toronto: Champlain Society, 1916; reprinted New York: Greenwood Press, 1968.

———, ed. *Journals of Samuel Hearne and Philip Turnor*. Toronto: Champlain Society, 1934.

Umfreville, Edward. *Present State of Hudson's Bay*. 1790. Edited by W.S. Wallace. Toronto: Ryerson Press, 1954.

Wallace, J.N. *The Wintering Partners on Red River from the Earliest Records to the Union in 1821*. Ottawa: Thorburn and Abbott, 1929.

Wallace, W. Stewart, ed. *Documents Relating to the Northwest Company*. Toronto: Champlain Society, 1934.

Williams, Glyndwr, ed. *Andrew Graham's Observations on Hudson's Bay 1767–91*. London: Hudson's Bay Record Society, 1969.

Zug, James, ed. *The Last Voyage of Captain Cook: The Collected Writings of John Ledyard.* Washington, DC: National Geographic Society, 1995.

6. Books

Abbott, Susan Woodruff. *Families of Early Milford, Conn*. Baltimore: Genealogical Publishing, 1979.

Adams, Percy G. *Travel and Travel Liars, 1660–1800*. Berkeley and Los Angeles: University of California Press, 1962.

Allen, John Logan, ed. *North American Exploration*. Vol. 1, *A New World Discovered.* Lincoln: University of Nebraska Press, 1997.

———, ed. *North American Exploration*. Vol. 2, *A Continent Defined*. Lincoln: University of Nebraska Press, 1997.

———. *Passage Through the Garden: Lewis and Clark and the Image of the American Northwest*. Urbana: University of Illinois Press, 1975.

Armour, David A., and Keith R. Widder. *At the Crossroads: Michilimackinac During the American Revolution*. Mackinac Island, MI: Mackinac Island State Park Commission, 1978.

Bailey, Thomas. *A Diplomatic History of the American People*. New York: F.S. Crofts, 1940.

Barry, James P. *Old Forts of the Great Lakes: Sentinels in the Wilderness*. Lansing, MI: Thunder Bay Press, 1994.

Baugh, Daniel. *The Global Seven Years War, 1754–1763*. Harlow, UK: Pearson, 2011.

Beer, George L. *British Colonial Policy, 1754–1765*. New York: 1907.

Belyea, Barbara. *Dark Storm Moving West*. Calgary: University of Calgary Press, 2007.

Binnema, Theodore. *Common and Contested Ground: A Human and Environmental History of the Northwestern Plains*. Norman: University of Oklahoma Press, 2001.

Brebner, John Bartlet. *Explorers of North America, 1492–1806*. New ed. London: Adam and Charles Black, 1964.

Brown, Jennifer. *Strangers in Blood: Fur Trade Families in Indian Country*. Vancouver: UBC Press, 1980.

Bumstead, J.M. *Fur Trade Wars: The Founding of Western Canada*. Winnipeg: Great Plains Publications, 1999.

Burpee, Lawrence J. *The Search for the Western Sea: The Story of the Exploration of North-western America*. 2 vols. Toronto: Macmillan of Canada, 1935.

Bushman, Richard. *From Puritan to Yankee: Character and the Social Order in Connecticut, 1690–1765*. Cambridge, MA: Harvard University Press, 1967.

Campbell, Marjorie Wilkins. *McGillivray, Lord of the Northwest*. Toronto: Clark, Irwin, 1962.

———. *The North West Company*. New York: St. Martin's Press, 1957.

Chalmers, John W., ed. *The Land of Peter Pond*. Edmonton: Boreal Institute for Northern Studies, University of Alberta, 1974.

Cline, Gloria Griffen. *Peter Skene Ogden and the Hudson's Bay Company*. Norman: University of Oklahoma Press, 1974.

Daniells, Roy. *Alexander Mackenzie and the North West*. London: Faber, 1969.

Davidson, George C. *The North West Company*. 1919. New York: Russell and Russell, 1967.

Denig, Edwin Thompson. *Five Indian Tribes of the Upper Missouri: Sioux, Arickaras, Assiniboines, Crees, Crows*. Edited by John C. Ewers. Norman: University of Oklahoma Press, 1961.

Doig, Ivan. *Winter Brothers: A Season at the Edge of America*. New York: Harvest/HBJ, 1980.

Fenn, Elizabeth A. *Pox Americana: The Great Smallpox Epidemic of 1775–82*. New York: Hill and Wang, 2001.

Fenton, William N. *The Great Law and the Longhouse: A Political History of the Iroquois Confederacy*. Norman: University of Oklahoma Press, 1998.

Fry, Howard T. Alexander Dalrymple (1738–1808) and the Expansion of British Trade. Buffalo and Toronto: University of Toronto Press, 1970.

Galbraith, John S. *The Hudson's Bay Company as an Imperial Factor, 1821–1869*. Berkeley and Los Angeles: University of California Press, 1957.

Gilman, Carolyn. *The Grand Portage Story*. St. Paul: Minnesota Historical Society Press, 1992.

Gipson, Lawrence H. *The Great War for the Empire: The Victorious Years, 1758–1760*. Vol. 7 of *The British Empire Before the American Revolution*. New York: Alfred A. Knopf, 1949.

Goetzmann, William H. *New Lands, New Men: America and the Second Great Age of Discovery*. New York: Viking Penguin, 1986.

Gough, Barry M. *Fighting Sail on Lake Huron and Georgian Bay: The War of 1812 and Its Aftermath*. Annapolis, MD: Naval Institute Press, 2002.

———. *First Across the Continent: Sir Alexander Mackenzie*. Norman/Toronto: University of Oklahoma Press/McClelland and Stewart, 1997.

———. *Fortune's a River: The Collision of Empires in Northwest America*. Madeira Park, BC: Harbour Publishing, 2007.

———. *Juan de Fuca's Strait: Voyages in the Waterway of Forgotten Dreams*. Madeira Park, BC: Harbour Publishing, 2012.

———. *The Northwest Coast: British Navigation, Trade, and Discoveries to 1812*. Vancouver: UBC Press, 1992.

Graham, Gerald S. *British Policy and Canada, 1774–1791: A Study in 18th Century Trade Policy*. London: Longmans, Green, 1930.

Gray, Edward G. *The Making of John Ledyard: Empire and Ambition in the Life of an Early American Traveler*. New Haven, CT: Yale University Press, 2007.

Hamelin, Louis-Edmond. *The Canadian North and Its Conceptual Referents*. Ottawa: Minister of Supply and Services, for Canadian Studies Directorate, Department of the Secretary of State for Canada, 1988.

Harlow, Vincent, and Frederick Madden, eds. *British Colonial Developments 1774–1834*. Oxford: Clarendon, 1953.

Helms, June. *Smithsonian Handbook of North American Indians*. Vol. 6, *Subarctic*. Washington, DC: Smithsonian Institution, 1981.

Hoxie, Frederick E., ed. *Encyclopedia of North American Indians*. Boston: Houghton Mifflin, 1996.

Huck, Barbara. *Exploring the Fur Trade Routes of North America: Discover the Highways That Opened a Continent*. Winnipeg: Heartland, 2000.

Innis, Harold A. *The Fur Trade in Canada: An Introduction to Canadian Economic History.* 1930. New edition with an introduction by Robin Winks. New Haven, CT: Yale University Press, 1956. Also University of Toronto edition, with an introduction by Arthur Ray.

———. *Peter Pond, Fur Trader and Adventurer.* Toronto: Irwin and Gordon, 1930.

Jackson, Harold McGill. *Rogers' Rangers: A History.* n.p. 1953.

Jacobs, James Ripley. *The Beginnings of the U.S. Army, 1783–1812.* Princeton, NJ: Princeton University Press, 1947.

Karklins, Karlis. *Trade Ornament Usage Among the Native Peoples of Canada: A Source Book.* Ottawa: National Historic Sites, Parks Service, Environment Canada, 1992.

Lawson, Philip. *The Imperial Challenge: Quebec and Britain in the Age of the American Revolution.* Montreal: McGill-Queen's University Press, 1989.

Leach, Douglas Edward. *Arms for Empire: A Military History of the British Colonies in North America, 1607–1763.* New York: Macmillan, 1973.

Litalien, Raymonde, Jean-François Palomino, and Denis Vaugeois. *Mapping a Continent: Historical Atlas of North America, 1492–1814.* Translated by Kathe Röth. (Montreal/Sillery, QC: McGill-Queen's University Press/Septentrion, 2007).

MacGregor, James G. *The Land of Twelve-Foot Davis: A History of the Peace River Country.* Edmonton: Institute of Applied Art, 1952.

MacKay, Douglas. *The Honourable Company: A History of the Hudson's Bay Company.* Rev. ed. Toronto: McClelland and Stewart, 1966.

MacLennan, Hugh. *Rivers of Canada.* Toronto: Macmillan of Canada, 1974.

McCart, Joyce and Peter. *On the Road with David Thompson.* Calgary: Fifth House, 2000.

Morse, Eric W. *Fur Trade Canoe Routes of Canada/Then and Now.* 2nd ed. Toronto: University of Toronto Press, 1979.

Morton, Arthur S. *A History of the Canadian West to 1870–71.* 2nd ed. Toronto: University of Toronto Press, 1973.

Nute, Grace Lee. *The Voyageur.* 1935. St. Paul: Minnesota Historical Society, 1955.

Parker, James. *Emporium of the North: Fort Chipewyan and the Fur Trade to 1835.* Regina: Alberta Culture and Multiculturalism and Canadian Plains Research Center, 1987.

Parkman, Francis. *France and England in North America.* Vol. 2, *Count Frontenac and New France Under Louis XIV, A Half-Century of Conflict, Montcalm and Wolfe.* New York: Library of America, 1983.

Phillips, Paul C. with J.W. Smurr. *The Fur Trade.* 2 vols. Norman: University of Oklahoma Press, 1961.

Rayburn, Alan. *Dictionary of Canadian Place Names.* Toronto: Oxford University Press, 1997.

Roberts, Kenneth. *Northwest Passage.* Chicago: J.G. Ferguson, 1936.

Rich, Edwin E. *The History of the Hudson's Bay Company.* 2 vols. London: Hudson's Bay Record Society, 1958–59.

———. *Montreal and the Fur Trade.* Montreal: McGill University Press, 1966.

Schwartz, Seymour I. *The French and Indian War, 1754–1763: The Imperial Struggle for North America.* Edison, NJ: Castle Books, 1994.

Smith, Alice E. *The History of Wisconsin.* Vol. 1, *From Exploration to Statehood.* Madison: State Historical Society of Wisconsin, 1973.

Smith, Alvy Ray. *Dr. John Durand of Derby, Connecticut, and His Family.* Boston: Newbury Street Press, 2003.

Smith, Arthur Britton. *Legend of the Lake: The 22-Gun Brig-Sloop* Ontario *1780.* Kingston: Quarry, 1997.

Sosin, Jack M. *Whitehall and the Wilderness: The Middle West in British Colonial Policy, 1760–1775.* Lincoln: University of Nebraska Press, 1961.

Stevens, Wayne E. *The Northwest Fur Trade, 1763–1800.* Urbana: Illinois Studies in the Social Sciences, University of Illinois Press, 1928.

Thistle, Paul C. *Indian-European Trade Relations in the Lower Saskatchewan River Region to 1840.* Winnipeg: University of Manitoba Press, 1986.

Timoney, Kevin P. *The Peace-Athabasca Delta: Portrait of a Dynamic Ecosystem.* Edmonton: University of Alberta Press, 2013.

Van Kirk, Sylvia. *Many Tender Ties: Women in Fur-Trade Society, 1670–1870.* Norman: University of Oklahoma Press, 1983.

Wagner, Henry R. *Peter Pond, Fur Trader and Explorer.* Western Historical Series No. 2. New Haven, CT: Yale University Library, 1955.

Wallace, W. Stewart. *The Pedlars from Quebec and Other Papers on the Nor'Westers.* Toronto: Ryerson Press, 1954. This contains "Was Peter Pond a Murderer?" as chapter 2, pp. 19–24.

Warkentin, Germaine. *Canadian Exploration Literature: An Anthology.* Toronto: Oxford University Press, 1993.

Warkentin, John, and Richard I. Ruggles, eds. *Manitoba Historical Atlas: A Selection of Facsimile Maps, Plans, and Sketches from 1612 to 1969.* Winnipeg: Historical and Scientific Society of Manitoba, 1970.

Watrous, Stephen D., ed. *John Ledyard's Journey Through Russia and Siberia, 1787–1788.* Madison: University of Wisconsin Press, 1966.

White, Richard. *The Middle Ground: Indians, Empires, and Republics in the Great Lakes Region, 1650–1815.* Cambridge: Cambridge University Press, 1991.

Williams, Glyndwr. *The British Search for the Northwest Passage in the Eighteenth Century.* London: Longmans, 1962.

———. *Voyages of Delusion: The Quest for the Northwest Passage.* New Haven, CT: Yale University Press, 2003.

7. Articles and Book Chapters

Alkon, Paul. "Did Minnesota Have an Eighteenth Century and If So, When?" In *Studies in Eighteenth-Century Culture*, edited by Patricia B. Craddock and Carla H. Hay, 267–88. N.p.: Colleagues Press, 1991.

Allen, John Logan. "To Unite the Discoveries: The American Response to the Early Exploration of Rupert's Land." In *Rupert's Land: A Cultural Tapestry*, edited by Richard C. Davis, 79–93. Waterloo, ON: Wilfrid Laurier University Press, 1988.

Anon. "The Ponds of Milford." *Connecticut Magazine,* 10 (1906): 161–76.

Briceland, Alan V. "British Exploration of the United States Interior." In *North American Exploration*. Vol. 2, *A Continent Defined*, edited by John Logan Allen, 269–327. Lincoln: University of Nebraska Press, 1997.

Brymner, Douglas. "Report on Canadian Archives." In *Report of Canadian Archives 1889* (Ottawa: Queen's Printer, 1890), xxxvi–xxxvii.

Buck, Solon J. "The Story of Grand Portage." *Minnesota History Magazine*, 5 (February 1923): 14–27.

Cooper, J.I. "Waddens (also Vaudens, Wadins), Jean-Étienne." In *Dictionary of Canadian Biography*, 4:757. Toronto/Laval: University of Toronto/Université Laval, 1979.

Decker, Jody F. "Tracing Historical Diffusion Patterns: The Case of the 1780–82 Smallpox Epidemic Among the Indians of Western Canada." *Native Studies Review*, 4, 1 and 2 (1988): 1–24.

Foster, Hamar. "Long-Distance Justice: The Criminal Jurisdiction of Canadian Courts West of the Canadas, 1763–1859." *American Journal of Legal History*, 34 (1990): 1–48.

Gough, Barry. "Innis and Northern Canada: Fur Trade and Nation." In *Innis and the North*, edited by William Buxton, 51–64. Montreal: McGill-Queen's University Press, 2013.

———. "Michilimackinac and Prairie du Chien: Northern Anchors of British Authority in the War of 1812." *Michigan Historical Review*, 38, 1 (September 2012): 83–105.

———. "Peter Pond." In *Dictionary of Canadian Biography*, 5:681–86. Toronto/ Laval: University of Toronto/ Université Laval, 1983.

———. "Peter Pond and Athabasca: Fur Trade, Discovery and Empire." Alberta, 1, 2 (1989): 1–18; reprinted in Gough, *Britain, Canada and the North Pacific: Maritime Enterprise and Dominion, 1778–1914,* chapter 8. Aldershot: Ashgate Variorum, 2004.

Greenfield, Bruce. "Creating the Distance of Print: The Memoir of Peter Pond, Fur Trader." *Early American Literature* 37, 3 (September 2002): 415–38.

Hamell, George. "Wampum." In Hoxie, *Encyclopedia of North American Indians*, 662–64.

Heyer, Paul. "Harold Innis, Peter Pond, and the Fur Trade." In *Innis and the North*, edited by William Buxton, 65–72. Montreal: McGill-Queen's University Press, 2013.

Innis, Harold A. "The North West Company." *Canadian Historical Review*, 8 (1927): 308–21.

———. "Peter Pond and the Influence of Capt. James Cook on Exploration in the Interior of North America." *Royal Society of Canada Transactions*, 3rd ser., 22 (1928), sect. ii: 131–41.

———. "Peter Pond in 1780." *Canadian Historical Review*, 9, 4 (December 1928): 333.

———. "Some Further Material on Peter Pond." *Canadian Historical Review* 16, 1 (1935): 61–64.

Kellogg, Louise Phelps. "Peter Pond." In *Dictionary of American Biography*, 15: 61. New York: Scribner's, 1935.

Lewis, G. Malcolm. "Changing National Perspectives and the Mapping of the Great Lakes Between 1755 and 1795." *Cartographica* ([Toronto]), 17, 3 (1980): 1–31.

Lone Hill, Karen D. "Sioux." In Hoxie, *Encyclopedia of North American Indians*, 590–93.

McLachlan, R.W. "Connecticut Adventurer Was a Founder of a Famous Fur Trust in 1783." *Connecticut Magazine* (New Haven), 10, 2 (1906): 236–37. This item and the next were published at the same time and as preliminaries to the first printing of the Pond journal.

Pond, Mrs. Nathan Gillette [Sophia Mooney]. "Journal of 'Sir' Peter Pond... Introductory." *Connecticut Magazine* (New Haven), 10, 2 (1906): 235–36.

Sloan, William. "The Native Response to the Extension of the European Traders into the Athabasca and Mackenzie Basin, 1770–1814." *Canadian Historical Review*, 60, 3 (1979): 281–99.

Spry, Irene M. "Matthew Cocking." In *Dictionary of Canadian Biography*, 4:156–58. Toronto/Laval: University of Toronto/Université Laval, 1979.

Wallace, W. Stewart. "Was Peter Pond a Murderer?" In *The Pedlars from Quebec and Other Papers on the Nor'Westers*, 19–24. Toronto: Ryerson Press, 1954.

Whyte, Jon. "Peter Pond, His True Confession." In *Stories from Western Canada*, edited by Rudy Wiebe. Toronto: Macmillan of Canada, 1972.

Young, Gregg A. "The Organization of the Transfer of Furs at Fort William: A Study in Historical Geography." *Thunder Bay Hist. Museum Society Papers and Records*, 2 (1974): 29–36.

Index

Page numbers in **bold** refer to illustrations.

Abercrombie (Abercromby), James, 22–25
Acadians, 17
Ageenaw (English Chief), 104, 117
Amherst, Jeffrey, 25–41
Arabasca. See Athabasca Fort
Arrowsmith, Aaron, ***ix***
Astor, John Jacob, 147, 179
Athabasca, 93–94, 98, 173–74, 182
Athabasca Fort, 100–103, 172–74
Athabasca River, **37, 95,** 97–105, 152, 170, 173
Athinnee, Mameek, 85

Bache, William, 158
Back, George, 173
Badelard, Philippe-Louis-François, 135
Baldwin, David, 18
Banks, Sir Joseph, 108, 130
Baptiste, Mr., 68
Barrington, Daines, 145
Basquiau, 88
Batt, Isaac, 82
Beaver Club, 119–21
Bentinck, Captain, 130
Bering, Vitus Jonassen (aka Ivan Ivanovich Bering), 122
Bigsby, John, 138
Birnie, Samuel, 158
Black, Samuel, 105, 181
Blondeau, Maurice, 121
Blue Jacket (Weyapiersenwah), 159
"Blue Laws," 12
Board of Trade, 40–44, 153
Bodega y Quadra, Juan Francisco de la, 157
Boscawen, Edward, 25
Boyer, Charles, 176
Braddock, Edward, 17
Bruce, William, 45
buffalo, 131–32
Bull, Mr., 29
Button, Thomas, 42

Cadotte, Etienne, 88–89
Cadotte (Cadot), Jean-Baptiste, 84, 89
Cadotte (Cadot), Jean Baptiste (son), 84
Cadotte (Cadot), Michel, 84
Campbell, Marjorie Wilkins, 169
Canada Jurisdiction Act (1803), 139–40
Carleton, Sir Guy. *See* Dorchester, Lord
Carteret, Sir George, 133
Carver, Jonathan, **15, 44,** 45–47, 64, 164, 176
Catholics and Catholicism, 14, 18, 53–57, 68
The Catt, 173
Chaboillez, Charles, 121
Champlain, Samuel de, 59
Chatique, 88–89
Churchill River, 94
Clark, William, **4,** 47, 64, 164–65
Clearwater River, **95,** 96–97
Cocking, Matthew, 81, 85–90
Cole, John, 86–89
Columbia River (River Oregan), **44,** 46–47, 178
Congregationalists, 12
Connecticut Colony, 12–14
Cook, James, *xviii,* 122–23, 130–35, 144–47, 154
Cook Inlet, 126, 145
Cook's River, 143–44
Corps of Discovery Expedition, **4**
Coteau des Prairies, 64–65
Cox, Ross, 109
Curry, Thomas, 79

Dalrymple, Alexander, 124–30, 144–45, 154–56, 168
De Peyster, Arent Schuyler, 69–73
Dean River, 177
Derry, Alexis, 176
Desrivieres, Hippolyte, 121
Dixon, George, 155
Dobbs, Arthur, 127
Dobie, Richard, 111
Dorchester, Lord, 43–47, 65, 132, 143–47
Duckworth, Harry, 91
Duncan, Charles, 156–57
Durand, Elizabeth. *See* Pond, Elizabeth (Betsey)

Easton, Pennsylvania, 26
Egremont, Lord, 41
Elk River. *See* Athabasca River
Ellis, William, 122
Enderby, Samuel, 145
English Chief. *See* Ageenaw (English Chief)
English River. *See* Churchill River
Ermatinger, Lawrence, 90

Fagniant, Joseph (aka Fagnant; Sagnant), 113–15
Fidler, Peter, 100–102, 138, 165
Finlay, James, 79, 89
Finlay, John, 105, 142
Finlay River, 181
First Nations. *See also* Métis
  alliances:
    with British, *xv,* 31, 179
    with French, *xv,* 26, 35–38
    of nations, 159
  annual rendezvous of nations, 66–67
  burial practices, 60–61
  calumet (emblem of peace), 120
  contributions to fur trade and exploration, **15,** 35, **55,** 118, **174**
  first council at Michilimackinac, 72
  hostilities to frontiersmen and traders, 109, 159–60
  hunting, 56
  influence of alcohol, 49, 117, 168
  interest in Lahontan's geographical methods, 163
  maps, 127
  Methye Portage, **95,** 97
  movements, 172
  murder of Montreal traders, 86

First Nations *(cont.)*
nations
Chipewyan (Dene; Northern Indians), 96
nations:
Algonquin, 59
Assiniboine, 81, 85, 139
Beaver (Dane-Zaa), 99, 102, 117, 174, 182
Blood, 139
Chipewyan (Dene; Northern Indians), 99–104, 134, 138, 173–74, 182
Chippewa, 162
Cordillera, 99
Cree (Knisteneaux), 81–89, 93, 98, 102–3, 109, 116, 139, 173, 182
Dakota, 64
Dakota Sioux, 110
Delaware, 26–27
Dogrib, 99
Fox, 45–46, 60, 63
Gens de Mer (Puant, Ounipigon, Winnebago), 59–60
Hare, 99
Huron, 35
Iroquois (Six Nations), 14, 17, 26, **27,** 28, 35, 51, 55, 160–63
Menominee, 59
Miami, 159–60
Mowachaht, 157
Muchalaht, 157
Nipissing, 50
Ojibwa (Chippewa), 65, 68, 71–73, 84
Onondaga, 26
Ottawa, 17, 28, 35, 39, 162
Pequot, 12
Plateau, 99
Potawatomi, 17, 162
Rapids (Gros Ventres), 139
Saulteaux, 50
Seneca, 26
Shawnee, 26, 159
Siksikas (Blackfeet), 81
Sioux, *xix,* 46, 63–73
Sioux: Yankton band, 70
Wabash, 160
Winnebago, 162
Yellowknife, 99, 104
pacification of, 158–62
peacemaking, 74
Proclamation of Indian Territory, 40–42
relationships with fur traders, 86, 106
river navigation, 178
smallpox, 109–10, 135–36, 173
stealing, 66
threats to traders, 88
title to land, 34, 40
trade with Hudson's Bay Company, 80–81
veneral disease, 136
wampum, 38–39
women's crops, 60–62
women's relationships with explorers and traders, 2, 47, 53, 57, 61, 82, 167, 173
Fonte, Admiral de, 154
Fort Carillon, 19, **21,** 22–25
Fort Chipewyan, 173, **174,** 175
Fort Dauphin, 89
Fort Duquesne, 25–26
Fort Edward, 21
Fort Edward Augustus, 39, 59
Fort Fork, 176
Fort Frontenac, 25
Fort Île-à-la-Crosse, **116**
Fort La Bay, 45
Fort Lévis, 31–32
Fort McMurray, 98, 168
Fort Niagara, 17, 26, **27,** 28–30
Fort Ontario, 30
Fort Oswego, 17, 27–30
Fort Pitt. *See* Fort Duquesne
Fort Pond, 64–65, 69
Fort Prince of Wales, 94
Fort Ticonderoga. *See* Fort Carillon
Fort William, 89

Fort William Henry, 29
Franklin, Benjamin, 124
Franklin, Sir John, 133, 151, 173
Fraser, Simon, 2–4, 178
Fraser River, 177–78
French and Indian War. *See* Seven Years' War
Frobisher, Benjamin, 79–83, 90–94, 112, 121, 125
Frobisher, Joseph, 79–84, 88–93, 112, 121, 125
Frobisher, Martin, 42
Frobisher, Thomas, 84, 88–94, 112, 170
Frontenac, Count, 163
Fuca, Juan de, 153–57
fur trade
 Albany–New York (Anglo-American), 51–52
 Athabasca, 102, 173
 beaver and beaver hats, **54,** 91–92, 97, 175
 challenges and considerations, 85, 94, 181
 with China, 125, 157
 effect of smallpox epidemic, 110
 exploration map, **76–77**
 First Nations partners, 38–42, 173
 French traders, 65–66
 historian, 166, 169
 Montreal "Pedlars," 80–87, 136
 northern forest zone, 91
 northwestern, 80
 Ottawa River–Lake Nipissing–French River route, 56
 partnerships of rivals, 4
 pemmican for food and trade, 78, 101–2, 170
 portages, **37**
 pragmatism, 2–3
 Saskatchewan Valley, 78, 111
 sea otter, 122, 125, 155, 157
 St. Lawrence–Lower Great Lakes route, 56
 tax revenue, 75
 trade of:
  alcohol and tobacco, 49–50, 109, 174
  European commodities, 74
  small items in demand, 52
 trade with *engagés,* 107
 traders' diet, 101–2, **174**
 transportation costs, 178
 tributary posts, 175–76
 use of:
  barges, 181
  bateau, 107–8
  canoes, 53, **54,** 58, **62,** 181
 violence, 139
 winter conditions, **116**

Gage, Thomas, 65
Gentleman's Magazine, 143, **144,** 145, 152–53
George III, 40
Goddard, James Stanley, 39, 45
Gorrell, James, 39–41
Graham, Andrew, 99
Graham, Felix, 50–51, 55, 67, 140
Grand Portage, 56, 74, 79, 89
Grand River. *See* Athabasca River
Grant, Charles, 107
Grant, Cuthbert, 100, 105, 116, 175
Grant, Robert, 90
Graves, Booty, 74, 108
Graves, Thomas, 46
Great Araubaskska. *See* Lake Athabasca
Great Athabasca River. *See* Athabasca River
Great Slave Lake, 126, 131, 143–45, 154, **174**
Green Bay, 59
Gregory, John, 136–37
Groseilliers, Médard des, 105

Hale, Nathan, 16
Hamilton, Henry, 125–26, **129**
Harmon, Daniel, **55,** 96–97, 139
Harrow, Alexander, 107–8
Hawthorne, Nathaniel, 18

Hearne, Samuel, *xviii,* 2, 85–87, 103–4, 123–27, 151, 154, 165
Henday, Anthony, 42, 53
Hennepin, Louis, 163
Henry, Alexander (the Elder), *xiv,* **15,** 121
account of Pond's travels, 108, 130
book of travels, **83**
canoes, 87
description of Chatique, 88–89
description of First Nations people, 39
home, 133
opinion of Pond, 125
trade at Michilmackinac, 51, 55
trading partners, 84–86
unacknowledged use of Pond's discoveries, 168
Henry, Alexander (the Younger), 103
Hezeta, Bruno de, 176
Holland, John Frederick, 156
Holland, Samuel, 156
Howard, John, 158
Howe, Lord William, 23
Hudson's Bay Company
Cumberland House, 84–85
dividends, 111
establishment and charter, 36, 80
monopoly over trade, 40–42
rivalry with Montreal traders, 85–87
rivalry with North West Company, 106, 126–27, 180
trading posts, 82, 134, 174
union with North West Company, 178–81
Hutchinson, Thomas, 35

Indians. *See* First Nations
Innis, Harold Adams, *xiv,* 115, 138, 151–52, 164, 169
Inuit, 99

Jacobs, Ferdinand, 81
Jay, John, 161
Jefferson, Thomas, **4,** 47, 161, 165
Jeffery, Thomas, 24
Johnson, Sir John, 121
Johnson, Sir William, 26, **27,** 29–31, 38, 41, 50, 121
Johnston, John, 28–30
Johnstown, Mohawk Valley, 28
Jolliet, Louis, 57–59
Jordan, Jacob, 158
Juan de Fuca Strait, 156

Kellogg, Louise Phelps, 169
Kelsey, Henry, 42
Kendrick, Captain, 153
King George's Sound Company, 155
Kirkland, Reverend, 160
Knox, Henry, 158

La Corne, Louis de, 42
La Galissonière, Roland-Michel Barrin de, 56
La Pérouse, Jean-François de, 94
La Rochefoucauld, Duc de, 168–69
La Salle, René-Robert Cavelier, sieur de, 43, 59
La Vérendrye, Pierre, sieur de, 35, 58, 121
Lac La Loche, 95–96
Lachine, 52
Lahontan, Louis-Armand, Baron de, 162–63
Lake Araubaska. *See* Great Slave Lake
Lake Athabasca, 4, 98–105, 143, 173, **174,** 175–76
Lake Athabasca River. *See* Clearwater River
"Lake of the Hills." *See* Lake Athabasca
Le Marchand de Lignery, Constant. *See* Lignery, Constant Le Marchand de
Ledyard, John, 122–23, 130, 147
Lesieur, Toussaint, 113–15
Lewis, Meriwether, **4,** 47, 64, 164–65
Lignery, Constant Le Marchand de, 57
Lindsey, Charles, 169

Little Athabasca River. *See* Clearwater River
Little River. *See* Clearwater River
Little Turtle (Michikinakoua), 159
Lok, Michael, 156
Long, John, 56, 63
Longmoor, Robert, 85, 90
Louisbourg, 16, 25
Lyman, Phineas, 25

Mackenzie, Sir Alexander
account of Waden's murder, 115
in Athabasca with Pond, 102–3
comments on First Nations hostilities to traders, 109
concerns for fur trade, 181
Cree woman, 173
descriptions of:
Athabasca oil sands, 98
Athabasca River, 97
canoes, 53
Methye Portage, 96
smallpox epidemic, 110
Sturgeon-weir River, 94
discovers route to Pacific Coast, 3, **4,** 145, 152, 176, **177,** 178
encounter with English Chief, 104
influence of Pond, *xiii,* 143, 169–71
influence on Lewis and Clark, 165
learns astronomical surveying, 146
map of explorations, ***ix***
medical mission to First Nations, 135
member of Beaver Club, 120
New North West Company, 179
North West Company, 133–41
opinion of Curry, 79
opinion of Pond, 112
river named for him, 105
trade with Chipewyans, 174–75
Mackenzie, Roderick, 104, 137, 140, 145, 166–68, 173
Mackenzie River, **95,** 105, 134, 143
MacLeod, Normand, 136–37
Maldonado, Lorenzo Ferrer, 154
Marquette, Jacques, 57–59
Matonabbee, 103–4
McBeath, George, 91, 108, 121
McGill, James, 52, 83, 90, 121
McGillivray, William, 135, 142, 147, 169
McKay, Alexander, *xiv*
McKay, Mr. (fur trader), 39
McKindlay, John, 111
McLachlan, R., 167
McTavish, Simon, 83, 90–93, 112, 135, 179
Meares, John, 2, 144, 153–54, 176
Methye Portage, **37, 95,** 96–98, 106–8, 168–70, 180–81
Methye River, 95
Métis, 2, 55, 117, 136, 167–68
Michilimackinac, 44, 52, 55–58, 69, **83,** 107
Middleton, Christopher, 42
Milford, Connecticut, 12–13
Minnesota River. *See* St. Peter's River
Molasses Act (1733), 13
Montcalm, Marquis de, 17, 20–24
Montreal, 32
Mooney, Sophia, 166–67
Morrison, Alan, 114

Native nations. *See* First Nations
Native people. *See* First Nations
Nepean, Evan, 145
Nestebeck. *See* Ageenaw (English Chief)
New France, 14–16. *See also* Quebec
New Haven Colony, 12–13
New North West Company (aka XY Company), 139, 179
Nicollet, Jean, 59
Nooth, John Mervin, 130–32, 168
Nootka, 153–57
North West Company
Chatique's demands, 88–89
deal with Hudson's Bay Company, 178
difficulties, 169
expansion, 172

North West Company *(cont.)*
flag, 101
genesis, 87, 170
interior posts, **116**
map of forts and trading realms, **129**
medicines for venereal disease, 135–36
memorandum requesting government support, 125–27
militia units, 179
partners, **83,** 90–93, 115
rivalry with:
Hudson's Bay Company, 180
Montreal traders, 135–37
New North West Company, 139, 179
route to Pacific Coast, 176
sale of Pond's share, 142
trading relations with First Nations, **55**
trading tokens, **90**
Northwest Passage, 3, 43–47, 127, 146, 153–54, 164, 169, 178

Oakes, Forrest, 112
Ogden, David, 133, 154
Ogden, Isaac, 133–35, 145, 168
Ogden, Peter Skene, 133, 181
Old Establishment. *See* Athabasca Fort

Pacific Fur Company, 179
Pangman, Peter, 89, 116, 136–38
Parsnip River, **95**
The Pas, 85
Paterson, Charles, 84, 89
Peace River, **95,** 105, 143, **177**
Péché, Mr. (aka Peshe; Piché), 137–38
Pelican River. *See* Clearwater River
Peter Pond Lake, 168
Peter Pond National Historic Site, 168
Petitot, Abbé Émile, 182
Pitt, William the Elder, 20
Polar Sea, 126
Pond, Charles, 15–16
Pond, Elizabeth (Betsey), 166
Pond, Mary (née Hubbard), 9, 19, 33
Pond, Peter
appearance and character, *xiii, xiv,* 6–11, 106, 119–21, 131
British agent, 47–48
British colonial soldier and scapegoat, 5
celebrity, **83,** 84
contemporary opinions of, **4,** 141–42, 155, 168–69
contributions to fur trade, *xv,* 3–5, 34, 49, 51, 59, 86–87, 170
correspondence, *xvi*
"country wife," 167
death, 166
descriptions of:
First Nations burial and culture, 60–62
Michilimackinac, 56
Sioux and Yankton Sioux, 70–71
diplomacy with First Nations, *xv,* 74
discoveries, *xviii,* 4, 94, 97, 104–8, 131, 170
duel with trader, 50
education, 1, 11, 31
emissary to the Sioux, 69
first council of First Nations at Michilimackinac, 72–74
first expedition for North West Company, 98–102
fleet of canoes, 58
friendship with French trader, 65–66
hope of route to Pacific, **177**
houses at:
Athabasca Fort, 101
Fort Pond, 64–65
humanitarian action, 135–36
influence:
diminished, 158
on Lewis and Clark, 165–66
on Mackenzie, **ix,** 143, 169–71
interest in voyageurs, 53–55
legacy, 167, 182–83

lineage, 9–13
map, *xvi*, ***xvii***, 5, 65, 76–77, 91, 100, 105, 121–23, **124**, 125–27, **128–29**, 132–34, 141–43, **144**, 145, 149–55, 165, 168–70
copied by St. John de Crevecoeur, 168
copied by Stiles, 151–52
marriage, children and grandchildren, 34, 166–67
meetings with:
Chatique, 88
Ezra Stiles, **149**, 150
member of Beaver Club, 119–21
memoir, *xvi*, 11, 162
memorandum requesting government support, 125–27, 181
military career, 5, 16–26, **27**, 28–32
murders of:
Ross, 137–38, 170
Waden, 113–15, 138, 170
opinion of Carver's narrative, 46, 64
partner in North West Company, 90–93, 115–16
partnerships with:
Cadotte, 84
Graham, 50–51
Graves, 74
Henry, 87
McBeath, 91
McBeath and Graves, 108
McTavish, 83
Waden, 112
Williams, 67
pemmican trade, 78, 170
post on Athabasca River, **37**
relationships with First Nations and English Chief, 99, 103–4, 117
religion, 11
residences listed by Stiles, 150–51
retirement from fur trade, 140, 146–47
rivalry with Montreal traders, 136
schools and heritage sites named for, 168
seafarer, **15**, 33, 50
second season in Athabasca, 107
secret agent for George Washington, 160–61
shoemaker, 33
statecraft, *xviii*
supply base, 89
Pond, Peter (Sr.), 9–10, 19, 33, 49
Pond, Peter (the third), 166
Pond, Samuel, 10, 13
Pond, Susanna (née Newell), 34, 166–67
Pond, William, 9
Pond, Winthrop, 119
Pond Inlet, 168
Pond's House. *See* Athabasca Fort
Pontiac, 39, **83**
Portage La Loche. *See* Methye Portage
Portlock, Nathaniel, 154–55
Pouchot, Pierre, 28–32
Prairie du Chien, 45–46, 63
Prideaux, John, 26–30
Prudden, Mr., 18
Puritans, 10

Quebec, 35, 40. *See also* New France

Radisson, Pierre-Esprit, 105
Rainy Lake, 79
Rich, Edwin E., 169
Richardson, John, 173
Richardson, Mr (Public Archives of Canada), 123–24
Rickman, John, 122
Riel, Louis, 136
River Oregan. *See* Columbia River (River Oregan)
Rogers, Robert, 6, 33, 41–47, 164
Ross, John, 112, 116, 136–40
Ross, Malcolm, 85
Royal Proclamation (1763), 40–41

St. Clair, Arthur, 159–60

St. John de Crevecoeur, J. Hector, 168
St. Peter's River, 63
Saskatchewan River, 78
Seven Years' War, 16–33
Shelburne, Lord, 43
Siegel, Mrs. S.E., 167
Simpson, Sir George, 180–81
Slave River, 105, 143
Small, Charlotte, 140
Small, Patrick, 140–41, 145, 169
smallpox, 109–10, 135
Smith, Sir Donald. *See* Strathcona, Lord
Snake River, 181
Steedman, William, 158–61
Stiles, Ezra, 105, **149,** 150–52, 162
Strathcona, Lord, 168
Stuart, John, 178
Sturgeon-weir River, 94
Swan River. *See* Clearwater River

Thodey, Michael, 30
Thompson, David
- account of Ross's murder, 138–40
- assessment of Pond, 5–6, 141–42, 169
- discovers Columbia River, 4, 178
- encounter with English Chief, 104
- mapmaker and explorer, 2
- maps, 165
- names Athabasca River, 100
- opinion of Pond's map, 123–25
- smallpox epidemic, 110

Todd, Isaac, 52, 90
Tomison, William, 81, 110
Treaty of Paris (1763), 39
Treaty of Utrecht (1713), 16
tribes. *See* First Nations
Turnbull, George, 60
Turnor, Philip, 137–38, 146
Tute, James, 44–47
Tyrell, Joseph, 124

Umfreville, Edward, 82
United States, 123–24, 157–59

Vancouver, George, 157
Vaudreuil, Marquis de, 32
voyageurs, 52–57
Vuadens, Adam Samuel, 111
Vuadens, Marie-Bernadine (née Ormond), 111

Waden, Jean-Étienne (aka Wadens, Waddens, Vuadens, Wadins, Dutchman), 111–14, 137, 140
Waden, Marie-Josephte (née Deguire), 111–14
Wagner, Henry Raup, 123–24
Walker, William, 106
Washington, George, 17, 159
Wayne, Anthony, 161
White Bird, 81
Whiting, Nathan, 20
Williams, Thomas, 67, 74
Winslow, John, 18
Winthrop, John, 9
Winthrop, John (Jr.), 12
Wistar, Caspar, 165–66
Wolfe, James, 25

Zimmerman, Henri, 122

SUPPOSED, the ICE SEA.
Here, according to the account of the Natives, the Water ebbs and flows, and they
Red Knife Lake
Red Knife PEOPLE
Slave Lake
HARE INDIANS
PIKE INDIANS
Prince Williams Sound as laid down by Capt Cook
River
Araubaska Lake
White
Stone Rr & Lake
PP Winter'd 1778 to 1784
River of Peace
BEAVER INDIANS
ARAUBASKA INDIANS
Great River Araubaska
a Carrying Place from the la Loch to this River
Lake la Loch
Beef Lake
Bear L.
1783 PP
Mr Thos Frobisher Wintered in 1777 on the Peninsula marked PP 1783
STRONG BOW INDIANS
COTTONOKIS
BEAVER RIVER INDIANS
Beaver River
Water Hen River
Assimpoil Lake
Pike Lake
Hudsons House
Sturgeon R. & Lake PP 1776 & 7
Assinboines of Canoes
RAPID INDIANS from a Rapid in this River
PACIFIC OCEAN
BEAVER INDIANS
King Georges Sound
Near these Mountains live the SWEET MOUTH. INDIANS
West River
The Indians who occupy this part of the Country are unknown to me.
The Indians who make War against them, say that they have seen amongst them People with long Beards
Leagues
23 46 69 92 115 138 161 184
69 138 207 276 345 414 483 552
Miles 69 to a Degree